CW00493864

THE HISTORY OF THE CHURCH

IN

PAUL PARISH

BY

G. M. TRELEASE

All proceeds from the sale of this book will be given to the Parochial Church Council of Paul Church, Penwith Deanery, towards the provision of a new organ, and to church funds in equal measure.

Dedication

This book is dedicated to my wonderful husband, and best friend
Trevor Hogben — Sidesman and P.C.C. member of Paul Church.

Published by:- Aurelian Publishing, 'Trelease', 5 Gloucester Road, Newlyn TR18 5DW.
Printed by: J. H. Haynes & Company Limited,
Sparkford, Yeovil, Somerset, BA22 7JJ.

Front cover illustration: Mr. Aidan Hicks, 2006.

FOREWORD

In the New Testament, the third Gospel, the Gospel according to St. Luke, begins with these words:-

"Inasmuch as many have undertaken to compile a narrative of the things which have been accomplished among us… it seemed good to me also having followed all things closely for some time past, to write an orderly account to you, most excellent Theophilus."

What follows is believed by scholars to be the most comprehensive and chronologically accurate account of the birth, life, teaching, death and resurrection of Jesus Christ. Its sequel, the Acts of the Apostles also accredited to St. Luke, is similarly concise, and comprehensive.

There have been several previous histories of Paul Church and Paul Parish. Each has its merits and has added to our knowledge and understanding of the development of the Church in this part of West Cornwall. However, a cursory glance at the bibliography at the end of this book will show that none has been as thorough or comprehensive as this current work. In writing this book, Jill has researched a wide range of records, historical documents, newspaper accounts, P.C.C. Minutes, etc., to produce the most comprehensive and thorough History of the Church in Paul Parish that has been written to date. In addition to spending countless hours in libraries and archives, consulting experts and professional people, by telephone and e-mail, and checking the information gleaned, Jill has interviewed more than a dozen older members of Paul Church, in order to get their perspective on the more recent history of the Church and the Community around it. Not content with this, Jill, with the help of her husband Trevor, has gone to great lengths to locate and incorporate in the book as many photographs and drawings as space would allow. These, together with some taken more recently, add much to the interest and appeal of the book.

I am pleased to write this Foreword introducing and commending 'A History of the Church in Paul Parish' to you. In doing so I would like to thank Jill and all who have assisted in the compilation and production of the book. It will, I am sure stand the test of time, and only need amending when another century or so has passed. Hopefully, by then another historian will emerge and do as thorough a job on a second edition as Jill has done on this one.

The Revd. G. J. Hansford
Vicar of Paul Church
The Vicarage
PAUL,
Cornwall, TR19 6US.

LIST OF THOSE KIND ENOUGH TO SUBSCRIBE TO THIS BOOK

Miss Eileen Andrews

Mrs. Phillipa Bailey

Sir Jeremy & Lady Alison Black

Mr. Roger & Mrs. Diane Bond

Mr. Rex & Mrs. Margaret Burfield

Mrs. Margaret Byrne

Mr. David & Mrs. Utee Carpenter

Mr. Olly Cooper & Ms. Corinne Hibbert

Mr. Barrie & Mrs. Jeanie Cox

Mr. Nigel Craig

Mr. John Dancy

Miss Margaret Dredge

Mr. Phillip & Mrs. Helen Freeman

Mrs. June Gibson

Mr. Stanley Gregory

Dr. Christine Hall

The Revd. Gordon & Mrs. Jean Hansford

Mr. Paul L. Harris

Mr. Robert & Mrs. Sue Harrison

Mrs. Marion Harvey

Mrs. Mary Harvey

Mr. Aidan Hicks

Mr. Donald & The Revd. Yvonne Hobson

Mr. Christopher Hogben

Mr. Nicholas Hogben

Mr. Trevor & Mrs. Gillian Hogben

Mr. James Howard

Susan Hoyle & Jeremy Knight

Ms. Jennifer Ingall

Mr. John Ingham & Mrs. Anjum Moon

Mrs. Pamela Jones

Mr. Timothy Le Grice

Mr. John & Mrs. Kath Matthews

Mr. E. Palmer

Mr. Richard Pentreath

Mr. Colin & Mrs. Evelyn Phillips

The Revd. Helen Poole

George Robinson & Marta Van Emden

Mrs. Nan Reeve

Mrs. Elizabeth Stubbings

Mr. John & Mrs. Judith Thomas

Mr. John Foster Tonkin

Miss Francesca Townsend

Miss Jessica Townsend

Mrs. Betty Trelease

Mr. Rod & Mrs. Sue Varlow

Dr. Frank & Mrs. Grace Vingoe

Mr. Eric & Mrs. Joan Williams

Mr. Robin & Mrs. Ingrid Young

PREFACE.

I was born in London, - an 'interloper' the Cornish may say, how dare she write a book about us! However, my Father was William Henry Trelease, born in Redruth, and brought up in Truro, and a Cathedral Chorister. So I was a Trelease too, and therefore half Cornish.

My Father loved Cornwall, and when I was young and hemmed in by suburban London, he used to speak at length of the fields, and streams, countryside and beaches of his youth, in fact he gave me an abiding love of a place I had never visited! He had paintings of Newquay on his walls, and spoke with a soft Cornish burr, which came out now and again through his public school accent. 'Directly' (Drekly) was his by word – and only by living in Cornwall can one comprehend the true local meaning of the word.

I came to Paul Church and Newlyn by accident, having the intention of living in Penzance. My husband Trevor (Paul P.C.C. member and a Sidesman), was made redundant from farming and he secured a job in Cornwall. We came down from Ilfracombe, North Devon, couldn't find a house in Penzance, and on our first trip we found a house in Newlyn, a place I had never visited. On the way home in the van I remembered something written in our family Bible. On checking it said on the flyleaf in sepia copper plate writing: *HENRY TONKIN, NEWLYN 1839*. This chap is my great-great-great Grandfather. So I am a Tonkin too! I was beginning to feel at home, then I found out that all my Tonkin and Banks relatives had been Christened, and Married in Paul Church, as far back as 1765, when Abraham

Tonkin married Elizabeth Tregurtha. Abraham Tonkin is my Great-great-great-great-Grandfather, but no connection to Henry as above! Tonkin connections *TWICE!* I was also related by marriage to the Branwell family of Penzance! As well as the Banks, Rowe, Rodda, and Pearce, and Tregurtha families!

I have Cornish blood in my veins, and thus have the cheek to write this book, the history of Paul Church, West Penwith, Cornwall.

G. M. TRELEASE, 2006

CONTENTS

Page Numbers

CHAPTER 1
The Early Church   1-5

CHAPTER 2
Hailes Abbey   6-10

CHAPTER 3
Architecture & Furniture   11-36

CHAPTER 4
Saints of Paul   37-46

CHAPTER 5
The Clergy & Vicarages of Paul   47-63

CHAPTER 6
Vestry Minutes   64-82

CHAPTER 7
Burials & The Crypt   83-108

CHAPTER 8
Crosses, Faculty Records, King's Letter   109-115

CHAPTER 9
Mousehole Chapels & The Lazar House   116-124

CHAPTER 10
The Reformation & The Spanish Raid   125-133

CHAPTER 11
Statistics & Sundial   134-140

CHAPTER 12
Choir & Bells   141-157

CHAPTER 13
The Churchyards & Various Burial places of Paul   158-168

CHAPTER 14
Glebe Terriers   169-173

CHAPTER 15
The Poor House & Church Hall   174-180

CHAPTER 16
Notes   181-195

CHAPTER 17
Magazine Notes   196-204

CHAPTER 18
Manors & Geology of Paul   205-216

CHAPTER 1 – EARLY YEARS OF CHRISTIANITY – IN CORNWALL

"History is not the past, but a map of the past drawn from a particular point to be useful to the modern traveller"   Henry Glassie, Historian.

The word 'church' is derived from the ancient word 'ciric' pronounced 'chirrich' which means holy ground or churchyard – a place of Christian worship. Cornish churches tell a tale of some 1300 years of history and social change, and are nearly always orientated to face east, as is Paul Church – towards Jerusalem and the rising sun. Cornwall is well known for its spirituality, and its Saints, although legend has it that even the devil said he had no wish to enter Cornwall, only to be turned into a Saint or a Pasty!

Paul Village c. 1980s © Simon Knight - permission for reproduction granted

Church buildings have always been a source of local pride, and villagers vied to outdo each other in the glory of their churches. They became the central pivot of village life, both spiritual, and secular, and were often sited in a pre-Christian area of special mystical significance, such as on a previous ancient burial site, or early Celtic place of worship. This is particularly true for churches with circular churchyards, although the plot of land on which Paul Church, and the old Vicarage and garden is sited, has a triangular shape. It is considered that straight lines may signify a Roman influence.

The Church is elevated above old Vicarage environs which, together with the lane running around the churchyard (once a through road), are on much lower levels. Thus, this raised sacred site upon a ridge would have had spiritual significance for eons. Paul Church was constructed to be visible, over-looking the Village of Mousehole or 'Porthenys' and Mount's Bay. The tower is perfectly apparent for miles around, and is a useful beacon for those at sea. However the early Church at Paul would not have had such a lofty tower, in fact, probably didn't have a tower at all.

The presence of an ancient stone cross head today set into the churchyard wall, may have been a meeting point for Christians even before any church was erected. Once, when it stood tall on its shaft, it would have been a sacred Standing Cross. These, also known as Preaching Crosses, were the first rallying point for those wishing to listen to the word of God. Churchyard crosses were also taken as collective memorials for all those buried around them. Here is a rubbing from the Celtic Cross shaft recently found in the north outer wall of Paul Church.

Early records of Christianity in Cornwall do exist, especially for Bodmin and St. German's Churches, and locally for St. Buryan, which was a Collegiate Church; unfortunately for Paul Church, there are none.

The conversion of Cornwall to Christianity is a subject veiled in obscurity. However, before the Gospel was preached here, or churches were founded, archaeology and local folklore all point to the practising of fire worship, with special reverence for heavenly bodies – chiefly the sun. The Beunans Meriasek or a play about the Patron Saint of Camborne St. Meriasek, discovered in 1504, shows that the chief gods were the Sun and Monfras (Whitley Stokes published this play in 1872). Monfras may simply be a corruption of 'big stone' Maen Vras. At Kerris there are two stones carved with a coil signifying the sun's rays; one is lost at present, but the other one may be seen set into the side of a farm building. The ancient custom of 'waving torches around the head' in Newlyn and Penzance, on Midsummer's eve, embodies pre-Christian worship of the sun, in a fire ritual.

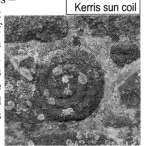

Kerris sun coil

The standing stones—or menhirs – were likely obelisks connected with pre-Christian worship, marking burials or simply places commemorating tribal battles. Sacred circles are now connected with sculpture, but may have been linked to Celtic rites of fire or sun worship. The Celts knew the abiding durability of granite, and used the natural stones in different ways, knowing that they would stand the test of time, eternal memorials to their way of life. Thus it seems a natural spiritualism already abounded in Cornwall before the coming of Christianity, and having created sacred sites, the most natural thing in the world was to honour the new religion of the Gospel of Christ by building Christian churches where they had already worshipped nature around them.

Tales are told, legends grew, superstition abounded, and the Cornish folk worshipped what they could see in the natural landscape around them. The rocks shaped by wind and waves, locally known as 'giants fingers', inspired legends of mermen and mermaids bringing them to life in the sighing of the waves, the mournful cries of seabirds and the odd seal or two. Cornwall in general, and West Penwith in particular, are very mystical and spiritual places, and it is easy to see how the early Celtic folk passed on tales of spirits, whether in the shape of the Cornish pisky, giants, mermaids or the Bucca-boo, all created from the elements of the largely wild and windy environment.

A Diversion into an early Celtic Tale concerning The Choir!

The following illustrates local folklore concerning a sea-god. A tale well known in the area of Paul and Newlyn is that of the 'Bucca-boo' (so called because he shouted 'Buckah!') and for which the annual 'Bucca's Fair' is named. Today also the 'Bucca's Four' is a male singing group, part of the Mousehole Male Voice Choir.

The Bucca-boo is a type of sea-god full of mischief, who one day saw the nets laid out on the beach at Newlyn to dry, having been newly mended, and stole them. Someone ran to Paul Church where the Choir were practising, and told the choristers, whereupon the whole Choir ran after the Bucca-boo singing the Apostles' Creed and the Lord's Prayer at the tops of their voices. This frightened the Bucca-boo and he took refuge in a tree at the top of the hill, however Paul Choir still sang, and chased him until he flew across the Coombe and turned the nets to stone at Tolcarne, where *'reticulations of the elvan'* are still supposed to be petrified nets of the unlucky fishermen of Newlyn.

I have come across this tale told in many different ways. One states that the year all this happened was 1592, and the Paul Choir members who ran after the Bucca-boo were: Shepherd Pentreath, Jacky Kelynack, Benny Downing, Dick Keigwin – among others! According to this version the Bucca-boo strode across the valley from the road behind Captain Bryn Tonkin's orchard. Mr. Bottrell writes in 1870: *'Every fishing boat 100 years ago in Newlyn set aside a portion of its catch, and left it on the beach to propitiate Bucca!'*

As a background to the early history of Paul Church, here is a little general Cornish Christian history:-

The Cornish did not give up their Celtic gods easily. The Gospel of Peace came slowly to Cornwall, taking at least two centuries, and is probably older than the conversion of England, which was largely suppressed by the Saxon conquest. Cornwall always remained Celtic. Those responsible for the conversion of the Cornish are more likely to be the Celtic Breton and Irish missionaries than St. Augustine, who landed far away in Kent to preach the Gospel of Christ.

It is likely that Cornwall was largely converted before the age of the Saints began, and before Christian Roman Emperors withdrew from Britain. The years from 500-600 A.D. is a period known as 'The Age of the Saints', and in 600 A.D. it is recorded that the earliest Cornish Christian Church opened at St. Piran's Oratory. A list of Cornish Saints, studied in an early 10th C manuscript, suggests that the parochial structure of Cornwall, as we know today, was already in existence at this time. There certainly were eight Bishops in West Cornwall in the early Celtic Church.

Cornwall became isolated after the formation of Wessex in 519, and its relations with Brittany (Amorica) were closer than with Saxonised Britain (see above). Celtic kinship between the Irish, Welsh and Bretons formed a link making conversion to the Christian faith acceptable as if between brothers. The Breton language is very similar to Cornish; therefore an understanding of the teachings of Christ would have stood a better chance than in English. Not only were the Bretons and Cornish one in origin, tradition and dialect, but they shared Celtic ideals of priestly religious life, and the early Saints were almost all of Celtic origin.

Christian missionaries may have lived in Cornwall since the time of Constantine the Great, but the process of converting the Cornish was not at all easy, and in 450 A.D. in Hayle and St. Ives, Christian missionaries were persecuted and hunted to death. In 664, the Synod of Whitby confirms England once again under the ecclesiastical jurisdiction of Rome, giving formal structure to parish and diocese. However once again Celtic Church of Dumnonia (the South West) remained monastic and refused to be subject to Roman structure. The Cornish Celts may have been rebels, but in terms of the provision of priests, much positive development occurred long before the Charter of 1050 (see below). The Cornish also had other things on their minds such as *'The Danes sailing about Penwith making foule havocke'* (Carew).

The legend of Paul Aurelian is discussed further, in Chapter 4, but I would mention in passing the method for consecration of a church as reported by Newlyn Vicar, the Revd. W. S. Lach-Szyrma. He states that the main method used, was in the fasting of the Saint, who would visit the area of the church in question, and stay for forty days, reflecting Jesus' fasting in the wilderness before His Ministry. The Saint, (and it seems to have been the same ritual for all of them), would only eat a little morsel of bread and an egg with a little milk and water every evening, except Sunday. During this time he prayed without ceasing for blessings to be poured on the area to be consecrated. This rite was finalised by the Saint who preached on the site, and then departed. The ritual being over, thus the church was considered founded, an interesting description of a rite of holy blessing, which may or may not have been correct! The aforementioned Reverend Lach-Szyrma was an exponent of Cornish Antiquities.

The See of Canterbury had no jurisdiction over Cornwall until the first Cornish Bishop, called Kenstec or Kenstet, accepted the supremacy. He was Bishop elect of the Cornish people, and possibly came from St. Germans near Falmouth. Bishop Kenstec made his obeisance to Archbishop Coehnoth in about A.D. 833. Cornwall was independent from England, and King Dungurth was King of Cornwall as late as A.D. 875. Cornwall was not annexed to England until King Athelstan's time.

However, Mr. Thomas Taylor, in his book 'Celtic Christianity of Cornwall', states that the reforms of Archbishop Theodore (689-690) resulted in the subdivisions of diocese and the formation of parishes, which were begun about seventy-five years later in England. Cornwall and Wales were untouched by reforms and did not acknowledge the Archbishop of Canterbury's jurisdiction until the days of Bishop Edbert (803-839).

King Edward the Elder, in 909, founded the See of Crediton in Devon, and commissioned Eadulf Bishop of Crediton to visit Cornwall annually and to bring the Cornish into the obedience of the Anglo-Saxon Church. This obedience continued until the first Bishop of the Cornish people, who seems to have been Conan, was consecrated in 931. Follwed by Aethelgeard in 946; Comoere – 959; Athelstan – 966; Wulfsige – 967-980; Ealdred – 993-1002; Aethelred; Buruhwold 1018 (records William of Malmsbury); Lyvingus (Saxon Chronicle); Leofric – 1046-1050 (Saxon Chronicle – moved the See to Exeter). Subsequently up to 1877-1883 Edward White Benson was the first Bishop of Cornwall in the newly-formed See of Truro.

However, once again there are anomalies in historical facts – a 13thC manuscript in the possession of the Dean and Chapter of Exeter (this from a History of St. Germans), speaks of eleven Bishops who sat in the Episcopal See of St. Germans from the time of King Edward, son of King Alfred to the time of King Cnut (Canute) the Dane. This list states the Bishops were: Athelstanus, Conanus, Raydoc (Ruydoc), Alfredus, Britwye, Wolsi, Woronus, Wolocis, Stidio, Adelfridus (of Adelredus), and Burwoldus. This list is a curious example of medieval forgery, the only correct names being Conan, Wulsi for Wulfsige, and Adelfridus for Ealdred.

Yet Mr. E. H. Pedlar, in his book on the Anglo-Saxon Episcopate of Cornwall, provides further enlightenment by stating that the Charter of King Edward the Confessor of 1050 united Devon and Cornwall under one Diocese with the See at Exeter. Leofric, being the first Bishop of the new See, was enthroned sixteen years before the Norman Conquest. Osbearne followed after Leofric who died in 1071. Someone called Florence of Worcester (who seems to have been male!) wrote his Chronicle shortly after the Norman Conquest, a contemporary of William of Malmsbury.

The authentic list of Cornish Bishops from the time of King Athelstan 925-940 when the See of Cornwall was created follows:-

1.	Conan	In book of St. Germans – 926 Athelstan
2.	Aethelgeard	Time of King Eadred 946-955
3.	Comoere or Cemoere	Time of King Eadgar 959-975
4.	Athelstan	Charter dated A.D. 966
5.	Wulfsige	Records of St. Petrockstowe
6.	Ealdred or Aethelred	Time of King Canute 1016-1035 –records Petrockstowe
	(probably the same person)	Charter dated 1001-1016-1035
7.	Buruhwold	In time of King Canute 1016-1035—records Petrockstowe
8.	Lyuing	Time of King Canute 1042-1066 died 1046 Florence of Worcester & William of Malmesbury
9.	Leofric	Died in reign of William I – A.D. 1071 (Bodlean ms)

The Anglo-Saxon Bishops of Cornwall had their See at Bodmin and later St. Germans, as Cornwall had no city with a cathedral. After the destruction of Bodmin by the Danes, in 981 it was certain that the See moved to St. Germans. It is reported that King Athelstan set up a Bishopric at St. Germans in 931, which lasted until 1042 when the See was united with the Bishopric of Crediton, Devon, and then on to unity under Exeter Diocese. In 1348-9 the Black Death visited Bodmin Priory, killing all but two of the thirteen Canons. Bodmin and St. Germans were Cornwall's Ecclesiastical Administration centres. St. Germans was the seat of the first Bishop of Cornwall Diocese, set up by Athelstan in 926.

Diocese of Exeter

A note about three early Bishops of Exeter. Bishop Bronescombe, consecrated in 1258 was a very active prelate whose registers of his good works are of great historical value. Bishop Stapledon was also an energetic prelate who encouraged and supported church restoration, and he wrote complaining of the state of many early Cornish Churches. Bishop Grandisson visited Paul Church in 1336; he also went to Land's End, consecrated the altar at Madron Church and preached at St. Buryan (see Chapter 3). Another important Exeter Bishop was Veysey who was consecrated in 1519; it was he who instituted the Parish Registers of birth, marriage and death throughout Cornwall, invaluable records for local historians.

There was difficulty in converting the Cornish to Christianity because not many could read or write; however, the Plen an Guare (*place of sport*), Cornish Miracle Plays, and Cornish Passion Plays were ways of spreading the Gospel to those who could not read or write. 'Passhyon Agan Arloedh' (c. 1375, The Passion of our Lord), The 'Cornish Ordinalia' (c. 1405), a drama in three parts, and the Bywans Meriasek (1504), brought the Gospel to life and made understanding Christianity more acceptable and easier for the local people. These plays taught the Cornish tinners, farmers and fisher folk of old the stories of the Bible. There were Plen an Guare sites at Marazion, Redruth St. Just and Perranzabuloe. The St. Just site is still very active today in 2006.

Diocese of Truro

Thus the very early Church of Paul grew from humble beginnings, and eventually became part of the Diocese of Exeter. In 1877 Paul became part of the Diocese of Truro, which in 2002 celebrated the 125 year Anniversary of its founding.

CHAPTER 2 – HAILES ABBEY & CONVENT, GLOUCESTERSHIRE

Richard, Earl of Cornwall

In this section I have taken notes from the Accounts of the lands and liberties held by Edmund Earl of Cornwall, in the year which ended at Michaelmas 1297. Also, from the lives of King John, King Henry III, and Edmund's Father, Richard, Earl of Cornwall. This history serves as a background to the whole story of Paul Church's early years.

Richard, the brother of Henry III, was born in 1209, the second son of King John (Lackland) and Isabella of Angouleme. Richard married three times in total, the first time to Isabella daughter of the 1st Earl of Pembroke in 1231. When she died, Richard married again to the Queen's sister Sanchia of Provence in 1243. Thus two brothers married sisters! In his later years on the death of Sanchia in 1261 he married yet again to Beatrice, daughter of Count Faulkenburg.

In 1225 Richard forced his brother King Henry III to grant him land and wealth he regarded as his right, and was granted the County of Cornwall with its tin rights and, two years later, the title of Earl of Cornwall. In his youth Richard showed little loyalty to his brother but with his marriage to Sanchia, sister to the Queen, it brought them closer, and he became one of King Henry's firmest supporters. The Manor of Alverton was among the land granted to the Richard, Earl of Cornwall, and at that time Paul Village (Brewinney), and Paul Church were within the bounds of this Manor.

Richard was quite a character, and wasn't averse to taking a bribe, and one of the earliest pieces of English satire was written about him:

'The Kyn of Alemaigne bi mi leaute
Thritti thousent pound askede he - for to make pees in the countre'.

Hailes Abbey

Richard made his headquarters at Launceston, in the old castle of Robert de Mortain, and later in 1236 by wrangling with Gervase de Hornicote secured the Castle of Tintagel, adding a wall and a great ward on the mainland linked to the island by a bridge. His lust for castles was not assuaged until in 1270, he secured Trematon Castle from Roger de Valletort.

I shall now enlarge on the Manor of Alverton by digressing for a moment and inserting a short extract from The Doomsday Book (section on Cornwall):-

Paul is not mentioned as a separate place, but the Manor of Alverton (Alwaretone) encompassed Paul, and Newlyn. Alfward – his name is remembered in 'Alverton' - held it before 1066 and paid tax for two hides: 3 hides there, however land for 60 ploughs, in lordship 3 ploughs, 11 slaves: ½ hide. 35 villagers and 25 smallholders, with 12 ploughs and 2½ hides. Meadows – 3 acres, pasture 2 leagues long and 1 league wide. Formerly £8 it now pays £20: 4 pigs 100 sheep, 17 unbroken mares, 1 cob, 9 cattle. (1 square kilometre = 247 acres – 2 hides; 12 acres to a hide.) Ermenhald holds Tolcarne (Newlyn) from Tavistock Church.

Hailes Abbey, Gloucester

To return to Earl Richard, he was also known as the 'King of the Romans'. This came about by his refusal of the Sicilian Crown offered to him by Pope Innocent IV. He went on to have himself elected in 1257, by a bare majority of German electors, to the title of 'King of the Romans' – he aspired to be Emperor Elect of the Holy Roman Empire; but together with another candidate he didn't make it to election to that title. He, however, used the subsidiary title 'King of the Romans' to placate himself no doubt for the disappointment he felt. He used this title at the desire of his brother, King Henry III, also because of his wealth (*money talks!*) and his very cordial relations with the Pope. He also had family connections with the Hohenstaufen family, and it was deemed probable that he would manage to unite all German parties under this title.

Richard's connection to Hailes Abbey and Convent is linked to a tale of him being at great peril in a storm at sea. According to Revd. Charles Henderson, in his 'Short History of Paul', this fearsome storm took place in 1246. He prayed that his life may be saved, promising to endow and found a religious house in thanksgiving. Richard was spared, and he gratefully honoured his pledge by founding the Monastery and Convent of Hailes in Gloucester, with the assistance of King Henry, who gave him the land of the Manor of Hailes on which to build the Cistercian Monastery.

Richard, Earl of Cornwall, began building Hailes Abbey in 1246, expanding 10,000 marks (one mark = 6/8d) which today would total just over £3,333, in finishing this Monastery. He had Hailes Abbey Church dedicated to St. Mary on 9th November, 1259 in the presence of the King and Queen with 300 knights, plus 13 Bishops, who were all entertained with '*incredible state and plenty*', and a good time was had by all!

Richard finally died on 2nd April, 1272, in his sixties, his end hastened by the grief felt on the murder of his first son (born of his first marriage), Henry of Almain, who was murdered in March, 1271. That left Richard's son Edmund, who then became his heir; and at the age of twenty-two, he received the lands and title of Earl of Cornwall, from his Uncle King Henry. Edmund became a knight on 13th October in the company of fifty other nobles, and at a solemn ceremony was invested with the sword of the County of Cornwall from which his Earldom took its name. Soon after this event on 16th November, 1272, Henry III died, succeeded by his son Edward, thus the two cousins Edmund, Earl of Cornwall and Edward I, King of England in synchronisation assumed their new responsibilities.

In 1289 and 1297 King Edward was abroad, and needed money to finance his 'arduous affairs'. He leant on his cousin Edmund during his life, and after his death, for loans to the sum of 27,300 marks (mark – 6/8d) or £18,200, an incredible amount in those days. These loans are reflected in the Stewards' Accounts of the Earldom of Cornwall, as in 1297 King Edward borrowed from Edmund the *whole of the output* of his tin mines of Cornwall and Devon, to satisfy certain men of Bayonne who were his creditors. The amount of tin was 100,000 in weight and its value was 7,000 marks.

Edmund had three castles at his disposal, Tintagel, Trematon and Restormel, the latter being his favourite. He decided to make Restormel the capital of Cornwall, and he constructed the wonderfully splendid 'Duchy Palace', making it equal to the County as the Palace of Westminster is to London, as a seat of Government.

The abiding interest of Edmund, Earl of Cornwall, was in the vigorous activity of founding and endowing religious houses and institutions. He earned the name of '*summus religiosorum patronus'* for so doing. Any account of his landed estates would not be complete without mentioning the way in which he carved up his inheritance for his charitable works. His first recorded act of piety was his donation of a portion of the blood of Christ (bought while in Germany with his Father) to the Cistercian Abbey of Hailes in Gloucester in 1270. This was famous enough to be mentioned in Chaucer's 'The Pardoner's Tale':

*'By God's precious heart and Passion, by God's nails
And by the Blood of Christ that is in Hailes'*

On 13th September, 1270 when Edmund was only 19, the relic was borne with great reverence to Hailes. The monks met the procession with a throng of people and a canopy of cloth of gold was erected over an altar so that the sacred relic could be displayed for veneration. Edmund also gave the Abbey a portion of the True Cross. In 1539 this phial of Holy Blood was removed to London at the Dissolution of the Monasteries, and found to be, unfortunately, a fake! It seems that Monasteries needed holy relics to give them credence, and to interest and attract pilgrims. They, in turn, gave funds for the upkeep of the Community; thus Edmund's donation of the holy relic, together with the advowsons of the churches mentioned below, supported the Cistercians and their prayerful, meditative, way of life. The fame of the relic of Holy Blood soon spread, and so did the scandal when it was found to be a fake! Bishop Hilsey mentions it in his sermon on 'feigned relics' on 24th November, 1538. In fact legends grew up around this relic, and at this time it was reported that when a Lollard priest attempted to say mass:

'The holy sacrament of Cristes owne blod there Reboyled anone up; unto the chalice brink.'

This strange boiling blood phenomenon is further reported in 'Richard Pynson & the Holy Blood of Hailes' by J. C. T. Oates. Boiling blood would seem to confirm without doubt that the relic was false; however, Richard Pynson in 1516 published a pamphlet to promote the 'Holy Blood of Hailes' designed to encourage pilgrimage to this Abbey, an early version of a travel brochure, perhaps, therefore swelling its coffers.

As the Abbey had been founded by his Father, Earl Richard, Edmund felt a strong responsibility to its Community, and he set about rebuilding a large part that had been destroyed by a devastating fire in 1271. This work was completed in 1277. Edmund then set about providing the monks with support, by granting to the Abbot and Convent the advowsons of the Churches of Hemel Hempstead in Hertfordshire, North Leigh in Oxford, and **Paul Church in Cornwall**. This endowment was made by **Edmund, and not his Father, Richard,** as was previously thought, and is mentioned in Oliver's Monasticon Anglic:-

' Firma Rectoris' for the Church of Paulyn was £41.

In a modern day Taxiato Database Paul Church comes under Benefice Code*: EX.CW.PE.04 taxation £9.6.8d—Grid Ref: SW465272 to Cistercian Monks of Hailes Abbey, Gloucester.* This was the *Taxiatio Ecclesiastica Angliae et Walliae auctoritate Pope Nicholai IV A.D. c. 1291.*

Edmund also donated land in Haughley, Suffolk, and in Helston-in-Kerrier, (Breage Church with its chapels in Cury and Gunwalloe, Cornwall), plus the manor of Longburgh, Park of Nether Swell, and the Manor of Lechlade in Gloucester; thus making Hailes Abbey very well off indeed. The first recorded Vicar of Paul Church was a Rector in his own right, appointed by Bishop Walter de Bronescombe of Exeter. However, after 1277, because of Edmund's gift of the Paul Church advowson, which carried on up to the Reformation, the Patrons of the Living of Paul Church (Rectors) were the Abbey and Convent of Hailes.

The title 'Earl of Cornwall' became extinct in 1305, upon the death of Edmund, the last Earl and only the second noble to bear this title. He was buried at Hailes Abbey near his second wife, Sanchia (although her heart was buried at Cirencester Abbey), and Henry, Edmund's step-brother and their father Richard. The title Earl of Cornwall was newly created for Piers

Gaveston (1307-12), who held it until his execution in 1312, and then to John of Eltham younger brother of Edward III (1328-36).

Subsequently in 1337, when he was only seven years old, Edward, The Black Prince was endowed with the title Duke of Cornwall, which still exists today in Prince Charles, Prince of Wales, and Duke of Cornwall, and has always been awarded to the monarch's eldest son.

CHAPTER 3 – ARCHITECTURE & FURNITURE

When researching through mounds of information, in order to write an accurate history, one invariably comes across a disparity in measurements in each historian's personal 'take' on a building, and Paul Church is no different. For instance the distance from Penzance to Paul Village is written in stone, yet different historians have described it as being 'two miles, two and a half miles, two and three-quarters of a mile, three miles', and 'a short distance' - the latter being a pretty safe statement. While Mousehole, is described as being one mile (approximately), by road from Paul Village.

J. J. T. Blight states in his 'Churches & Antiquities of Cornwall' (1885) that Paul Church *'Possesses few architectural features of interest, for it is the most sadly disfigured Church in West Cornwall'*.

Paul Village c. 1950

To commence writing about the architecture of Paul Church, one has to go back to the very early days. The landscape would have been very bare, and in the mind's eye one has to imagine nothing of modern times, simply open countryside, with tiny fields and wooded areas. The modest, first early Church, with ancient cross and a few houses clustered around, would have resembled a mother hen with her brood. It would have looked a little like a barn, no more than 16-17 feet in length, quite crudely built of stone, as in St. Piran's Oratory, or maybe it was even more simply constructed of cob, wattle, or wood, with a thatched roof and tiny slit windows to keep out the cold winds. Just a simple place of shelter, for the gathering of local people drawn to the cross, and the peace and love of God found in the new Christian religion.

It was not until the Normans invaded England that larger stone churches were commonly built. They were prolific builders; they built 135 churches in Cornwall alone. In fact, in 1259, when the Plantagenet King Henry II came to the throne, a total of 19 Cornish parishes were preparing for the dedication of their churches, and in 1259 Paul Church received its first (recorded) Priest.

The key is as follows: 1. Large stones 0.07-0.08 beneath floor. 2.Loose s. stones, brown earth + slates//pier (4). 3. Stones in line, laid 0.17 below top of (1) cut by (1). Clay/earth, orange mortar, irregular stones. 4. 0.17 of layer of lime mortar & slate, then on to (3). 5. 0.33 height of old wall—3 courses. 6. Higher stone lost, wall continues. 7. Loose ground. Includes bones and 1737 coffin lid.

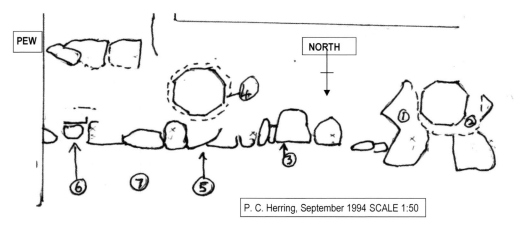

PEW

NORTH

P. C. Herring, September 1994 SCALE 1:50

Fifty years later Paul Church had four newly made altars, and they awaited consecration. This would indicate that before 1315 there was enlarging and rebuilding carried out, and the altars could indicate the presence of transepts. Or the two aisles, north and south, could have been added together, although it was more usual for one aisle to be added first. The north aisle with its altar, would by tradition, be dedicated to the Virgin Mary in pre-Reformation times. The small piscina in the south wall of the south aisle, is today, set lower than normal indicating floor level changes; this may be linked to the large crypt underneath. The piscina also indicates the presence of an altar, and dates from the pre-fire pre-Reformation Church. One concludes, therefore, that in the south aisle, east end, a fragment of pre-fire church (lower) wall remained. One has to act in the mode of Sherlock Holmes in Paul Church - but the clues to the past are there to be found, if not immediately obvious.

During the restoration of the floor in 1994, part of an old wall was discovered under the floor at the west end of the church. I was informed that no official archaeologist had investigated this area, as the builders were in a hurry to replace the floor. However, John George, Churchwarden, had had the foresight to record this wall with his camera. The photos are rather unclear, but then I was also lucky enough to find that Peter Herring, Archaeologist, had privately visited the Church whilst under restoration, had taken notes and drawn the wall (see above). This is part of his report:- *'Most of the church floor appears to have been disturbed during the extensive 19th c restorations (1828, 1864, 1873). Most important for understanding the development of the church was the length of foundation walling 20 m wide with only crudely finished large granite stones. This walling lay beneath the two western piers of the north aisle. It was not a foundation for the piers which were supported here, and elsewhere in the church by surprisingly uneven heaps of large stones, overlying the foundation wall. Rather, the foundations were for continuous masonry, most likely the early Nave wall. It seems likely that at some stage (probably Norman) the church either had a simple chancel and nave or was cruciform, with transepts at the junction of chancel and nave. Unfortunately these fragments of walling were not sufficient to determine which was the case.'*

The only way to understand the Herring drawing is to stand in the north aisle looking towards the south door, with the back of the last pew (of the row to the left of the nave), to your left. You can now see that the wall stretched from the second pillar from the back of the Church up to the pew. The wall does continue under the pew, but that is as far as was excavated at that time. Therefore, it seems that we could have had a sturdy Norman Church at Paul, possibly replacing an earlier simple Church building.

The celebrated Mr. Edmund H. Sedding in his book 'Norman Architecture in Cornwall' states *'one pier of the 14c arcade was worked in at the rebuild (1600), the rest of the Church is 16c and there is no sign of Norman Masonry'*. He, of course, did not have access under the floor!

In the main, Norman churches had thick walls of stone, round arches and small round arched windows. Although the Norman buildings were substantial, they generally built their churches of softer stone than granite, as the working of granite in those days was only crudely executed; softer stone was easier to carve.

The north wall of the old nave, left of the altar, lines up with part of the old wall (above ground) remaining at the back of the church, in which the last arcade pillar is embedded – a respond. It also lines up with the walling as illustrated. In fact at both sides of the altar there are thick walls in which arcade piers (responds) are embedded. These alignments indicate that the Church of Paul, existing in the time of the Plantagenet Kings, had an extraordinarily long nave that ran into a chancel and sanctuary. The nave and chancel of today have no visible distinction, such as a chancel arch to indicate where one ends and the other begins, other than the chancel step. The step position holds no clue either, as it was moved forward to give more room in the choir area in 1987. The pre-1987 line of the chancel step may still be seen in the position of the north aisle step; although, in the plan of 1873 illustrated later, there seems to be no definite chancel step present. The pre-Reformation rood screen would have provided the separation of nave and chancel. An interior photo (c.1960 p. 22) showing the spandrels, does have a line on the ceiling which could indicate the demarcation line between chancel and nave.

The early 14th century building would have been much more substantial than the original tiny Church, and it may have had transepts (ref: P. C. Herring), making it cruciform in shape. These date from the 1300s. The height of the walls to either side of the altar would indicate that the early wall plates of the roof would have been lower than in the present Church.

The pre-1595 pillars of catacleuse stone, fluted and decorated, with horizontal banding just below their capitals (examples may be seen in the small pillars at the 'little arch'), may have run in arcades from the west end to the east end, as the present arcades. Again, there is nothing to prove that the earlier arcades of the aisles were larger or smaller. The presence of the wall under the floor near the north aisle, does indicate that it may be older than the south aisle. The present circa 1600 capitals are plain, without decoration, topping the monolith octagonal granite pillars, supporting nine double chamfered arches. Curiously, the granite used for the pillars is much rougher and more weathered than that of the tooled and finer granite of some of the arches; this is especially apparent at the east end of the south aisle. As the pillars were severely damaged by the fire, the granite pillars of today only date from the rebuild, which was completed by 1600; there once being an inscription in the Church to this effect. The pre-fire pillars so fashioned as to be in keeping with a more ornate interior can be seen at the little arch in the chancel. This arch has been patched together, in a probable attempt to re-create what was there previously. The earlier stone (catacleuse) is much softer than granite, and when heated at high temperatures, I am reliably informed, explodes into pieces.

There is no evidence in the base of the Paul Church tower to prove that there was an earlier tower. In fact the tower stands squarely supported on the base raft, built to last, even the dreadful ravages of fire. Mr. Gilbert in his 'Survey of Cornwall' states that the walls and tower of Paul – as we see them today - were erected in the early part of the 15th century. About the tower he is correct, but incorrect about the walls (see Chapter 12).

INTERIOR 1910 CHOIR AREA - note different Reredos

It makes it rather frustrating not to be able to put a definite date on early Paul Church construction, and no local families are recorded as being involved with financing Church construction or embellishment. Hailes Abbey was the owner of the Rectorial tithes; one can wonder who would have paid for the erection of the tower. This would have been no mean feat in those days: before modern cranes, the layers of granite blocks would have been placed in position using horse or mule power, and winches used to elevate the huge stones to the top. Without any early records to enlighten the historian, one has to think logically about the sequence of events. Paul tower could be connected with the loss of a daughter chapel at Mousehole, which was used as a 'sea-mark'. In 1414, maybe the parishioners and Bishop Stafford realised that if a tower was constructed at Paul Church, standing where it does, it would be seen for miles. Therefore its construction could be placed sometime after this date. The transomed mullioned windows in the tower give no clue, as they were added later. The Mousehole Chapel was eventually reconstructed away from the shore-line, in a safer position, no longer needed as a sea-mark.

In August, 1315, there must have been some unrest in Paul Church, plus there were difficulties in communicating with Hailes Abbey. As on 22nd August, Brother Richard De Gloucestre, Proctor of the Abbey of Hailes appeared before Bishop Walter Stapledon (1308-1326), and begged him in the name of the Abbey and Parishioners of Paul, to consecrate four new altars in Paul Church. The Bishop sent word that he did not have the time on that occasion. He complained that as there

STAPLEDON

were no good roads, he began to suffer '*weariness and painfulness*' during his visits to the locality. This quote gives an insight into the humanity of a long dead Bishop, and one can just imagine the poor man wanting to go home, and still having to travel for days to get to Exeter.

INTERIOR c. 1905-10
Note the flue on the right from the 'heating apparatus', also the lectern on its plinth in the middle of the aisle.

Bishop Stapledon founded Exeter College Oxford in 1314. His successor Bishop James Berkeley died fourteen weeks into his pontificate, and was succeeded by Bishop John de Grandisson, who was inordinately interested in keeping the fabric of churches in his Diocese up to scratch. He insisted on reports being made on the fabric of churches in his See, and was not pleased with the state of some Cornish Churches (ref: Bishop's Register).

GRANDISSON

Eventually, Bishop Grandisson visited Paul Church while the Revd. John Bosevaran was the incumbent, and he consecrated the high altar on 11th July, 1336; although no mention is made of the other four altars, one would presume that having travelled so far, he would dedicate those concurrently. Nothing is recorded in his Registers to state to which Saint Paul (*Ecclesiastic Sancte Paulini*) the Church was **already** dedicated. He certainly could have put to rest much conjecture by recording which Saint Paul was correct. Two days later Bishop Grandisson consecrated the high altar at Madron (13th July, 1336), thus making full use of his presence in the vicinity.

The 1400s, generally, were a time for embellishing and beautifying churches throughout England. Early churches were very plain on the whole, and people wanted to let light into their buildings and made the windows larger, and they added decorative stone carving. Most churches before the Reformation would have had beautifully carved and painted wooden rood screens stretching across the aisles and nave, at the chancel step. The word 'rood' derives from the Anglo-Saxon 'rode' or 'rod' meaning 'cross'. The screen at Paul Church is likely have been intricately and fantastically carved with fruit and flowers, animals, birds and symbols of Christian worship. Rood screens had gilded and carved cornices, and lower panelling, usually beautifully painted and decorated with images of the Apostles or Saints, and the whole thing would have been a blaze of colour. Rood screens separated the congregation from the sanctuary or chancel and 'holy of holies' the sanctuary and main altar. When the doctrine of transubstantiation (*the belief that Christ was physically present in the consecrated Host*), was adopted in the second half of the 12th century by the church, the open chancel was enclosed behind this screen as being a too sacred for the ordinary congregation. Before rood screens were erected, a large painted cloth was tied across the chancel for the 40 days of Lent, to screen off the sanctuary and altar.

c.1817 note lowered left window and moved memorials

Interior of Paul Church
H P Trenerweirerae

During Lent the rood screen would often be covered with a veil or rood cloth, in black or violet, sometimes marked with a white cross. An acolyte would, at certain times of the year, read portions of the service from the rood loft, and sometimes, if the loft was of particularly large or substantial construction, musicians and singers would perform parts of the service from the top. If the rood loft was of lesser substance, only the '*rood man*' would go up the steps to light the candles illuminating the cross or rood above. He would have to be fairly slim to get through the '*creeps*' or hollowed out areas in the arcade spandrels, from one part of the rood loft in one aisle to the nave where the rood stood. The rood itself would take the form of Christ crucified on the cross (rood) with Mary His Mother at His right, and St. John at on His left. These figures again would be skilfully carved, making good use of local wood carvers.

The rood screen of Paul Church would have been similar to that at St. Buryan, and even in churches where the screen had been removed, evidence for its position may be seen in two doors in the walls of the north aisle. These tiny doors would lead to a curved staircase, which in turn would open out on to the top of the rood screen. Early doors always seem so small to us today; the tower door leading to the ringing chamber, up to the clock mechanism, tower roof and look-out turret, is really tiny. With centuries of good nutrition the human race has grown in stature.

The rood screen played a significant part in the ceremonial procession on Palm Sunday in the Middle Ages. Everyone was involved: the priests, acolytes and servers, and all the local village, would have been in the congregation. In fact, if people did not take Holy Communion they were not acceptable in society, and in the case of doctors and professional people, were not allowed to follow their profession. Thus a very colourful Procession would proceed out of the south door of Paul Church carrying torches and chanting. A standing cross in the churchyard (as we know Paul Church possessed), would also be very important on Palm Sunday, and would have been near the south door.

During the procession the cross would be a point of worship. The people would circumnavigate the Church in a clockwise (right) direction to the north side, which was where they believed the devil lived. At the north door the Priest would read the Litany, and then the whole procession would carry on to the west door, which was only used on important Holy days. The west door would then be slammed shut, and a ceremony similar to that on the opening of Parliament (Black Rod) would take place. The crucifer would knock on the west door three times using the large ceremonial cross (all churches would have had one of these, much larger than today's processional cross). The crucifer would demand entry for Christ (present in the pyx) into his church, whereupon the door was flung open. Two Priests would have stood by the west door with the consecrated host elevated in a pyx (Paul Church owned a silver pyx). The Procession would then bow down their heads to the Host, and pass through into the church where the black cloths were removed from the rood, and all would kneel on the floor for the next part of the service.

Belfry window, with empty niches

Holy Communion was taken with a housel-cloth stretched out underneath the Host preventing accidental slips. Palm Sunday Ceremony was very important liturgically as it marked the beginning of Holy Week. Today at Paul Church on Palm Sunday, the congregation, clergy and choir process up from the centre of the village to the Church singing 'Hosanna' and waving palms.

To return to the architecture. The word 'nave' comes from 'navis', a Latin word meaning a ship. Barrel vaulted or round ceilings are supposed to resemble upturned boats, or the Ark of Noah, especially when the roof rafters are showing. The whole nave then symbolises the church being a ship in which Christians sail to heaven. If one stands in the nave of Paul Church, and looks to the ringing chamber and choir vestry, the tower alignment as it abuts the nave is quite obviously off-centre, a fascinating detail! The mis-alignment of the nave and tower may be traced back to a possible cruciform early church. These were built off-centre from the central cell, in order to represent, if looking down from above, the lolling to one side of Christ's head in death on the cross. This was supposed to remind God of the sacrifice made by His Son, church architecture replicating the crucifixion. However, in the case of Paul Church, it may be that the post-1595 builders were in such a hurry to replace their burnt church, that they miscalculated and produced this anomaly.

The evidence for one high altar, and four smaller altars in Paul Church, lies in the amount of plate in its possession. There is a fuller list in Chapter 5, but Paul Church possessed five chalices and patens, one set for each altar! The rood screen could have contained altars situated on the west side of the screen facing east, on either side of the aisle. These small altars would be used for private devotions, or weekly offices, with the focus always being on the high altar for Sunday and Feast services.

The Spanish firing of Paul Church (described in Chapter 10) took place after the Reformation had commenced. Therefore it may be surmised that the church had already been defaced, the rood pulled down, and probably broken. Often the faces of Saints or Apostles were crudely scratched out and obliterated, and the painted walls whitewashed out. The three empty niches on the tower (see Chapter 12) would have contained figures of Saints and the Virgin Mary. The sign 'M' (or a fleur de lis) may still be seen where her statue would have stood, but with the coming of the Church of England under Henry VIII, all previous Catholic icons were removed by force. However the letters I.H.C. survived, and are translated in the Chapter 12.

Some churches managed to hide their precious pictures, icons and Catholic artefacts. Together with other churches in the district Paul's valuable silver Communion plate was taken to St. Mawes for safety. Fowey and Paul were the only Churches to possess a silver incense boat weighing 10 oz. (a full list of Paul Church plate with photo is listed in Chapter 5). In Queen Mary's time Paul is mentioned as '*one of the richest Parishes in the Deanery of Penwith*', and having seen the lists of other church possessions, Paul was very well endowed.

Richard Carew in his 'Survey of Cornwall' of 1603 mentions the Spanish Raid and states '*burnd not only the houses as they went by (Spaniards) but also the Parish Church of Paul – the force of the fire being such it utterly ruined all the great stone pillars thereof*'. Well, thank goodness for Richard Carew; he was a good friend of Sir Francis Godolphin, who engaged in combat with the Spaniards on West Penzance Green (see Chapter 10) and he received a first hand report of the whole raid from Sir Francis.

The almost complete demolition of the Church with the roof collapsing, and virtually all the pillars disintegrating, paints a picture of utter devastation. The people of Paul must have been heartbroken to lose not only their homes, but also their place of worship. Nevertheless, the Vicar, the Revd. John Tremearne (from 1581) had a stout heart. He was living in the western portion of his burnt Vicarage, and only had a small part of Paul Church in which to carry out his duties, but the Registers state that services of Baptism, Marriage and Burial were still being carried out from 23rd July, 1595.

The fact that the Vicar carried on taking Services to the best of his ability under really difficult circumstances must have lifted the spirits of the villagers of Paul. Their houses were also destroyed by fire, and the Vicar's undaunted fortitude must have given them the heart to carry on and rebuild their lives and homes. The tower being stoutly constructed didn't suffer much fire damage, apart from losing its bells and bell frame. During subsequent restoration smoke-blackened timbers were found in the tower, and the south porch, on being repaired in 1807, was found to contain a charred portion of the woodwork.

THE SITUATION OF THE CHURCH

Paul Church, built on a ridge, having a long central nave with two side aisles to north and south, with a magnificent tower and turret, presents an edifice of impressive portions, dwarfing the village in its grandeur. It is certainly is certainly imposing, and much to be envied; it is not hidden in any way, and was constructed to be seen, and admired from across Mount's Bay and for miles around (see Chapter 12 for details of the tower). It is not overly decorated with carvings, but is fashioned in a way to withstand the rigours of Cornish wind and precipitation, storms and squalls. A solid and true building – mirroring the 'no-nonsense or fuss' attitude in its sturdy construction. The outer walls are many feet thick, with deep windows and stout doors. The remaining antiquities are the tower; the Celtic cross head, and a shaft set in the outside wall at the north east end of the church; and possibly the lower part of the outside walls, particularly the west end of the north aisle. Also the north door (see below), the holy water recess in the south porch and the piscina in the south aisle. The rest of the building dates mainly from the 1600 rebuild but also has had many and varied restorations, therefore it is not an easy Church to read architecturally; in fact, it is an enigma!

Paul Church is very long! The chancel, nave and sanctuary together are 101 feet long by 20 feet wide, the north and south aisles being two feet shorter than the nave, and 15 ft 3 inches in width.

The nave has a marked slope down to the chancel steps; this runs parallel with the road outside. During an earlier restoration it was decided to *'keep the inclination of the Nave'*. Before 1873 the altar was raised up on three steps, and was in a much higher position than today, and the slope down would have made the main altar seem very elevated indeed.

The aisles were known as 'Newlyn' the north aisle, and 'Mousehole' the south aisle, with Paul villagers in the middle. The congregations for each aisle, from each district (before the construction of St. Peters, Newlyn), entered Paul Church in their corresponding door. Mousehole people came in the south aisle doors, and Newlyn people came up the round steps of the north west gate and into the Church by the old north door, or the west tower door. The tower is thirteen foot square inside (ref: VCH 1906).

South Porch Door

ENTRANCES

Today, the church is entered at the narthex, or vestibule (south porch), but would have once had its main ceremonial door at the west entrance of the tower. The west door of all churches was significant before the Reformation, for ceremonial processional entry during Christian Festivals. The west door is no longer used and its inner side has become a storage area in the choir vestry. The entrance steps are still in place.

The south porch is built for liturgical use, not just as a shelter to the south entrance or narthex. It was used particularly for parts of the wedding ceremony; these were performed by the Priest, before the Bride and Groom entered the main body of the Church to continue the ceremony. Surrounding the inner south porch door there is a magnificent specimen of Tudor workmanship: the carved dark catacleuse stone is wonderfully fluted and carved with pointed feet, is extremely handsome, and adds great importance to the entrance to Paul Church. The catacleuse stone is possibly the same material used for the original pre-1595 carved pillars at the 'arch' in the nave. It is covered with graffiti listed below:-

On the left side of the Door	On the right side of the Door
WD, JTR, RE, R, WH 1777,	ER, PD, EG, WL, TM,
William Maddern Oct 1752,	? ?703, WC, RH, P,
M, AR, RH,	John Marram or Mappam
AH – 1675	June 1738
RW – 17--	Richard Hodge 1738

The oldest of these carvings is 1675; these were probably made by children or young people waiting for their parents to come out of church. They certainly must have waited for a long time, as the carving is carefully executed in some cases and would have taken quite a while to perfect. Although the stone is much softer than granite, persistence would still have been employed to produce the end result – their marks, for posterity!

There is an empty support over this fine inner door, indicating a possible niche under the plaster; this would have held a statue in pre-Reformation times, of the Virgin Mary. Charred timbers were discovered in 1807, during repairs; this again indicates that this area was not ruined by the fire of 1595. Over the outside of the narthex is a sundial, described in Chapter 11.

The south aisle window and door have swapped places.
Note the curved altar table and side of block built Reredos.

The holy water stoop inset (right of photo porch door) was discovered under the plaster, whilst the porch was undergoing renovation during Revd. G. Harper's incumbency. Before the Reformation all members of the congregation would dip into the holy water and make the sign of the cross, before entering the church. These stoops were usually filled in and the original stoop taken out, pending a visit from the Commissioners of King Edward VI in 1549, or in late 1600s, if a Parliamentarian visit was expected. The corn measure (ref: Dr. J. Mattingly) which now sits in the original stoop surround, was discovered by Janie Curnow in a hole under a cobbled floor while workmen were working in Duck Street, Mousehole.

The inner north door now painted green dates from before 1873. Over both the north and south (east end) doors were internal porches and curtains, to keep out drafts. The small south door had a large water tank over its porch, supplying the heating system hidden in wooden casing.

There were grand designs for the doors at this time (1873) but it seems that they were not carried out. The small south aisle door, at the east end, was merely for the Priest to slip into and out of his Church without mixing with the ordinary people. This door gave access to the area east of the rood screen, the most holy part of the Church. Often the Priest would store his vestments near the altar and robe in this area before taking Mass. Today this door has a filigree wrought iron gate on the outside, and is mainly used to keep the Church cool in summer during Services, or for disabled access. It was once situated to the right of its present position (see H. P. Tremenheere's watercolour, above).

The north door would often be used at funerals: it led to the north side of the Church, the place where the sun did not shine. Traditionally this was the place where the devil dwelt, and where the churchyard was used for less important burials or miscreants of the Parish. Paul had very little burial space actually surrounding the Church, therefore the north side would have been as important as any other burial place near the building. The outer frame of the north door at Paul is also of great antiquity; it survived the Spanish raid, and is decorated with early Tudor hood moulding, containing decorated spandrels. North doors were significant during Baptism (see 'Font' section). Steps lead down into the Church from the narthex and also from the north door.

THE FONT

On the immediate left of the south door is the granite font. It is a modern copy of a font in the north of Cornwall. In 1865 it was reported that a more modern font should be made to replace the earlier one. The old font appears, on architectural drawings of 1873 (Salter & Pellow in the C.R.O.). Therefore a date after 1873 may be given for the introduction of the new granite font into Paul Church. As no plaque records this event, a definite date for the advent of this font cannot be given. The new font was certainly in place in 1912 as Mr. Charles Cox mentions a fine granite font to the left of the south entrance, in his book 'The Churches of Cornwall' published in that year.

In C. Aitken's Church History (1910) when discussing earlier restorations, he describes the old font:
'the font was very small and on a plain stone pedestal with a square top – with a depression capable of holding as much water as an ordinary basin'.

He omits to describe the modern font; this may be because he also knew no definite date for its erection.

The old font used to stand in the middle of the nave, at the back of the Church, in line with the north door and the second pillar from the back (see illustration: Salter & Pellow 1873). It is now in the new Vicarage garden; its curved stone base is flattened on one side as if it once was attached to something else. It really could be mistaken for a pedestal, or chimney pot (!) and looks quite at home in a garden.

Fonts are placed near the main entrance of churches, usually to the left, signifying the entrance by Baptism into the Christian Faith. Previously the modern font had a plain round wooden cover, described as *'extremely heavy'*. The present ornate wooden font cover was the gift of Mr. and Mrs. Albert Waters, who donated the money in memory of their son Laurence who was killed during the Second World War on 23rd November, 1944, aged 31.   Laurence was a driver in the Royal Army Service Corps. He was the second son of Albert George and Clara Bertha Waters of Middle Kemyel, and the husband of Aubreen Waters. He is buried in Leopoldsburg War Cemetery, Belgium (research: Bob Harrison).

The present Font

A word about Baptisms in the pre-Reformation times: the font, would have been big enough to totally immerse the infant. During the ceremony the baby would be immersed on one side, and turned over, again immersed on the other side, then the infant would be totally immersed face downwards!

This cannot have been a pleasant experience as the child would probably have screamed with fright, and it has been reported that many of the babies actually died from the cold caught during Baptism. It was firmly believed in the Middle Ages, (as mentioned above) that the Devil was present at a Baptism, and in order to let him out to 'his' part of the churchyard, the north door was always left open during a Christening Service.

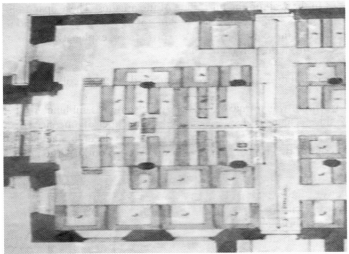

The old font may just be seen near to the pillar mid Nave. Note the Harmonium, Children's seating and the steps each side of this area, leading up to the back of both aisles which were on the same level as the Tower door c. 1873.

Natural cross

THE LECTERN

The Lectern in the shape of an eagle with wings outstretched is made of brass, and was presented by the 'Ladies of the Church in 1904'. It used to stand in the middle of the nave, on a granite plinth cut in the same pattern as that on which the font now stands. This plinth is presently leaning up against the churchyard wall. It was an anonymous gift to Paul Church on 24th April, 1905. The lectern plinth contains a small Cross of feldspar twinned crystal – described as a:
    '*natural production untouched by tools*'.

Lectern plinth

ARCADES, SPANDRELS & INCLINATION

The nave and aisles are connected by nine arches on each side. The third arch is much smaller and is of rather disjointed construction, and is the subject of much conjecture, discussed below. The stone arches incline distinctly to the north and south of the nave, and iron braces, bolted through the spandrels between the arches, control the movement. There use to be at least six of these but today there are three. The inclination of the pillars is open to much speculation; a well-respected architect visited Paul Church some years before 1910, and had the strong opinion that the pillars were purposely built with a slant in opposite directions. This theory is supported by the fact that the pillars at St. Keverne in the Lizard are built in a similar fashion. However, others firmly believe that their lean is due to insufficient foundation support.

The iron braces, according to J. T. Blight, were in place holding the north and south arcade walls together before 1885. Some have been removed (1987), especially at the chancel end of the nave, where one can see the ties in the wall on the outer side of the arcades. These spandrels prevent further movement of the pillars, which is mainly due to the lack of substantial foundations under the piers, and ensure the church walls stay firm. Two explanations, from Revd. Aitken, for the pillars' departure from the perpendicular:-

1. In all very widely arched buildings there is really more danger of collapse than expansion.
2. In some churches the intention was to make the Nave bear some resemblance to the shape of a ship or Ark sides. The capitals were evidently cut deeper on one side than the other so as to throw the top wall perpendicular. The whole arch, facing the western door, is formed out of two stone blocks; these are worked out of large pieces of granite.

Five Spandrels or braces c. 1950s

The braces, although not attractive, have their uses as for hanging decorations such as at Paul Feast or Christmas, and the brilliantly colourful felt and embroidered banner produced for the May Fest 2002.

GALLERIES

The Royal Cornwall Guardian of 28th April, 1865, proved that Paul Church did possess two adjoining galleries. '*The orchestra and a curious flower stand gallery at the west end, erected by the late Vicar have been removed*'. The late Vicar could be Revd. C. G. Ruddock Festing or Revd. John Garrett.

One gallery stretched across the nave from the back of the Church to the second pillars of the arcade. This gallery probably carried on across to the north aisle wall, where some supports still may be seen: one in the present vestry, one on the wall, and two near the north door.

The gallery across the rear of the Church was for the 'orchestra', which presumably supplied music for services before the first harmonium/organ was installed. Apparently the congregation would turn to the galleries when music was sung or played, and thus the origin of the expression 'face the music' was born! The cut notches in the capitals over the pillars along the right side of the nave, would have been the slots for wooden gallery supports. This has always been puzzling as the right hand side cut marks continue down to the fourth pillar, but only on this side! It is presumed that a single gallery extended up to the fourth pillar on the south side of the nave, which was probably attached to the main gallery at the back. The steps or stairs to these galleries were probably made of wood, like the galleries themselves, and were also removed.

A second '*flower stand gallery*' seems a little odd, but knowing how much the Victorians loved large floral displays and utilised flower stands, this would have been a good place to store them. All galleries were removed during the sweeping changes of Revd. Dr. W. Carpenter Vicar (1864-1865).

THE ARCH

H. P. Tremenheere, watercolour - early 19th C

This small arch has been the subject of much speculation and conjecture. The main fact remains that no-one really knows the answer for its existence. Theories that abound are many, including that it could be a Sepulchral Arch, used when the coffin came into the church through the north door carried by Priests or Acolytes. Bearers would have passed it through this arch to the sanctuary for the Service of Committal. After the Service, it would have been ceremoniously passed back through the arch from Priests to Pall-bearers, and out of the north door, thence to the graveside. This last passing through the arch signified the passing from this transitory life, to life everlasting.

Or it could be a joining feature of nave and chancel (see earlier chancel step reference), two different parts of the body of the Church. Another theory is that, pre-Reformation, it was some sort of hagioscope, or squint, from the north aisle or north transept, enabling those to see the main altar and the elevation of the Host. Some say it was connected to the rood screen, however that does not seem really feasible. Was it merely constructed out of pieces left after the fire for sentimental value? Does it echo a feature that existed before the fire? Conjecture reigns but uncertainty rules!

There was a thought that the pillar to the left of the arch could still be in its original position, before the collapse of the Church. Unfortunately, looking at its plinth, the angle of the pillar base and the pillar itself, it is obvious that they do not correspond (ref: Eric Berry). Yet another theory is that the pulpit arch had to be slightly wider to accommodate the pulpit (perhaps with a sounding board), and in order to line up the pillars in an orderly and aesthetically pleasing way to the altar, a small arch was constructed, allowing the next two pillars to be in parallel across the chancel.

It is highly likely that Paul villagers wanted to incorporate their ruined Church into the architecture of the new building of 1600, and thus salvaged pieces from the ruined pillars, as the majority exploded under the heat of the fire. One piece of old pillar may still be seen outside at the bottom of the churchyard wall, near the south churchyard gate. These old pillars are similar to those in the south aisle of Truro Cathedral (St. Mary's Church), and their decoration of bands at the top is quite unusual. They may be dated to the reign of Henry II (1154-1189). This could indicate that the second Church of St. Paul was of an even earlier date than the 14th century.

The arch was known in the 20th century as 'The Memorial Arch', as the list of those killed in the First and Second World Wars used to hang in the middle of it, and flowers were always placed beneath the names on the Roll of Honour. In fact, until recently, flowers were always placed in the middle of the arch by a kind member of the congregation and ex-choir lady, Dawn Pentreath.

I recently discovered three watercolours of Paul Church interior painted by Mr. Henry Pendarves Tremenheere; these pose some more interesting questions about this area.

Henry Tremenheere was born in Penzance in 1775, and he lived in his deceased wife's home of Treneere House at Madron until his death at the house 26th February, 1841, aged 66. There is a monumental window dedicated to him in Madron Church. In 1817 he retired from the sea as a Captain, and it is likely that he painted these pictures after this date. Only the dates of his life and death are on the watercolours. Three of these paintings are in this Chapter.

The large stone that makes up the bottom of the arch stands 3'6" above the ground and is shaped very much like the top of an old stone coffin. It has a cemented recess in its top surface. This once carried a wall (see the watercolour) and there is no sign of the arch above. This poses the question, why was the arch covered up by plaster, and the Godolphin Memorial placed on top (now in the north aisle east end)? The painting also shows the whitewash that was on the pillars of the church before 1864. The pieces of pillars making up the arch are said to be 'smoke-blackened' from the fire. I have consulted several experts (Eric Berry, David Scott) on this phenomenon, and they have assured me that the popular local myth of smoke-blackening from the 1595 fire is not possible, as this stone is naturally dark.

The explanation for the 'mottled' appearance has finally been discovered. In The Royal Cornwall Gazette of 1865, it was reported that during the incumbency of the Revd. Dr. W. Carpenter (1864-65), he had all the whitewash removed from the granite pillars, and everywhere else, in the Church. The dark pillars of the arch, being of softer catacleuse stone than the granite pillars, absorbed the whitewash making it impossible to remove, and it stained the stone a shade lighter. These old pillar fragments, and the tops of their capitals, still show flecks of white, making the illusion of smoke blackening; the original pillars were naturally as dark as the Tudor surround of the south porch entrance.

It is highly likely that when the whitewash was being removed from the pillars in 1865, that the large Godolphin memorial was moved to the north aisle, and the Hutchens' memorial moved to the south aisle. The arch would then have been uncovered, maybe by accidental damage to this area, and the whole area opened up again, as at the re-build of 1600.

PEWS & SEATING

Pews were common in churches after the Reformation, but before this time there was very little seating, only a few seats around the pillars for the old and infirm, hence *'the weakest to the wall'* where people would lean. During the reign of Queen Elizabeth very long sermons lasting several hours were introduced, and the need for pews for the comfort of the congregation became vital. The Tremenheere paintings also show the many large 'horse box' pews abounding in Paul Church, each of its occupants was firmly held in a little area of their own. The occupants often were seated facing each other.

In Paul Church, before the 1873 restoration, the church was bursting with pews. Again, during the 1987 restoration more pews were removed from the back of the Church, and from the south aisle east end, where the pews turned towards the chancel and altar, and those pews at the back of the Church were placed in tiers. There was an area of tiered pews in the side aisles that were elevated; this may be seen on the interior drawing in the 'Font' section of this Chapter. Pew rentals were sources of income for the Church, although those who collected them took their cut as perks. Pew disputes – legal and 'friendly'- are discussed in other Chapters of this book.

This is the format of a Pew rental ticket:

	PAUL CHURCH PEW RENTS
…………...19……..	……………………………………………...19…….
Received from	**Received from**…………………………………………………….
………………………….	*The sum of*…………………………………………………………*Pounds*
No…………………..	…………………………………………*shillings and* …………………… *Pence*
Sittings………………	**Seat No.** ……………….*Sittings*……………. ………..Half 19………….
	£…………………………………………….. ………………………

Before 1873, the choir pews were large with large carved fleur de lis *'poppy heads'* ends. They had very sensible book rests, and kneelers. These continued in use until the restoration of the Church in 1987. Revd. Tyrrell (Vicar 1960-66) was a talented artist and carved a new choir pew to resemble the others, with trefoil inserts. In 1873, when the Church was being

re-ordered, on the Architectural plans was written:

'n.b. the <u>entire</u> west end and all the <u>north</u> aisle seats will be declared free and un-appropriated'

Choir after Evensong: 5th April 1983 - note old choir pews

However in the Vestry Minutes of 17th November, 1873 at the re-opening of the newly refurbished church it was reported that:

'All seats should be free on a first come first served basis. Appropriation of Sittings – All Sittings in the Nave of the church should be charged 9d per quarter, and all sittings in the aisles at 6d per quarter.' An Amendment was passed *'All sitting in the pews in the aisles which join the pews in the nave 8d per quarter. Southern aisle or elsewhere next to the wall – 6d (Mousehole side) sittings in the North aisle or Newlyn side – 6d.'*

In 1875 it was 'resolved that in future Churchwardens would receive 5% of the amount of the pew rents instead of seven shillings each. The Churchwardens changed every year, one acted as a Vicar's Warden, and one as a Parish Warden. Pew disputes were common and some are reported elsewhere in this book, see the Vestry Minutes (Chapter 6).

WINDOWS

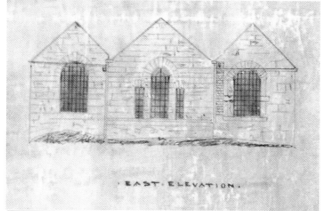

Hutchens' House stone tracery in the wall, possibly from 1600

Paul Church unfortunately does not contain any medieval stained glass, owing to the rebuild of 1600. However there are old pieces of stone (granite) tracery, the same as the top of the tower windows, set into the side of Hutchens' House.

East Window 1873 - note only three lights in the main nave window, note unchanged right window

The Tremenheere paintings depict the windows without stained glass, making the Church very light, especially in the Sanctuary; despite the presence of a large reredos behind the altar, the large eastern plain glass window still allowed lots of sunlight to penetrate the interior. This east window of five lights was inserted 29th March, 1875, designed by Mr. Sedding, as was the Tower west window. Some windows are in different places than may be seen today. One notable window has swapped places with today's door in the south aisle, next to the piscina.

The present windows are in need of restoration: the mullions are crumbling due to the force of the rain and wind on the polyphant stone. Other windows were of plain glass, as described by the Revd. Aitken in 1910, as 'churchwarden' or 'Engine House' plain Georgian windows. 'Engine House' windows are so named as they are reminiscent of those in mine engine houses, and one of these windows still remains at the east end of the north aisle. Some windows have hood mouldings and some are unprotected. At this time the stained glass in the south aisle east window 'Ascension' was inserted, dedicated to the Revd. R. Malone. Most of the other windows were subsequently replaced with polyphant stone tracery and mullions, returning the Church to the look of the original granite mullioned windows of the middle ages. There are inconsistencies in the window design: some are rounded and some pointed.

Wooden window, north aisle east end

On Monday 21st June, 1875, Messrs. Bone of Liskeard commenced work in placing two new windows (ref: 'Cornish Telegraph', it doesn't mention which windows). It was proposed to replace all the windows as funds allowed.

The second sky-light

One window in the north aisle is very much lower than its neighbour; in this area today one can see a stone sill, protruding in the north wall, marking its original position. Mr. Tremenheere's painting shows the lower window, which would have been removed and replaced by the higher 'Tonkin' window after the restoration of the walls after a storm in 1828.

The stained glass was all put in after 1873, and the windows are described in Chapter 7, as they are all memorials to people of the Parish. There is an interesting window in the Vicar's Vestry – from the outside can be seen that its tracery is constructed of wood; this window is not that old, and dates from post 1873 (see photo on preceding page).

There are parts of very old granite mullions lying in the churchyard, and one ancient corbel in the crypt - these would have been part of the windows of pre-Georgian times, and may even date to before the fire in 1595.

THE ROOF

In the Diary of William Williams of Newlyn, (who was mainly concerned with weather forecasts and fishing) under the heading 'Remarkable Occurrences or Principal Events', he writes:

> *'1780 – Paul church timbred lafted and plaistred as Compass roof in 1778'*

Old roof timbers

A compass roof has a ridge in the centre, and has rafters or ties where components of the structure form an arch on the underside (taken from J. Curls' 1992 Encyclopaedia of Architectural Terms). The original roof of the Church in 15th C would have been a wagon roof plastered in sections leaving moulded purlins, principal rafters and wallplates exposed. After the fire in 1595 the roof was restored thus. Many original principal rafters survived, as did many purlins in the south aisle. Further, the vast majority of purlins and principal rafters are *moulded to be exposed* as in a wagon roof. There are two or three pre-1595 timbers left in the north aisle for future architectural interest; this fact has been confirmed by Scott & Company, who undertook the restoration. As the photo shows there was a second sky-light in the roof opposite the remaining sky-light which lights the Pulpit; the second would have thrown light on to the Clerk's Desk.

1777 The woodwork of roof had become so patched, and decayed, the solution was made to put in a barrel ceiling with cornices for two reasons: One, architectural, and fashion. Two, the financial saving.

On 8th December, 1828, James Harvey and Alexander Berryman wrote a letter on the state of the Church. Following a severe gale the Church was *'rendered wholly unsafe and unfit for worship'*. It states that the south wall of the south aisle is in a very dilapidated state, leaning outwards nearly one inch to every foot in height, and appears to be going further. The north wall of the north aisle is particularly perilous, and if the roof should be shaken by a storm it would fall without the least warning, as there is tremendous pressure against the walls. This rendered the Church in a dangerous state and the letters asked for permission to licence the School Room for Divine Service while repairs are carried out.

The roof slates are described as *'rotten, being laid several times, the laths tolerably good but the nails are done – the deal rafters laid on the circular ribs of the former old roof about 25 years ago (1797) has added much weight on the ceilings. The plaster is done and the earth mortar is spent having no strength to hold to its key and must be all done new, the plaster on the side walls is weak also, in consequence of the failure of the walls'.*

On 14th April, 1884 under the Revd. Aitken the roof was reported to be *'unsatisfactory and unsafe, owing to weakness'.* 1st July, 1894, restoration of the roof is complete. Again, in 1910, the Revd. Aitken stated that *'the whole of the roof has been strengthened, and re-slated.'* It seems an ongoing problem, which is hopefully now in 2006 – solved!

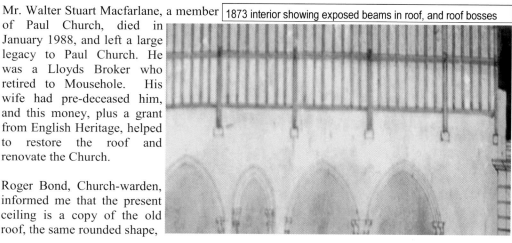

Eric Harvey, Churchwarden for 25 years

At Eric Harvey's funeral in 1986, Phillip Stephens, a builder from Mousehole, noticed dry rot in the roof at the end of the south aisle, and said it needed urgent attention. Also in 1986, after a concert in Church, a piece of cornice fell on the Vicar's stall, both dry and wet rot were discovered in the roof after an inspection. In 1989, as the roof timbers *'are good and sound'*, and in better condition than at any time for a good 300 years, it seemed logical to leave some timbers exposed. A Petition was started by John George for the return of the roof to an open timbered structure, but English Heritage would not allow this to happen, and insisted that the plaster ceilings be reinstated. These ceilings give Paul Church its remarkable acoustics.

1873 interior showing exposed beams in roof, and roof bosses

Mr. Walter Stuart Macfarlane, a member of Paul Church, died in January 1988, and left a large legacy to Paul Church. He was a Lloyds Broker who retired to Mousehole. His wife had pre-deceased him, and this money, plus a grant from English Heritage, helped to restore the roof and renovate the Church.

Roger Bond, Church-warden, informed me that the present ceiling is a copy of the old roof, the same rounded shape, and when it was renewed split chestnut laths and an old method of plastering was tried, but unfortunately did not work. The ceiling was plastered onto wire mesh in a more modern fashion. The walls were once painted yellow ochre and the wall plate was brown, and latterly dark turquoise. The Church had a darker interior than today, mainly due to dark décor and the presence of the reredos and many stained glass windows (see 1905 interior photo).

C. Aitken states in 1910 *'the whole of the roof has been strengthened, and re-slated'*, but the roof problems were ongoing, largely due to the exposed position of the Church to winter gales.

Old pulpit c. 1905-10

In 1994 the restoration of what, in effect, were three separate roofs of the nave and both aisles, plus the renewal of the floor, was an enormous undertaking. Services carried on as normal – underneath the scaffolding, for roughly two to three years. The roof was the first to be renewed, followed by the renovation of the floor, which was completed in sections so as to cause less disruption. A time capsule was placed in the roof over the Sanctuary, in the form of a pot thrown by potter, John Swan (choir member and bell ringer) containing a rough history of the Church.

PULPITS

Proposed wooden pulpit 1873 next to small arch

Pre-Reformation pulpits were used, not for sermons, but for exhorting the congregation to prayer. Well off parishioners would pay for prayers to be said for their souls; this could carry on for many years, with the church receiving fees for same. It wasn't until Thomas Cranmer's time (1485-1556) that preaching from a pulpit based on his Book of Homilies largely came into being.

No doubt Paul Church once had a massive wooden pulpit with a sounding board, as those possessed by many churches. In a 1905-1910 photo, there may be seen a carved octagonal wooden pulpit, in roughly the same position as the granite pulpit of the present time. The very old wooden pulpit was rumoured to have had a cantilever floor, this sounds like pure conjecture, but I was informed that it could be moved up and down by a lever to accommodate short and tall Clergy alike!

Apparently, one Vicar said the words of Jesus to His disciples (St. John 16.16)

Pulpit in correct position as photo, c. 1905/10

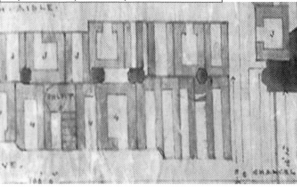

'A little while and ye shall not see me; and again, a little while and ye shall see me', there was a crack, and the floor went down, and he did too! Who knows if that is true or not, but it's fun, and is just one of the rich tapestry of tales I have come across whilst researching!

In 1873 there was a plan to have a new pulpit with access steps cut through the memorial arch, as you can see from the architectural drawing. This did not happen, and a new granite carved octagonal pulpit was placed in the church in memory of Revd. Robert Wesley Aitken in 1911, as is carved on the stone steps. This pulpit was carved in 1910 to a design by Mr. Sedding, by Arnold Snell, stonemason, and Grandfather to Steve Snell. The brass candlesticks and book rest were inherited from the old pulpit, and they very much enhance the preaching area.

REREDOS

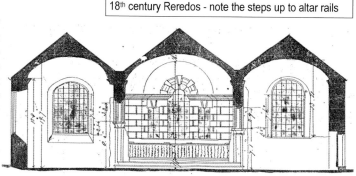

18th century Reredos - note the steps up to altar rails

In 1873, there was a very large reredos stretching across the substantial plain glass east window. It was built up in courses, carrying on to the side walls of the sanctuary, (see drawing) and quite plain.

The reredos was broken by a gap in the middle and smaller slits for light penetration on either side. The smooth tapering of the plaster on top of the two memorials either side of the altar today, indicates where part of the reredos reached over these monuments, forming a projecting lintel. The top of the Pendarves memorial, today echoes the shape of the lintel.   This could indicate that this first reredos was erected in Revd. H. Pendarves' time, c. 1694-1739, as the Vicarage was also built (1726) and new bells put in the tower (1727). During his incumbency there seemed to be plenty of money around to get things done. Part of this reredos may be seen in the Tremenheere painting, also in the architectural sketch by Messrs. Salter & Perrow.

Although this reredos was sizeable, the window behind was larger, with one principal and two small lights. The clear glass, and openings in the reredos, meant that the sunlight could still pour into the body of the church. This was replaced in 1888 by another gothic-shaped reredos of white and pink alabaster. It had a large pointed central panel and two smaller pointed side panels. It was erected by Revd. Malone in memory of his Father, the Vicar of Pendeen. Presumably this reredos was removed when the Bolitho window was erected after 1915. It may just be seen in the background of the photo of the church interior (1910). Parts of this reredos were subsequently stored in the boiler room, but are no longer there today.

There were gothic shaped boards, known as Decalogues, removed in 1972, which used to stand either side of the altar.   On these were written the Ten Commandments. Their large predecessors are now either side of the tower arch, at the rear of the church. Canon H. Miles Brown, on writing about Paul Church, dates these boards at the back from 1716 (see photos at end of Chapter). Another board hung at the back of the church with the psalm the 'Venite' thereon. These decorated boards were often hung to replace pictures of Holy icons taken down at the Reformation.

SANCTUARY & ALTAR

The Tremenheere paintings show the old sanctuary with mahogany turned communion rails stretching across from pillar to pillar. The Revd. Aitken describes our communion rails as '*curious*', as there are few examples of such '*thickly set and massive*' communion rails.

On examination of the present communion rails, one can see that these are, indeed, the original rails with extensions bringing them forward to the arrangement of today. The post-1873 joins are evident. This enables the dating of the handsome mahogany rails, with their rounded corners, to well before 1817.

There were two steps for kneeling at the communion rails, and the altar was elevated up another step, probably to enable those in high-sided pews to see the Vicar at the altar. The watercolours show an altar table bare of vestments, with curved decoration; no description exists to indicate the type of wood of which it was made. There is now only one step up into the sanctuary. This area today contains two prie-dieux, and two oak decorated chairs for visiting clergy. Mrs. Conrad Barber gave these to Paul Church in the 1970s (Faculty dated 5th October, 1975), to replace two chairs that had seen better days.

ORGANS & HARMONIUM

There was an harmonium at the back of Paul Church (see drawing in 'Font' section) - but as these two conflicting newspapers report - it could have been present *as well as* an organ.

In the 'Cornish Telegraph' dated 1878, the harmonium was reported to have been '*admirably played by a Mr. F. H. Griffin in Paul Church*'. This caused me some consternation when I read the following for 1865, some thirteen years earlier. I can only surmise that both were in place for a while. Or the writer could have been mistaking an harmonium for an organ; with both authentic newspaper dates, it's hard to imagine what was really going on. The Royal Cornwall Gazette, 28[th]April, 1865:- the Vicar (Revd. Dr. W. Carpenter) '*has also supplied funds for a new organ which is to be placed in the Church in early May*'.

R.C.G. – Friday 19th May, 1865 – '*On Sunday a new organ presented to this Church, by Revd. W. Carpenter, the worthy Vicar, was opened. The Church both morning and evening was crammed to excess and many were unavoidably excluded. The organ, which is gothic style of pattern, intended to correspond with the interior of the Church, was designed by Mr. Sedding architect of Penzance, and was built by Mr. James Verran of Penzance. It consists of the full stops First Open Diapason CC, Second Stopt Diapason CC, third Dulciana, CC, Fourth Principal CC, fifth 15th CC, sixth Twelfth CC, Seventh the pedal Bourdais CC, twelve note spare slider for a trumpet and two composition pedals – the fine toned instrument has the great advantage of being built entirely damp proof. On Sunday sermons were preached by the Reverend W. Carpenter after which a collection was made in aid of the Parochial School amounting to £2.10.0d in addition to a donation of £2 from a friend in Manchester. In the evening a collection amounted to £10 – total for school £20. Mr. Henry Viner late Organist to St. Paul's Church Penzance, presided at the instrument – the following was the music: 'Gloria in Excelsis' by Pergolesi, 'Awake the Harp' Haydn, 'Hallelujah' by Handel. The anthem was 147th psalm in the morning and 24th psalm in the evening – 'The earth is the Lords'. We understand that Mr. Richard Berryman of Halwyn, Paul is appointed the Organist.*'

There was a Bill for the repair of an 'organ' from Easter 1876-1877 totalling £1.10.0d. This organ was pumped by hand as described in Chapter 12. The organ was thoroughly restored again by Hele & Company, on 1st July, 1894 at a cost of £45. On 10th July, 1939, the sum of £30 was set aside for a new organ fund; at that time the organ was in the north aisle, and the console was behind a wooden parclose screen which was erected in 1964. The organist sat with his back to the choir, until the console was moved in 1962, to its present site in the south aisle, and electric wires transferred signals from the keyboard to the pipes across the chancel under the floor.

On 19th May, 1941 the organ was insured against war damage for £250, and on 27th May, 1949 an electric blower was inserted for the organ, and Joe Llewellyn the organ 'pumper' was very grateful to Mr. Bath's generosity! More about Joe in Chapter 3.

This organ was not so large as its successor, and it did not obscure the 'Richards Bath' window. There is a Faculty for the works on the installation of a new pipe organ in 1962. The second pipe organ of Paul Church came from St. Michael's Church in Newquay. On Saturday 6th October, 1962 there was a Service held for the Dedication of the new organ taken by the Assistant Bishop of Truro. This may be viewed in full in the C.R.O. The Vicar of Paul, the Revd. J. H. Tyrell, wrote:

'The members of Paul Church express their grateful thanks to Canon C. K. Peeke and the P.C.C. of Newquay for donating to us their old organ. It has been rebuilt by Hele & Company Ltd., of Plymouth, and we express our thanks to them for all the care and trouble they have taken to provide the best instrument with the money available. The new organ replaces an instrument of uncertain origin, which was in use for approx. 150 years. It became badly worm eaten and no longer tuneable. All must agree that the new organ proves a very beautiful addition to the Church, and we are most grateful to those who gave so generously towards the cost of rebuilding and to those who laboured in the Church preparing the site.'

In the Parish Magazine for April 1985 it is reported that the Organ had been valued at: £40,000 (in March 1985). In 1988 when the roof had to undergo a complete rebuild, this organ was dismantled in order to obtain access to the roof and walls. A faculty for the removal of the pipe organ was posted in the porch. It was intended to restore the organ when the roof was renewed and decorated, however it was found that it needed some renovation. An electronic organ was purchased as a 'short-term' measure (ref: letter Diocesan Secretary: C. B. Gorton, 7th December, 1988). There were objections when it was discovered in the Parish that the pipe organ was not going to be returned, and it remained in storage. These objections, together with a Petition, were taken to two Hearings in Truro. The objections were defeated, and subsequently the P.C.C. passed a resolution to dispose of the pipe organ on 24th April, 1990. The temporary organ was placed on the same spot as the previous organ console, and the pipe organ was sold on to St. Sampson's Church, Golant, and remains there today, although in a slightly smaller modified version.

Correspondence on this matter appeared in 'The Cornishman' for November 1990. The Revd. Fr. Denys Griffin of Goldsithney wrote expressing his dismay at the removal of the pipe organ on 1st November. On 8th November, Mr. Vaughan L. Tregenza of Mousehole replied in strong terms extolling the 'fine organ' and supporting Revd. Griffin. The following week the Revd. G. Harper wrote in reply, welcoming the interest, and defending the replacement of a pipe organ with an electronic organ. Mr. John Harry, our present Organist, also wrote a letter that appeared in 'The Cornishman' supporting the virtues of the pipe organ.

Today in 2006, Paul Church members are undertaking to raise the money to replace the electronic organ with a modern digital instrument. Half of the proceeds of the sale of this book will go into the new organ fund. The new instrument will enhance the music of the services, and the many concerts which now take place at Paul Church, a Church well known for its spirituality, acoustics, choir and music.

FLOOR & LIGHTING

As with the Church roof, floors also cause problems, and in 1872 the floor was renovated and encaustic tiles in the sanctuary were to be taken away, but more were to be placed in the '*chancel passage*'.

There have always been steps leading down from the west door into the tower chamber, as the slope of the hill outside means one had to step down from the west end. Outside the tower chamber door the floor remained level as one entered the Church, and a level floor carried on into the back of both the north and south aisles. These steps lead to the many pews at the back of the aisles, all numbered and arranged in tiers. From these side aisle areas there were two steps down each side, roughly in line with the arcades leading down to the level of today's compass round, where the children's seating, the harmonium and old font stood. This may be seen on the floor plan of Salter & Perrow (1873) at the end of this book in the References.

In September 1930, the floor collapsed in the *'Free Seats area'* at the back of the Church, owing to dry rot. The tiled floor of today dates from the restoration of 1987, replacing a similar tiled floor, interspersed with blue/grey slate slabs. The Tremenheere paintings show large flagstones in place between 1774-1841.

The floor is full of intramural burials and vaults – these are described in the Burials Chapter. Today, more floor space than ever is exposed to view; pre-1873 very little of the floor could be seen, with a narrow main aisle, narrow side aisles, and pews covering all. In fact, as stated, in the Burials Chapter, the parishioners were very surprised at the cracked state of the floor when some pews were removed and renewed. It was only then they realised they were in danger from noxious fumes and infection from those buried beneath their feet. There are no records of a new floor; maybe they just repaired the cracks. However, new encaustic floor tiles were laid in the chancel and the baptistery by 31st October, 1899. By the communion rails in the south aisle are the initials 'J.J.' embedded in the grey slate, a maker's mark perhaps.

Scott & Company designed the present round decoration in front of the Choir Vestry. It is constructed of slate and granite, and breaks up, and adds interest to, the quarry tiled areas. The round resembles a compass, but was not intended as such, despite the maritime links of Paul Church. It is not fixed on any particular orientation. Its purpose is to open up in a circular format the processional route between west to east emphasising, and focusing on, an area for gathering and then dispersing, from that point after a Service.

There was a renovation in 1910 reported by the Vicar of Paul at that time the Revd. Aitken. He states: '*the regard for economy necessitated by the 'limited means of the parishioners' is to be expected in a Parish whose inhabitants with few exceptions depend upon their own exertions for an honourable livelihood. The work done is solid and creditable but the pews were of the kind known as 'horse boxes' and the windows were more suitable for public offices than the home of sacred worship.*'

The many restorations were begun by volunteer parishioners and landowners, and carried on through the incumbencies of Revd. Dr. Carpenter, Revd. Garrett and the Revd. R. Malone.

In Revd. Aitken's time the Church was lit with *'oil lamps'* and he reports that *'at Evening Service each of the congregation had to bring his own 'dip' for the pews, and those more enterprising worshippers were privileged to snuff with their fingers when necessary'*.

Presumably using the light from their neighbour's 'dip'! Oil-lamps were removed from the church, and electricity installed 6th November, 1930.

Paul Church has two handsome brass 'spider' chandeliers, one is engraved:

'The Gift of Edward Tonkin 1765'

and the other, rather more ornate with flames at the top and decorated with three shells underneath is engraved:-

'In the year of our Lord 1777 Bryan Tonkin'.

One presently hangs over the open area at the back of the church, and the other hangs over the choir stalls in the chancel.

VICARS' AND CHOIR VESTRIES

Before the 1873 restoration the incumbent at that time, the Revd. Malone had a small robing area (see Chapter 12 for picture) at the east end of the north aisle which was panelled and hidden from view by the organ and choir pews. He wanted a rod and curtain for this area, and one was obtained from St. Paul's Church, Penzance. He said, this was *'owing to the inconvenience of the Vestry Room being so far from the Reading Desk'*. The choir sat in this area (east end north aisle) at that time, but when they moved to the chancel after the restoration, a larger robing area was made in the east end of the north aisle for the clergy and choir, with a small Vicar's Vestry. Additional choir seats were placed in the chancel in 1888, made by John James Downing of Mousehole for the princely sum of 13/6d!

In the 1940s and 50s there was wooden-partitioned vestry for male choir members and the clergy, at the east end of the north aisle. In those days there were no robes for the ladies of the choir, who wore their ordinary clothes, or Sunday best. The Vestry was smaller than the present arrangement. Later the male choir moved to a small Vestry at the back of this aisle and the Vicar's Vestry remained in situ at the east end south aisle.

In 1968 the present Choir Vestry was built in the tower, at a cost of £2,000, utilising the west tower arch, in which was inserted a screen and a door, sealing off this area. It was dedicated by the Archdeacon of Cornwall.

At the time of the 1980s restoration a new Vicar's Vestry and kitchen area was constructed in the north aisle, west end, replacing pews and the small vestry as above. It cleverly utilises one outer wall of the vestry with two large opening doors, housing a sink, cupboards, and electricity supply for boiling kettles and preparing coffee after Services. The Vicar's Vestry is well supplied with useful cupboards and a wardrobe for robes and vestments.

The Reading Desk was very large and was also known as the '*Clerk of the Council's Desk*'. It was situated in the area of the Vicar's desk and chair at the present time. According to the Royal Cornwall Gazette on Friday 28th April, 1865 it was reported:-
'*great alterations have been carried out in the Parish Church of St. Paul almost immediately of his appointment, the much respected Vicar Dr. Carpenter set to work to repair and reduce the height of the huge square boxes which cover the body of the Church. To scrape the whitewash off the columns and arches, to provide lamps and matting etc.*' (This produced the mottled effect at the 'little Arch' mentioned earlier.)

A meeting of the parishioners was held and a Committee formed and £60 subscribed towards further improvements. One of the most interesting of which was that the partition of lath and plaster, which existed between the tower and the nave, was demolished, the fine arch opened to view, and the interior of the tower cleaned and repaired. The next bit is interesting: '*the west door and floor of the tower lowered to their original level*'. As there are steps up to the west door today this seems a little obscure, however in 1873 there **were no steps** into the church from the tower: the floor was level to the back of both north and south aisles. The upper ringing chamber may have been accessed via the gallery. More about Bells and Tower in Chapter 12.

The old huge square 'horse box' pews were either removed or reduced in height, and '*new open seats have been erected at the west end of the nave, and a new font of granite is to be added.*'

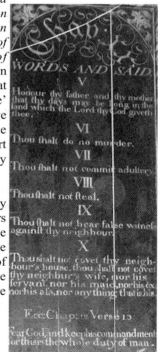

The tower floor and space around the font are to be laid with Minton tiles – these alterations have been carried out under the direction of Mr. Sedding Architect of Penzance'. The anomaly is that in l910, Cecil Aitken reports that there were still 'horse box-type' pews, presumably some must have been left in place after the renovation of 1865, but the report above gives one the idea that they were all taken out.

Church fabric is constantly changing as the need for repairs and renewals arise; no doubt in the future there will be more restorations to report. Spring of 2006 - new runners are on the pews, for the comfort of the congregation.

The Decalogues used to hang in the 'Osborne' Chapel

CHAPTER 4 – THE SAINTS OF PAUL CHURCH

The lives of the Saints are largely wrapped up in folklore, legend and stories. Saints were like badges with which folk identified themselves within their Parishes; this culminated in the Feast celebrations, which are now largely confined to Cornwall, but would have once happened all over England. As for Paul Church and its dedicatee, this Chapter could well be entitled 'What is in a Name?', as there are three contenders:- Paulinus of York, Paul Aurelian, or *even perhaps* the Apostle St. Paul. Richard Carew the historian of the sixteenth century calls Paul Church '*St. Pawle*'. Thus, after the re-build of the fire-destroyed Church in 1600, the new Church was called 'St. Pawle'.

To commence this Chapter, the following is a list of historical references to Paul Church, taken from Gover's place names of Cornwall index in the C.R.O., some O.S. maps, and from the registers of the Bishops of Exeter. This indicates the name of Paul Church through the ages commencing in 1259:-

		Anno Domini
Ecclesie Sancti Paulini (first recorded Priest)	*Bishop Bronescombe*	2nd *May, 1259*
Ecclesia Sancti Paulini (taxation Pope Nicholas)		*1291*
Ecclesie Sancti Pauli-Vicar: J. de Bosevoran	*Feet of Fines*	*1317*
St. Paul de Bruony		*1308*
St. Paul de Breweny	*Royal Writ*	*1329*
St. Paul (Vulgo'Paul' Sancti Paul in Cornubia):		
Installed as Priest: Sir John de Bosevaron		26th *March, 1317*
Sancti Pauli (hodie Paul) dedication high altar	*Bishop Grandisson*	11th *July, 1336*
Ecclesie Sancti Pawle		*1475*
Ecclesie Sancti Paulini		*1494*
Reg. Warnham Vol 1. f 205	*Bishop Warnham*	*1504*
Saynt Paul of Borweny		*1540*
St. Pawle – Richard Carew	*historian*	*1595*
'Paul'- John Speede	*(map 1610)*	*1610*
St. Paule	*(map Joel Gascoigne)*	*1699*
Paulinus	*(Willis:168)*	*1733*
Paul		*1742*
Paulinus, Bishop of Rochester	*(Lysons:255)*	*1814*
Paulinus	*(Oliver)*	*1846*
St. Paulinus Church	*(map 1876)*	*1876*
St. Paul	*(map 1878)*	*1878*
St. Paulinus	*O.S. map 1880*	*1880*
Paul	*Milestone (Sennen)*	*1834*
The first mention of 'Pol-de-Leon'	*(O.S. map 1907)*	*1907*
St. Pol-de-Leon Charles Henderson, historian		*1925*

The above list demonstrates that the earliest recorded reference to 'Paul' as a name for our Church is that of 1259. This was when the Bishop of Exeter, Walter de Bronescombe by the '*Ordinacio Ecclesiae Sancti Paulini*' dated at London on 2nd May, 1259 confirmed the arrangement for the first recorded Vicar of Paul Church (see Chapter Five on the Vicars of Paul). The term '*Ecclesiae*' indicates that our Church had full parochial rights, and *Paulini* is Latin for Paul.

This table also demonstrates that Paul Church **was not named 'St. Pol-de-Leon' until 1907**, and a plausible reason for this change of name, after some eight hundred years of being known as 'Paul Church', ensues.

Joel Gascoyne 1696 - ST. PAULE

It is highly likely that the 'Celtic' resurgence, which was both political and religious, and linked to the high church or Anglo Catholic revival of the early 20th century, was responsible for the name change. This 'revival' was spearheaded by a Mr. Henry Jenner (1848-1934), a Cornish man born in St. Columb Major. Other members of the group were Canon Gilbert Hunter Doble and Charles Henderson.

In 1877 Henry Jenner, then a young man, discovered a scrap of Middle Cornish the 'Charter Fragment' at the British Museum. This inspired him to find out more about Cornwall and its Celtic roots, in fact he wanted to banish 'Englishness' from Cornwall's shores. On 15th August, 1901 the short-lived Celtic-Cornish Society (Cowethas Kelto-Kernuak) was formed, with Jenner as its Vice-President. He had a great affinity for Brittany, and its Saint Paul-of-Leon. He acknowledged Breton as the language closest to Cornish, and he published a Cornish Dictionary in 1904. This all led to an upsurge of Cornish nationalism and fostered links with Ireland, Wales and Brittany. At an address to a meeting of the Royal Institute of Cornwall Henry Jenner said:- *that it is desirable that the Royal Institute of Cornwall take steps towards promoting a systematic general survey and collection of Cornish place and family names with a view to correct interpretation'.* Previously to this Henry Jenner and W. C. Borlase, at the Cornish Manuscript Society of 1876, decided there was a *need to establish correct and consistent spelling of Cornish place names for Ordinance Survey maps'.*

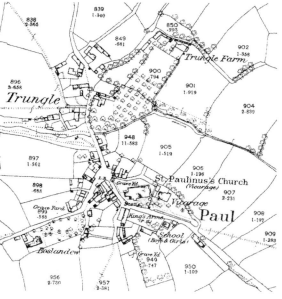

O.S. MAP 1880 - reproduction permission granted ST. PAULINUS'S CHURCH

Henry Jenner visited Paul to see Dolly Pentreath's memorial, as she was reputedly the last Cornish monoglot. The Revd. Wadislas Somerville Lach-Szyrma, Vicar of St. Peters Church, Newlyn, accompanied Jenner. These two spent a lot of time together investigating the Cornish dialect of Newlyn. The Revd. Lach-Szyrma also threw himself into discovering and interpreting Cornish antiquities, and it was he who organised the Celebration on the Centenary of Dolly's death on 27th December, 1877, in Paul. After the celebration he gave two further lectures in an effort to teach the Cornish about their own language and encourage its resurgence.

The question is: did both of these fervent 'Celtic revivalists' visit the Vicar, Revd. Aitken, or the Revd. Prideaux his successor, and influence one of them to change the name of Paul Church? The dates would point to Revd. Aitken, but then his son Cecil Aitken's history book is dated 1910 and is called 'The Ancient Church of Paul'. There is no sign of the name 'Pol-de-Leon' in his book.

The Revd. Aitken preached on Feast Sunday 9th October, 1877 stating that the origins of 'Feast' were to be found in Jewish traditions of the Old Testament. It does seem that he was not to be influenced by Revd. Lach-Szyrma into changing the name of Paul Church.

O.S. 1907 permission granted for reproduction
ST. POL-DE-LEON'S CHURCH

Meanwhile Jenner in 1903 was admitted as 'Gwaz Mikael' (Servant of Michael) into the recently formed Gorsedd of Brittany, over which he ruled as 'Grand Bard'. His main aim, as that of Revd. Lach-Szyrma, was to rouse Cornish people from their indifference to their own heritage. He presided over a Celtic Congress in Truro and tried to influence all to his ideal of Cornwall as a Celtic Nation. Shortly afterwards, the Bretonic French name of 'St. Pol-de-Leon' appeared on the 1907 O.S. Map.

There is a fascinating statement by Mr. R. Pentreath in the Vestry Minutes 11th April, 1908, *that there are the wrong number of 'bezants' (10 instead of 15), on the Cornish shield in the window depicting Paulus of Leon'*. This minuted discrepancy would indicate that the window had only lately been inserted, again tying up with the map dates on the following O.S. maps which tell the story graphically. On the map of 1696 the Church and Village are called 'St. Paule', in 1880 the Victorian map depicts the Church as 'St. Paulinus' Church', and finally – in O.S. map of 1907 – it is called St. Pol-de-Leon. Therefore it is only in **between the dates 1880 and 1907** that Paul Church was given the French name of 'St. Pol-de-Leon'. I have checked recently with the Diocesan Office, and they have no record of date for the name change of Paul Church.

The Parish Church of Staverton in Devon also claims St. Paul of Leon as their patron Saint, and has done so since 1926. This claim to Paul Aurelian is also very tenuous, and is mainly due to the romantic fancy of the Vicar the Revd. E. D. Drake-Brockman (ref: Prof. N. I. Orme). Interestingly, this occurred some nineteen years after the name 'Pol-de-Leon' became to be an alternate name for 'Paul Church'; there could be a link, but I have not discovered one.

The Latin (*Ecclesie Sancti Paulini - Church of St. Paul)* **also** demonstrates that the Church may well have originally been called 'Saint Paul' (as 'St. Pawle' in 16th C), and somewhere along the way lost the title 'Saint.' In fact, the Village was also marked as being called 'St. Paul', on a map dated 1808. This could give credence to some historians who believe that the Apostle St. Paul was the dedicatee of our Church; however, once again, there is no evidence to prove that either.

I found a reference to the Cornish language (Kernewek), in which is stated that the Cornish did not use the prefix 'Saint' and would call their Saint just by his name e.g. 'Piran'. Thus the Village and Church were both known as 'Paul', as depicted on a map of Cornwall by John Speede dated 1610. I have always been fascinated by this, and am very glad to have come across a reason!

The correct dedicatee, and all the confusion, might well have been settled by ancient documents that subsequently perished in the burning of Church and Vicarage in 1595. The Spaniards took away more than the fabric of the Church – all the pre-1595 records were lost too. Luckily we do have the Registers of the various Bishops of Exeter, which are pretty accurate records of the ecclesiastical business of the Diocese (see below).

Paul Village is likely to have had a different name to that of the Church, as it would have pre-dated any church building. There are many pointers towards the original Village name being 'Brewinney', as this name is mentioned more than once in records – coupled with 'Paul Churchtown'. For example: on 5th June, 1605 – a marriage settlement for 'Jasper's House' in Brewinny *alias Paul Church Town*. The area of Brewinney encompasses land in front of the Church, stretching up to Trungle (another early Village), and on to Sheffield Village. As the Church gradually grew in its midst, the Village took its name from the centre of worship (see Chapter 18).

The three Saints (one of whom may be a dedicatee of Paul Church), have no authentic rights to the title in any existing documentation, and historians cannot prove their claims!! Past historians of Paul Church have disputed this mystery, some report in favour of Paul Aurelian, and others support St. Paulinus of York, with the latter being the overall favourite (refs: Gilberts, Tonkins and Lakes Histories). One or two support the Apostle, St. Paul.

The Church sports stained glass windows depicting both Saints, so those who made the windows weren't taking any chances! A window in the north aisle shows St. Paulinus of York baptising King Edwin of Northumberland in a smaller pane underneath the main Saint's image. Paul Aurelian is in the south aisle window, as 'St. Paulinus of Leon'. In this window is a small depiction of a pelican feeding her chicks with blood from her breast. This is a religious symbol of Christ the Redeemer, in self-sacrifice, but also has heraldic significance.

Mr. Hope Moncrieff states that '*the south aisle only of Paul Church is dedicated to Paul Aurelian, the Breton Bishop'*, an entirely incorrect statement. This statement could have been misinterpreted by the presence of the Saint's window as mentioned above. A Mr. Penn writes '*I am not aware that this 'Saint' was ever in Cornwall, but on the Continent he was a great celebrity.'*

Again, written in a 'Cornish Church Guide' by Charles Henderson in 1925, he states: '*The Church was dedicated to St. Paulinus of York 1259 – and again dedicated to St. Paulus (Aurelian) in 1315.'* (!!!) This statement is purely fabricated, the dates mean nothing, and this leads to a lot of misunderstanding. The authorities for such sweeping dated claims should be found in the Registers of the various Bishops of Exeter, Bronescombe, Grandisson, Stapledon, who being enthroned in the Sees, in their time, had all of their ecclesiastical matters recorded meticulously therein (see above). Unfortunately, there is *nothing* documented even in these Registers that lists the true dedication of 'a Saint Paul' to this Church. When Bishop John de Grandisson came to Paul Church on 11th July, 1336, *he dedicated (consecrated)* only the new high altar, in a Church which already had the name of

'Saint Paul', unfortunately omitting to add further details:-

> '*1336 item xi die Julii, Dominus dedicavit majus altare ecclesie Sancti Pauli
> (hodie 'Paul') in Cornubia'.*

'Hodie' means today, or this day, and was added by F. Hingston-Randolph when he transcribed the Bishops' Registers.

In Tonkin's History of Cornwall of 1739, he states that Paul Church is '*only dedicated to St. Paulinus of York;* this is repeated in Lakes Parochial History of 1868. In 'The Churches of Cornwall' by Mr. J. Charles Cox, again he states that the Church was '*Re-dedicated to St. Paulinus of York in 1336'.* These chaps all seem pretty sure, maybe one copied the other, with no real documented evidence, as unfortunately happens with **some** historians!

Even the dates are completely confused. For instance, the 10th October, celebrated in Paul Church today as 'The Feast Day of Paul Aurelian' is really the date of the death of 'St. Paulinus of York'! Thus 10th October is the Feast Day of Paulinus, Bishop of York. Paul Aurelian's true Feast Day is 12th March, on the day of his death. One can understand therefore that this fact seemed to point to St. Paulinus of York being the true dedicatee of Paul Church, but *then,* I came across something else of interest.

This was: the fact that Henry VIII, after his break from Rome in 1536, abolished most of the Feast Days of the Church in general. He decided that too much time was spent away from work (such as milking, feeding livestock, general farming and fishing), while the workers celebrated Holy Feast Days. This legislation against Feast Days caused widespread discontent, and many continued unheeded. It was called the Act '*for the abrogation of certain holydays'* mentioning the sin of excess, and riot as the people were '*being entysed by the lycencyous vacacyon and lybertye of those holydays.'*

Henry's Chancellor, Cromwell, sent spies into Cornwall visiting monasteries (such as they were at that time, just before the dissolution) and churches alike. However, such was the unrest caused by abolishing Feast Days, that special dispensation was secured to allow the celebration of Cornish Patronal Festivals – or 'Feasts' - mainly because so many of the Cornish Saints were Celtic in origin. This good news was to the '*marvellous pleasure'* of the people.

However, the Cornish being rebels continued with their other Holy Days, as well. Bishop Veysey of Exeter circulated an angry reprimand to the clergy of his Diocese, complaining not only of the continued observation of Holy Days, but a widespread abstention from work, from noon on the eves of Feast Days. Crops were being lost as a result of the superstitious reluctance to work on Feast Days, so it was quite a problem for the economy.

The King, in his new self-proclaimed office of Supreme Head of the Church of England, decreed that from henceforth the Feast of the Church dedication should be kept everywhere **on the first Sunday in October!** This may be the real reason for the Feast of St. Paul Aurelian being kept on 10th October.

Feast Celebrations in Cornwall are unique. There is such a strong affinity in the Celtic roots of the Cornish that link with legends of the Celtic Saints, and their celebrations today are still lively, great fun and fiercely protected. All sorts of fun and games were to be had, especially for the children. In 1878 during Paul Feast, a greasy pole was erected over the sea, with a leg of mutton and a bunch of parsnips tied to the end; much laughter was generated when a portly gentleman had a go, and fell in the sea! It was eventually conquered by a lighter Mr. William Henry Smith of Tolcarne.

The enthusiasm and fun of 'Feast' was beautifully expressed in October 1981, when the Revd. R.H Cadman, Vicar of Paul Church, gleefully wrote in the Church Magazine:

'*Dear Fellow Feasters,*

Paul Feast is in the air and on the breeze. "If it's fine for Paul, it's fine for all!" whatever that means, it certainly denotes the supreme confidence of Paul Folk in their Patron Saint and their happiness in living and worshipping in Paul Parish. Paul Feast means the scent of Autumn, brown leaves lying on the ground, fine rain, encircling mist, a lighted Cross high up in the sky, Paul Church lit up, Feast pudding,

Paul Strick & David Harvey 'The Ventriloquist'

Saffron Cake, the Cornish Family connection and Cornish Pixies. Long may the Feast spirit live on in Penwith. ------- The essence of Paul Feast is "the Praise of the Lord" and its H.Q. is Paul Church on Paul Feast Sunday.------So, fellow-Feasters, "Let us Keep the Feast."'

Paul Feast 1880:—

'*By this time the usual Monday night carousal after the Western Hunt Meeting at the public house has given place to Church and Chapel teas, followed by concerts in the School room. Although there are still stalls (standing) in the streets for the sale of gingerbread, fairings etc., and swings for the children.*'

This epitomises the local feeling for Feast Week very clearly. Feast Week will always be celebrated in October, no matter which Saint is the true dedicatee, and this fact will never detract from the lively celebrations at Paul.

PAUL AURELIAN - BISHOP OF LEON

St. Paulus of Leon window in the south aisle

I will now tell a little of the life of Paul Aurelian, as he is much loved as a Saint in Paul Church: in Wales he was known as the Welsh '*Pawl Hen*' or '*Polin Eagob*', and in Breton '*Kastell-Paol*'.

His life is based on the writings of Wrmonoc, (also known as 'Uurmonoc') who wrote the '*Vita Sancti Pauli Episcope Leonensis in Britannia Minori Auctore - Wormonoco*' in the A.D. 884, from a Monastery in Landevennec, in Brittany. This writing was published by Dom. Plaine in the 'Analecta Bollandiana' of 1882 Vol. I Page 208-58. Also by M. Charles Cuissard in his 'La Revue Celtique' Vol. V in 1883.

Wrmonoc himself gives credence to an earlier writing on the Life of Paul Aurelian, which survived in two texts, one of the 10th century, and one of the late 11th or early 12th century. Wrmonoc wrote about Paul Aurelian **400 years after his death**, reputedly in A.D. 884, therefore his integrity will be more than a little in question. Wrmonoc himself acknowledges the authority for his writings as being shaky owing to '*the immense space of time which had passed*' since Paul Aurelian lived. Wrmonoc had never been abroad, and had little knowledge of Cornwall or Wales. He appears to have had some access to material from Britain, but had used it imprecisely, as his British geography was so vague.

Nicholas Roscarrock also wrote 'The Lives of the Saints of Cornwall', completed in 1610-1620. Professor Nicholas Orme of Exeter University published a book on the Saints of Cornwall, and he edited Roscarrock's book. Albert Le Grand wrote a 'Further Life of Paul' in the 17th century, but he only reproduced the information from Wrmonoc's text.

The Revd. Gilbert Doble writes '*The reader will now understand that it is useless to look to Wrmonoc's writing for an accurate account of the life and labours of the founder of the French Diocese of Leon. The ideas of the 9th Century on the subject of writing of history were not ours (1941).*'

Thus it is clear that only a few fragments of the true story of St. Paul Aurelian himself had been handed down. Nevertheless he must have been a remarkable character; he had a powerful personality, which ensured that his influence was felt throughout the whole of Brittany.

Wrmonoc records that Paul Aurelian was born A.D. 490, the son of a Count Periphius (or Porphius) of Pennohen in Wales; he was of Romano-British stock. He had eight brothers and three sisters. Baring-Gould states he was born at Cowbridge in Glamorgan. As a young man he studied under St. Illtud at Llantwit Major, Glamorganshire, with other candidates for Sainthood, Samson, David and Gildas. Paul Aurelian is reported as acting as spiritual director to his nephew Saint Joavan.

While Paul was studying it is reported by Wrmonoc that the young teenage Paul managed to repel the sea from the monastery, and drove some birds, which were being a nuisance and feeding on the crops, into a barn, and they were only released when Illtud allowed them to leave. Paul received a strong calling to take on the life of a hermit or recluse. He was only sixteen at the time, and – knowing teenage boys – his conviction must have been very positive, and he acted on it steadfastly.

As a recluse or hermit, his fame seems to have spread abroad until it reached the ears of a certain Quonomorius or King Mark (Marcus). This King wanted to strengthen the faith of those in his country, and the only clue we have to its whereabouts is that his people spoke four languages. This is an extremely vague reference – however a King Mark is linked with Fowey, and has connections with the story of Tristran and Isolde. Therefore, from this tenuous reason, it has been stated that the Caer Banhead or Villa Banhedos is the place to which Paul Aurelian travelled next in the company of twelve priests. He could, of course, have been as old as thirty by then, as there is no reference to the length of his time as a recluse, only that his fame went before him. Two of Paul's brothers were: Notolius, Potolius and one sister was Sitofolla. His Father wanted him to marry and procreate, but Paul renounced earthly hopes and consecrated himself to the service of God.

'Paul's Path – *Semita Pauli* – or 'Hent-Saint-Paul'. There is a legend that when Paul was fitting out his ship for his journey to Brittany his sister Sitofolla wanted the land enlarged. Paul Aurelian, in the story, placed pebbles at low tide; these were supposed to become huge columns, and Paul's Path between the columns came into existence. No such geographical feature is known on the north coast of the English Channel, and this story has been described as '*a literary device to bring both Brother and Sister together'.*

A similar miracle was reported at the Monastery of St. Illtud at Llanilltud Fawr on the Welsh mainland. Paul Aurelian remained at Caer Banhead for a while, preaching and living a Christian life, but again he was called to become a Bishop in France, and left the land of King Mark – travelling by sea to Brittany where he founded churches at St. Pol-de-Leon and the adjoining Ile-de-Batz. He arrived as Paul Aurelian, and he took on the Bretonic French 'Pol-de-Leon' – Paul of Leon, as did the Cathedral he founded.

Now to the question of Paul's sister Sitofolla. Marazion Church has a reference in its Church History which is also undocumented, stating that 'Satirola' lived at St. Michael's Mount. Professor Nicholas Orme states that Sitofolla may be linked to the Exeter Saint of Sidwell. It is interesting that St. Michael's Mount also lays a claim to her legend.

Paul lived a prayerful life of a Christian Bishop, and it is said he died at the ripe old age 104, which says a lot about the way of life of a fervent Christian! Paul's death date was 12th March, 572, making him really only 82, still pretty old for that time. The story does not end there, nevertheless, as his body was claimed by both the priests of St. Pol-de-Leon, and the monks of Ile-de-Batz. They could not decide who should have Paul's body. The status that such a Saint's tomb would give to a place of worship, meant much financial advantage, as it would draw many pilgrims. Nicholas Roscarrock in the seventeenth century sets the scene thus:

'Two close wagons to be brought into the place where his body was, and a yoake of oxen to eyther of them, and placed in such sort at the one bended towarde the towne, and the other towards the monastery, and set the body iuste betwixt them, which suddenly vanished, no man perceiving how, so as both parties drove ther oxen homewards, hoping they had him, but these of the monastery found ther wagon empty and these of the towne the body in ther wagon, which they burye with great solemnity.'

Thus St. Paul of Leon was buried in the church that bore his name. After his death, a story arose that a monk called Felix was lying ill at Fleury, and saw in a vision the blessed Bishop Paul standing resplendent in light at his bed-side. Paul proceeded to remove his diseased rib.

In the Church of Lampaul-Guimiliau, in Brittany, there is a 16th century Banner showing St. Paul holding a crozier and trampling the serpent, and it is very much akin to the Banner in our Church today. He also has a long beard! Also in this church in the porch is a statue of St. Paul and the dragon dated 1533. St. Pol-de-Leon is known in Brittany as one of the 'Seven Saints of Brittany', although he is not widely known throughout France. St. Pol-de-Leon Cathedral is a popular visiting place for pilgrims, where the Saint's relics are now venerated in a gilded reliquary, and they consist of the Saint's head, a bone of one of his arms, and a finger bone. Wrmonoc states that there are certain charters stored close to the Saint's head. John Harry, our present Church organist, has travelled to see the Saint's relics, and will be pleased to describe them to anyone interested!

Bell Hir-glas

Wrmonoc also reports that he could describe the serpent's cave clearly, from personal observation, and knew exactly where the incidents recorded in the legend about it took place. Wrmonoc also informs us of St. Paul's famous Bell and gives it the name of 'Hir-glas.' One Sunday in each year, after Vespers, all the people of the Cathedral of Pol-de-Leon kneel at the Communion Rails to have this Bell placed on their heads! He also had a book, which was probably the Bible; it was bound in silver gilt, with the arms of

Rochefort and Leon by Guillaume de Rochfort, Bishop of Leon in 1352.

To conclude on Paul Aurelian, here is a very nice little coincidence:- the *last* Bishop of Leon, M. de La Marche, was driven out of his Diocese by the French Revolution in 1791. He landed in Mount's Bay to take refuge in England on 3rd March, 1791!

ST. PAULINUS—BISHOP OF YORK

Many earlier historians of Paul Church have thought that Saint Paulinus of York is the correct Saint to whom the Church of Paul is dedicated. His Feast Day is on *10th October*, and this fact seems to be at the heart of the mystery. He was born in A.D. 584 in Rome *(Baring-Gould states he was born A.D. 644)*. He was a monk at St. Andrew's Monastery in Rome, and became a missionary to the Anglo-Saxons in 601 sent by Pope St. Gregory the Great, to follow shortly after the mission of the great St. Augustine. The Venerable Bede wrote about St. Paulinus as did other writers and the following is taken from various notes on his life.

Bede describes him as '*a tall man with a slight stoop, with black hair and a thin face and narrow aquiline nose, his presence being venerable and awe-inspiring*'. He worked with St. Augustine, St. Justus and Saint Mellitus, all from Canterbury. He evangelised in Kent for 24 years. Paulinus was consecrated Bishop by Archbishop Justus on 21st July, 625. He then went north, and became the first missionary to Northumbria, converting thousands including King Edwin in 627. The King was battling against pagan Mercians, who defeated Edwin's forces in 633.

Paulinus gave the King Edwin instruction in the Faith, and he promised to abandon idol worship. However Paulinus found it difficult to bring the King's proud mind to accept the humility of the way of salvation. The King used to sit alone for hours deliberating on which religion to follow. Finally the teaching of Paulinus convinced Edwin, and he was Baptised with the nobles of his court, and a large number of humbler folk at York on Easter Day at the Church of St. Peter, which the King hastily constructed of timber. After the Baptism Paulinus suggested a larger oratory of stone be built on the spot. There is a stained glass window in the north aisle of Paul Church showing Paulinus baptising King Edwin; it is situated under a larger depiction of St. Paulinus.

Paulinus then moved on to Lindsey south of the Humber River, and continued his Christian work. Bishop Honorius sent Paulinus the Pallium to wear at his consecration because of his many converts to Christianity. A Pallium of the 6th century was a long wide white band ornamented with black or red crosses finished with tassels. It was draped around the shoulders and breast and formed a V in the front with the ends hanging down from the left shoulder – one in front and one behind. Its use was reserved for the Pope and archbishops, but bishops sometimes received the Pallium as a mark of special favour – but it does not increase their power or jurisdiction nor give them any precedence. The Pope has the absolute right to wear the Pallium.

Paulinus retreated to Kent with the remaining Royal Family, and became Bishop of Rochester in A.D. 633. St. Paulinus speaking in Northumbria said:-

'This is how the present life of man on earth, or a King, appears to me in comparison with that time which is unknown to us. You are sitting feasting with your eldormen and thiegns in wintertime, the fire is burning on the hearth in the middle of the hall, all is warm inside while outside wintry storms of rain and snow are raging, and a sparrow flies swiftly in at one door and quickly flies out at the other – for the few moments it is inside the storm and wintry tempest cannot touch it, but after the briefest of calm it flies from your sight, out of the wintry storms and into it again. So this life of man appears but for a moment – what follows or indeed, what went before, we know not at all. That is what life is like, at birth we emerge from the unknown and for a brief while we are here on earth with a fair amount of comfort and happiness – then we fly out of the window into the cold and dark and unknown future, if the new religion can lighten that darkness for us then let us follow it.'

Pope Saint Honorius 1st recognised Paulinus as Archbishop of York. He administered the See of Rochester for ten years (Attwath, Benedictines, Delaney Encyclopaedia). St. Paulinus died on 10th October, A.D. 642 in Rochester of natural causes.

Well, there are the facts, and the reader may make of them what they will! Personally, I find it very interesting that the two main contenders:- 1. St. Paulinus was Italian, and 2. St. Paul Aurelian was born in Wales, supposedly of Romano/British origin (Italian), therefore both Saints were connected with Italy, and not a Cornishman among them!

As a postscript: the website for the Diocese of Truro recognises Paul Aurelian on his Feast day of 12th March.

CHAPTER 5 - THE CLERGY & VICARAGES OF PAUL

There certainly would have been earlier Priests for Paul Church, but there are no records documenting them so I have to commence with the earliest recorded Priest. Not all the dates for institution or resignation/retirement are available.

A LIST OF PAUL CLERGY

The only **Rector of Paul** in his own right -Roger de Sancto Constantino (Reg. Bishop Bronescombe)	Temp in charge 3rd May to Michaelmas 1259 Then instituted 11th July, 1259 – left by 17th April, 1283
No Vicar reported, John Heym had gone	12th April, 1297
The first **Vicar:**	In charge as Vicar with Hailes Abbey as Patrons
'John' Instituted (Reg. Bishop Stafford)	27th November, 1308 - 26th March, 1317 Palm Sunday 1317
Sir John Bosevaran	Instituted 1st May, 1317
Sir William Polgrim also Vicar of Ilfracombe	Resigned 31st January, 1360
Sir John de Trewroneke	Instituted 1st March, 1360
Odo Bost paid clerical subsidy in:	1410, resigned 1418
Sir John Patry	Instituted 26th February, 1417 - resigned 1439
Sir Thomas Mata	Instituted 16th September, 1439
Sir John Martyn de Pensans	Died 1493
Sir Thomas Godolhan (maybe Godolphin?)	26th July, 1493
Sir William Nedercote	8th July, 1504
Master John Mockryche	1523
Master Olyver Smith	resigned 1530
Master Martin James (Curate Sir John Hancoke)	August, 1537
John Tremearne Vicar during the Spanish Raid	1581-1624 Patron Queen Elizabeth I
Thomas Harries, M.A.	1624 died 1661
William Badcock	1653 Patron Parliament (under Cromwell)
John Smith	1661 Patron the Lord Chancellor
Henry Pendarves Vicar 58 years, died 14th June, 1739	1694-1739
Henry Penneck	1739-1771
John Allen, B.A.	1771-1802
G. J. Scobell	November, 1786
Charles Valentine Le Grice	1799
Richard Gurney (nominally his son was Curate)	1786-1825
Died 17th May, 1825 age 77	1815-1825 presented by Eldon Lord Chancellor
Warwick Oben Gurney, B.A was Curate	admitted 13th March, 1802
of Paul Church for 47 years	died August, 1849 age 70
Charles George Ruddock Festing, M.A.	1827-1857
John Garrett	1857-1864
William Carpenter Doctor of Divinity	1864-1865
Richard Malone	1866-1876
Robert Wesley Aitken	1876-1911
Frederick Joseph Prideaux, M.A.	1911-1938 (died)
Frederick Charles Eddy- Parish population 3,000 souls	1939-1942
William Valentine Wagner, B.A.	1942-1953 (died)
Deryck Harry Percival Davey, B.A.	1953-1960
John Herbert Tyrrell	1960-1966
Reginald Hugh Cadman, L.L.M. Rural Dean of Penwith	1966-1982
Geoffrey Harper, M.A.	1982-1999
Gordon John Hansford, B.Sc.	1999-present day

I compiled the list as above. I then discovered that the Revd. Charles Valentine Le Grice (1799) and the Revd. G. J. Scobell (November 1786) were mentioned in documents of the time as being Vicars at Paul. This presents a puzzle as there were already Vicars during that time – Revd. John Allen and Revd. Richard Gurney.

Thus, when two Vicars were listed at the same time, one could have been a Curate, which were more than Vicars in Training, i.e. young Priests. In the 18/19th Centuries it was usual to have a 'Curate' who was an assistant Vicar, as often the main Priest would have more than one Parish, a 'pluralist', and he needed a Priest in the Parish at all times while he was away. This was a type of shared Ministry (plurality).

Plurality also occurred under Revd. C. G. Ruddock Festing, (details later on in this Chapter). It was against the Decrees of the Council of Lyons passed in the 13th century, however so many priests were involved that it was largely ignored. Often Parish Clerks went on to train for the ministry and become curates.

This situation occurs again with the Revd. Richard Gurney and his son, the Revd. Warwick Oben Gurney, who was at Paul Church for forty-seven years, but is only mentioned as a 'Curate'. I have recently discovered that the Revd. C.V. Le Grice was, in fact, Vicar of St. Mary's Church Penzance, and was a Curate at Paul Church, his first post after being ordained.

In 1310, it was considered that £42 paid four times a year was enough to support a knight, but this amount was needed twelve times a year in order to support a Vicar! As far as possible, I will now try to discuss the lives of the Vicars, some Curates and one Rector of Paul.

In Dugdale's Monasticon Anglic., under Hailes Abbey it shows that the amount of money received for the Church of Paulyn was £41. That is a great deal of money for those times, Paul was a rich Parish. At the time of this endowment of Paul Church to the Abbey and Convent of Hailes, in Gloucester, two clerics claimed to be the '*Rector Ecclesiae Sancti Paulini*', they were: **Roger de Sancto Constantino** (*aliquando Canonicus Ecclesie de Glasneya*) and **John Heym.** In 1277 the first recorded Priest of nearby Perranuthnoe Church was called Adam Heym; there may be a link between these two clergymen.

In Bishop Bronescombe's Register it states '*A die sabbati proxima ante dominicam in ramis palmarum*' – 26th March (Sunday nearest to Palm Sunday). Roger de Sancto Constantino was installed as Priest at Paul on 11th July, 1259 as he had been appointed to the charge of this Parish from 3rd May to Michaelmas 1259. Roger of St. Constantine had been temporarily appointed in charge of the parish from 3rd May to Michaelmas 1259 on condition that he paid the John Heym an annual pension of 60s. He was Vicar of Lanreath in 1263, and went on to be Rector of Silverton Church in Devon on 8th September, 1309 and was Canon of Glasney. Bishop Bronescombe founded Glasney College in 1265, at Penryn. It held twenty-six Clerics, and in 1349 suffered from the black death or bubonic plague, reducing its inmates considerably, it recovered, but was eventually closed during the Reformation.

Bishop Walter de Bronescombe of Exeter confirmed the pension, dated at London 2nd May, 1259 by the *Ordinacio Ecclesiae Sancti Paulini*. Apparently the Bishop tried to sort things out between the two Priests, and alluded to the Church as '*super Ecclesia Beati Pauli in Cornubia*' with '*Sancti Paulini*' written in the margin. He decided that '*the said Roger shall have the same Church, with all its appurtenances and with the cure of souls, and shall pay to the said John*

Heym sixty shillings from the goods of the said Church every year, at the Feast of the Blessed Michael and Easter, on pain of paying us (the Bishop) a mark for every default.' On condition, however that when *'either of them decease or resign the Church with all its appurtenances shall belong to the survivor'.* Roger was to be responsible for burdens on the living as if he were *'the Rector, thereof'.*

Roger of St. Constantine was duly instituted in 1259, as above, in respect of this agreement. He seems to have been a distinguished man, although he was a pluralist as he was also instituted to the Rectory of Landreath in 1263, and admitted to a portion of two marks in Church of St. Neuline in 1264. In the Charter Rolls it mentions that he was one of the Kings Clerks, 'Roger de Sancto Constantino, King's Clerk and Parson of St. Paulinus, had licence in 1266 for a yearly fair at St. Paulinus on the Vigil, Feast and Morrow of St. Paulinus'. (*No date for this unfortunately, that would have been too helpful to historians*!) He obtained a Charter for a weekly market on Thursday in his Manor of Portheness (Mousehole), and a yearly fair there at the Feast of St. Matthias.

The weekly markets were very important to the financial stability of the local people, being the place where they would sell their produce, animals, and fish, a bit like the Farmers' Markets of today. Therefore obtaining this Charter would have made Roger very popular and ensured the financial stability of the area. The yearly Fair would also have been looked forward to with great glee, as it was usually a time of roistering and merriment, as well as another chance to make some money for the local folk (see also Chapter 9).

After Roger, there were no more Rectors at Paul, the Abbot and Convent of Hailes became the Rectors given by Edmund, Earl of Cornwall, and they appointed a 'Vicar' to have the cure of Paul souls. A document dated 17th April, 1283 speaks of Roger in the past tense, thus perhaps **John Heym** waiting in the wings had his turn as Vicar, but there are no documents to prove this! In the Taxation of Pope Nicholas IV begun in 1288, and completed 1291, the value of Ecclesia Sancti Paulini was £9.6.8d Decima 8/7d.

John Heym, however, was up to no good, as on 17th April, 1297 an order was sent to the Sheriff of Cornwall by the King *'to release John, Vicar of St. Paul'* as he had been thrown into a prison at *Launceveton* with thirty-three other Cornish clergymen, for the publication of a Papal letter. This Vicar was full of passion and of violent disposition, as again on 26th October, 1308, the King had to issue a writ to the Bishop of Exeter complaining that Ralph de Kerris had summoned John, Vicar of *St. Paul of Bruony* to explain an alleged assault *'beating and wounding'* Ralph at Mousehole and removing certain muniments. The Bishop ordered John the Vicar to pay one mark (6/8d). This was not the only occasion when he was punished for violent conduct, unbecoming to a man of the cloth!

He also was one of ten West Cornwall Parsons who, because the Dean of St. Buryan wouldn't allow the Bishop to hold a visitation in that Church, showed their sympathy with the Bishop by marching to St. Buryan, breaking into the Church, and holding a visitation there by force! The King came out on the side of the Dean of Buryan and *'John the Vicar of the Church of St. Paulinus'* was summoned to appear before the Royal Court, and the Bishop was made to take a sequestration (or confiscation) of 10s from the goods of the Church of *'Johannis, Vicarii Ecclesia Sancti Paulini'*

Remarkably, this chap was not finished! As it is reported that on 21st June, 1311 a Royal Writ was issued to the Bishop in which our John *'Vicar of the Church of Brewony'* (Village) was summoned on a charge of beating Alan Wolwayne at Brewoni with arms (as in clubs, or maybe even swords) in his hands! Again the Bishop had to impose a sequestration to the value of one mark. So the Church of St. Paul actually lost money every time the Vicar was in a fight. There is a wonderful description of this Vicar John — he was *'a bellicose disciple of the Prince of Peace!'*

It seems that restoration work was carried out in the Church even in the fourteenth century. For on 22nd August, 1315 Brother Richard De Gloucestre, Proctor of the Abbey of Hailes appeared before Bishop Stapeldon, and begged him in the name of the Abbey and Parishioners of Paul to come and consecrate four newly made altars in the Church. The Bishop said he did not have the time on that occasion (see Chapter 4).

On Palm Sunday 1317 Paul Church was reported as having no Vicar: perhaps John must have resigned, or died on the Saturday before, records are not clear as to what happened. In the 'Feet of Fines' for Paul it just records *'Paul Vicar 1317 – John de Bosvoran' (also spelt Bosvuragh).*

According to the Register of the Bishop of Exeter, Stafford: in *'Sancti Pauli in Cornubia'* on 27th November, 1308 someone just called John was installed as the Vicar of Paul until 26th March, 1317.

Sir John Bosevaran, Priest Instituted on 1st May. Patrons: Abbot (Fr. John) and Convent of Hailes (ref: Cadman). Thus on 1st May, 1317 the next Vicar Sir John Bosevaran, Priest, was instituted to the Vicarage of Paul. Licence was given to the Abbot of Hailes on 1st August, 1317, to put the benefice of St. Paul to farm for one year from Michaelmas, and again on 3rd August, 1320 for two years to Michaelmas to Richard de Trewarveneth, Clerk.

On 24th May, 1329 a Royal Writ was issued to the Bishop to cause John Bosevaran Vicar of the Church of St. Paul de Breweney to attend and answer Benedict le Bray for his debt of 40s, arrears of the annual rent of 6/8d. The Bishop again sequestered the benefice to the value of 60s. Seven years later in 1336, Bishop Grandisson came to consecrate the Church, 'on 11th July the Lord Bishop dedicated the High altar of the Church of St. Paul in Cornwall'. Also in 1336, it was noted that the Abbot and Convent of Hailes did not pay 4/8d due to the Procurations of the Cardinals for their Church of St. Paul.

The next Vicar is unclear, but **Sir William Polgrim**, who was also Rector of Ilfracombe Church in North Devon, resigned the living of *'Sancti Pauli juxta Mousehole in Penwythe'* on 31st January, 1360, therefore it must have been this very Sir William.

On 1st March, 1360 **Sir John de Trewroneke**, Priest was instituted to Paul Church (at Chudleigh, Devon) – he was appointed a penitentiary in the Archdeaconry of Cornwall on 17th February, 1373. These institutions must have occurred in Devon because we came under the Diocese of the Bishop of Exeter, and rather than the Bishop travelling to Cornwall, the prospective incumbent probably had to travel to wherever he was holding institutions.

The next Vicar comes with the curious name of **Odo Bost**, who paid the Clerical Subsidy in 1410. Then under Bishop Stafford, Odo resigned and:-

Sir John Patry Chaplain, who had been Vicar of Newlyn East in 1234, was instituted Vicar of

Paul, on 26th February, 1417.   Interestingly, a licence was issued to him at Marghasyow (Marazion) on 17th April, 1425 for his Service in two Chapels in his Parish. There were at least two Chapels in the Parish of Paul - more about those in Chapter 9. On Sir John's resignation: under Bishop Lacy:-

Sir Thomas Mata, Chaplain, was instituted Vicar of Paul on 16th September, 1439 (at Radeway), again a great distance in those days.   This clerical chap described as *'Vicar of Paule'* formed part of a jury which met in 1461, in St. Ermet's Chapel at Markusiowe. This was for an *'Inquisition de jure patronatus'* of the Rectory of Redruth, to which John Bassett, Esq. had presented Sir William Hoigg, and again he was a juror in a similar case of St. Martin of Camborne. So perhaps he was a very learned fellow!

In 1469 it is reported that a Bristol chap, John Nancothan left 20s to the fabric of the Church of St. Paul *'juxta Porthynes',* which was very kind of him, 20s being a lot of money in the fifteenth century. It would be interesting to know why – but maybe he had relatives in Cornwall or just liked the church!

Next comes **Sir John Martyn de Pensans**, a chaplain, and an important sounding person; Paul Church seemed to have a plethora of knighted Vicars in those days. The reason being that before the Reformation the prefix 'Sir' before the name of these Priests, was a courtesy title only, much akin to the word 'Sire', and was dropped in 1535.

Another reason for knighted priests was that second or third sons of the gentry send to 'take the cloth'; as was the custom, first sons inherited, second sons went into one of the services and the third son went into the Church. This would certainly explain a curate with a title, as it would have been inherited from his Father, if he had no elder brothers. The patronage of the Church was often in the hands of the local Lord of the Manor, who would give his son a large house and land for a Vicarage; thus, especially in the eighteenth century, there were very many palatial vicarages, and the clergy lived very well with servants and plenty of land on which to keep their horses.

John Martyn de Pensans was also a member of a jury which met *'in capella de Redruth'* for an Inquisition in 1493 into the right of patronage of Illogan. He died in this year, and he was followed by:-

Sir Thomas Godolhan (Godolphin) who was instituted on 26th July, 1493. Then came:-

Sir William Nedercote, Clerk – 8th July, 1504 instituted Vicar of St. Paulinus. This Vicar of Paul, whose possessions did not exceed above 20 marks, (one mark = 6/8d roughly) was directed by the Abbot of Tavistock to pay £5.5.8d! This was reported in the *Valor* of the diocese made by Bishop Vesey in the 14th year of the reign of Henry VIII. No mention is made of why he had to pay so much, when he had so little.

Then came Master **John Mockryche** of whom nothing appears to be known. In fact he is very much left out altogether, maybe he was merely a Curate, as it is reported that upon Sir William's death the next Vicar appointed was **Olyver Smith,** and on his resignation **Martin James** was instituted. In the Valuation of the Archdeaconry of Cornwall in August 1537 *The Vicar of Powle* was assessed at 3s and the assistant Curate who went by the grand name of **Sir John Hancoke** assessed at only 20d.

There was a case tried in the famous Star Chamber in which, in the year 1540, **Martin Jamys** the

Vicar of *Saynt Paule of Borweny* complained that John Godoltam probably a different form of Godolphin, (the family established themselves at Trewarveneth in the 17th century) had violently dispossessed him of a messuage called the Vicarage, together with a parcel of ground there 70ft by 63ft, in the town of *Borweny.* Previous Vicars had always held this land in the right of Paul Church. In addition Godoltham had confederated (conspired?) with the wife of Thomas Richards called Alice Richards, a parishioner, to bring him to disgrace by accusing Vicar Martin James of incontinence. Sounds like another dirty deed to me, in other words she maybe had to make up tales of the Vicar lusting after her in order to disgrace him.

John Godolgham (the spelling of his name keeps changing) stated that he was the lessee of the Rectory of Paul by grant from the late Abbot of '*Haylez*' (Hailes) and that the above premises were included in his lease. The outcome of the Trial is not known. At this time the troubles of the Reformation and plunder of churches begun by Henry VIII reached the Parish of Paul. Further confiscations of property, given to churches by the piety of earlier generations, were carried out by the Government of his son Edward VI. Most parish churches lost all their ornaments, and a list of Cornish church plate taken and sent to St. Mawes Castle showed that Paul was the richest Parish in the Deanery of Penwith. The Church plate was restored to Paul Church upon the accession of Queen Mary Tudor, and is listed thus:

ST. PAULLE – CHURCH PLATE

5 chalices and patens	Weight 101 oz
A lytell crosse of sylver gilt	" 12 oz
A schippe (incense boat) of silver	" 10¼ oz
A sensor of silver	" 35 oz
A Pyx of silver	Weight 158¼ oz

This photo shows an example of a silver incense boat, so named as it resembles small boat. Although alluded to above as a 'schippe'. The lid is open to show the space inside for the incense, and it is beautifully engraved.

Paul Church had high status Church plate. This would give credence to the fact that the pre-Reformation Church, destroyed by the fire in 1595, would have been beautifully decorated and ornate, in line with this status. Paul and Fowey Churches were the only ones to possess incense boats.

In January 1971 a silver flagon owned by Paul Church was valued at £1,000 by W. B. Mitchell, Jewellers; it is inscribed with the date 1695 and weighs 60 oz.

Queen Elizabeth seized and confiscated both the Chapels of Newlyn and Mousehole, within which the Latin Catholic mass would have been heard. Both Chapels came under the Church of St. Paul, and they were both desecrated; this caused the growth of dissent in West Cornwall.

The next Vicar in 1581 was **John Tremearne**, and now the Patron is the Queen herself; since

Henry VIII's dissolution of the monasteries the patronage passed to the Queen, as the Abbey and Monastery of Hailes in Gloucester was no more. John Tremearne was the Vicar who made a note in the beginning of the Parish register, after the violence and burning of the Church Vicarage and Village by the Spanish raid of 1595.

John Tremearne tried manfully to carry out his duties of Marriage, Christenings and Burials in the portion of the church that was left after the burning. He also tried to live in the western end of his burnt vicarage, in the kitchens, which still stand today (more of that under Vicarages - this Chapter) but it all was too much for him and he gave up.

On his resignation, the next vicar was the **Revd. Thomas Harries, M.A.** He was instituted in 1624, and he died in 1661. At that time part of the pre-fire Vicarage was still standing, but by now was probably uninhabitable – this Vicar could have resided somewhere else in the Parish or even been a Vicar *in absentia.*

A few gaps appear here as some of the Vicars do not seem to have any documentary information listed.

The **Revd. Henry Pendarves** (1694-1739) descended from the Pendarves family of Roscrow and died 14th June, 1739, as stated on his large memorial tablet on the left of the altar. At this time there was a letter written to all Parishes under the Patronage of the Prince of Wales, with a list of said Parishes; Paul was one of them – the letter from the Prince of Wales' Office at Pall Mall dated 21st April, 1787 states:

'We are directed to enter a Caveat in the Court of the Bishops of Exeter, to the effect that no Institution may take place in consequence of any Presentation to such livings unless from the Prince himself.'

The letter goes on to ask what form this caveat should be presented, the reply came probably from the Bishop's office that the caveat should be entered into the Book of Office in the usual form. Original documents to this effect are in the Devon Record Office. The Revd. Pendarves was the first Vicar to live in the newly built vicarage of 1726. More about Revd. Pendarves in Chapters 7 and 3 respectively.

Revd. Henry Penneck (1739-1771) was the second son of Charles Penneck of Tregembo in St. Hilary, and became Rector of Cheriton Fitzpaine in Devon, after being Vicar of Paul. He died on 23rd August, 1784 and was brought back to Paul, a Parish he loved dearly, to be buried under the altar. On 7th July, 1807 some thirty-six years after her husband left Paul Church as Vicar, Mrs. Juliana Penneck, then his widow, died aged 76. Her body was also brought to Paul, to be buried with her husband under the altar.

According to the Revd. Gilbert Doble, in reply to a questionnaire sent to all incumbents in the Diocese by the Bishop *'have you any Chapels in this parish*?' the Revd. Henry Penneck wrote *'We have some old walls here and there that ye people call chapels and which were so, if at all, before ye Reformation'.* Another mystery! One could have been a Chapel at Newlyn desecrated by Queen Elizabeth I.

Revd. John Allen, (1771-1802), Vicar of Paul, died in his Parish of South Moulton and was buried in the chancel of that Church *'A man of whom iniquity was not imputed and in whose spirit there was no guile.'*

Revd. G. J. Scobell (November 1786). This man must have been another Curate under the
Revd. R. Gurney, as their dates are concurrent, as are those of:-

Revd. C. V. Le Grice

Revd. Charles Valentine Le Grice (1799). The Revd. Le
Grice, was the son of the clergyman the Revd. Charles Le
Grice. He lived at 'Trereife Park' and was a noted poet and
writer. He was a friend of the poet Coleridge, both being
fellow students of Christ's Hospital School and Cambridge
University. He obtained his B.A. in 1796, and returned to
Cornwall to tutor William John Godophin Nicholls, son of
the widowed Mary Nicholls of Trereife, whom he married on
16th May, 1799. They subsequently had a son of their own,
Day Perry Le Grice. Shortly after his marriage he was
ordained, and began his ecclesiastical career as Vicar of
Paul Church.

Although the Revd. Le Grice is reported as 'Vicar' of Paul,
(this being his first experience of priesthood), he would
probably have only served as a Curate, assisting Revd. Richard Gurney, and possibly his son
the Revd. W. O. Gurney. Then in 1806 he went on to be perpetual Curate of St. Mary's
Church, Penzance. He did not bandy words and preached against the 'danger' of Methodist
revivalism in 1814. He died in 1832 and is buried in Madron Church.

It seems that the Revd. W. O. Gurney was such a good Curate of Paul that Vicars came and
went and seem to overlap at this time, and he presumably held the fort; there is very little
written about the Revds. John Allen, and J. Scobell who also served Paul Church during his
incumbency.

Revd. Richard Gurney (1786-1825). Father of long term Curate the Revd. W. O. Gurney.
Richard died 17th May, 1825 aged 77. He wrote in 1821 in a report for the Visitation of Bishop
Carey, that there were 800 families and no Papists, but many dissenters in his Parish. There
were no residential teachers, two Methodist Meeting Houses, one Baptist and one Independent
Chapel, all licensed. He was residing in Tregony, at St. James. The Curate at Paul was his son
Revd. W. O. Gurney, who did not live in the Vicarage, but in his own house (Trungle) near the
Church; his salary was £70. There was no instruction of youth but a common school where
rudiments of religion was taught. He was Ordained July 1773 and was instituted to the Vicarage
of Paul, in 1786. (Thus no Sunday School in 1821!)

Revd. Warwick Oben Gurney – admitted 13th March, 1802. He was officially only the Curate
of Paul Church, but he carried out this office for a long period of 47 years. He was also a
qualified solicitor and acted when various deeds were drawn up for land for the Cholera Ground
in 1817, and again on 18th May, 1852 for the land for the new church burial ground behind the
Church Hall.

A mystery arose around an old water colour painting now owned by the Roger Bond,
Churchwarden, (present owner of Trungle House), and entitled 'The Vicarage'. This was
eventually made clear, knowing the length of time the Revd. W. O. Gurney held the Curacy of
Paul, as the painting does not depict the old Vicarage, but Trungle House (see 'Vicarages' in
this Chapter). A letter written by his nephew states that his Aunt lived in Trungle House and it
seems that his Uncle Warwick sometimes separately lived in the Vicarage.

Presumably he retired to his own house when a new Vicar was instituted. He is described as a '*kind but melancholy man, deeply inbred with Calvinism.*' His sermons were described as '*eloquent*', and he spoke without notes.

He had a standing feud with his Father the Vicar of Paul and Rector of Tregony, in doctrinal matters, and would fulminate against him in the words of St. James '*Shew me they faith without thy works, and I will* shew *thee my faith by my works*'. He was seen pacing and meditating in the Vicarage garden many times. The nephew also wrote '*lest I should be thought irreverent, that nobody called the parish of Paul – St. Paul in those days.*' This was written during his Uncle's incumbency.

Revd. Warwick O. Gurney was an energetic fellow and, in 1843, was also the Rector of Aston Botterell Near Bridgend and Rector of a Parish near Bridgenorth. The Revd. Gurney must have had to travel between the Parishes, but settled mainly in Paul. His children were Oben, John, William, Nanny and Agnes. Agnes died of consumption aged only 13, and is buried under the altar. Revd. Gurney died in August, 1849 aged 70 was buried in Paul Church.

Revd. Charles George Ruddock Festing was presented by the Lord Chancellor Eldon, and admitted to Paul Church 14th August, 1827 - formerly of St. John's College Cambridge. He was Vicar of Paul Church for 30 years. He was a pluralist, (holding two Livings, see above W.O. Gurney) which was obviously quite a common occurrence in 19th century, and he was also appointed to Witham Friary, Somerset, in 1822 for 35 years. He moved into the Vicarage at Witham Friary, Somerset, in 1822, and shortly afterwards married Miss Louisa Seagram, and they had a son and daughter. As his predecessor, the Revd. W. O. Gurney, he probably commuted between the two Parishes, finally coming to live in Paul in 1850. He died on 30th August, 1857 and his body was returned to burial in the churchyard at Witham Friary, where an east window was erected to his memory. It is said that *he also* lived at Trungle House. This Vicar was probably responsible for erecting the galleries in church.

Revd. John Garrett (1857) about whom, unfortunately, nothing is known.

Revd. W. Carpenter, Doctor of Divinity, was born in Ireland in 1806, and had originally intended to become a lawyer. He eloped to marry the daughter of Sir William Forbes! He was Curate of Odogh, Co. Kilkenny (1831-32) where he was very popular. Then Curate of St. Barnabas Isle of Man (1832-1845) and Vicar of St. Jude's Church, Liverpool (1849-50), where his evangelical tone and anti-Catholic feelings caused problems. He came to Paul in 1864 from Christ Church, Moss-side Manchester, where '*his counsel was ever needed and as readily given*'. He moved to Paul because of ill-health, and was Vicar of Paul Church for only one year, and died on 24th December, 1865. His flock erected a memorial tablet to him, as a '*mark of affectionate remembrance*'. He is buried in the School Burial Ground. The Revd. Carpenter made his mark upon Paul Church by carrying out sweeping restorations to the fabric, as detailed in Chapter 3, although he only ministered at Paul for a short time

Revd. Malone

Revd. Richard Malone who was instituted 13th March, 1866, had a reredos erected in Paul Church in memory of his Father, Revd. Edmund Malone, the Vicar of Pendeen. He also arranged for the tower belfry windows to be replaced with authentic pierced protective frames, which came from another church, and replaced the rubble that previously filled these windows (see Chapter 12). On 16th May, 1876 Revd. Malone accepted the living of Upton in Bucks and left Paul shortly after (ref: Cornish Telegraph). In the 1873 Vestry Minutes one can read about Paul Church under the guidance of the two Vicars, the Revds. Richard Malone, and Robert Aitken (Chapter 6). From now on I am lucky to have photos of the ensuing Vicars.

Revd. Robert Wesley Aitken, (1876-1911). The Cornish Telegraph records that on two Feast Sundays, in both 1877 and in 1878, Revd. R. W. Aitken preached at Paul. The Revd. Aitken was the younger brother of the famous Canon William Hay McDowall Hunter Aitken, and the son of the Vicar of Pendeen, the Revd. Robert Aitken. Thus both Vicars of Paul, Malone and Aitken, had coincidentally paternal Clergymen of Pendeen! The Revd. R. W. Aitken was Priested in the Diocese of York in 1859 and held Curacies in York and on the Isle of Man. He was Vicar of St. Paul's Church Penzance from 1862-1869.

His mother was rather renowned for her advocacy of corporal punishment, especially across her knee with the '*lid of a skillet!*' In Pendeen, mothers were known to admonish their children with: '*Mind now, or Mrs. Aitken will warm 'ee!*' His wife was called Mary and he had seven daughters Mary, Beatrice, Mabel, Lilian, Helen, Treur, Theodora and one son Cecil.

Cecil Aitken composed carols for Christmas, and wrote a booklet called 'The Ancient Church of Paul, Cornwall' in January, 1910. Cecil writes highly of his father for allowing him to write the booklet, and the Revd. Aitken wrote a forward to the publication. This stated that he wanted the Church to be freely accessible to the visiting public and wrote that the Caretaker of the Church had the key should it be closed. Mabel Georgina Aitken, the Revd. Aitken's daughter, married Dr. Ashley T. Jago (see Chapter 16). Their son also Dr. Jago lived at Penolva and read the Lessons in Paul Church, (in a memorable voice) many years later. The granite pulpit was erected in the memory of Revd. R. W. Aitken in 1911.

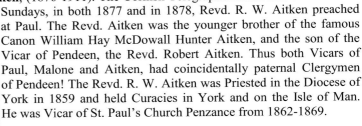
Revd. Prideaux

In the P.C.C. Minutes the **Revd. Frederick Joseph Prideaux**, (1911-1938) who died 15th September, 1938 is reported as being '*a perfect gentleman in every respect*'. He was very musical, and his wife sang in the choir. He was described as a wonderful man with a small beard, quite tall and grey haired. He had one daughter known as '*Miss Betty*'. He was a well to do Vicar with many servants, two gardeners and a chauffeur. One such gardener was called Luther Maddern who helped out when he was a young man, as did Timmy Trenoweth. The gates to the old Vicarage were in pristine condition in those days, and would swing open to allow the Revd. Prideaux to sweep up the drive to the front of the Vicarage. The Vicarage garden was used a lot for garden parties, and concerts for the children, and the lawns and flower beds were immaculate.

He was a very kind gentleman, although not a great preacher, nor a good parish visitor, and he was always smoking! Often when he threw cigarette butts down, Paul village children would follow him and smoke them after him! He would come out of the Vicarage in a cloud of smoke and if he saw children sitting on the 'Green' wall, would come over and say 'Morning Girls,' and give them sixpence each, which was a fortune in those days. He always had a kindly smile, but his wife was more reserved. There were Firework displays in the orchard at the back of the Vicarage garden, and the Vicar grew lots of gooseberries, which were shared out amongst the children during outings.

The Revd. Prideaux would often choose the choir boys, and called George Prowse and Charlie his brother down to the Vicarage to hear their voices. He told George 'I'll have this one' but Charlie was told 'you can go home!' George Prowse sang in the choir from that moment on for sixty years (see also Chapter 12). When Revd. Prideaux died his Parishioners gave the present Vicar's desk and chair, carved with angels, in his memory (see Chapter 7).

Revd. F. E. Eddy, (1939-42) during whose incumbency there were 3,000 souls in the Parish of Paul. He is described as a small man, with fairish hair, and much loved, as he was a good Vicar. His brother was an architect, and he studied to become an architect before he took the cloth. He had a servant who came from the Bernardos Homes. Mrs. Eddy and her daughter carried out war work at the Vicarage, as agents for charities. They addressed 1,000 envelopes for 10/-, and her daughter bought her first pair of blue shoes with her pay.

Revd. Eddy

Revd. William Valentine Wagner, (1942-1953) who is described as a 'dear chap', tall and imposing and 'looked like a Vicar'. He was a good preacher, and it seems his only down side was that he 'could not sing'! He officiated at the marriage of Marion and Eric Harvey in 1948, also Mary and Billy Barnes in 1944. In the Revd. Wagner's time Church Parade was a regular Service attended by Guides and Scouts. Merelle Wagner, the Vicar's daughter, was a Girl Guide Leader, and was known by all as 'Miss Merelle'. Merelle Wagner kept the Vicarage going, and acted as a housekeeper for her parents. She moved to Penzance when her parents died.

Revd. Wagner arranged for a new Priest's Stall to be added to the Church in memory of the Revd. Prideaux on 23rd June, 1942.

Mary's sister Ellen and Harold Gruzelier were married by Canon Oatey, brother of Miss Oatey, Organist and Choir Mistress; later Ellen was married to Thornley Renfree. The Revd. Wagner was very popular as a Vicar, a 'steady chap.' He was a good preacher and a very gentle man, and was described as 'kind and compassionate'. Mrs. Wagner was described as 'a gentlewoman'. She was a plumpish lady, extremely smart at all times, and often wore fur coats, and hats. She also wore a chunky gold charm bracelet which rattled as she walked; the children were in awe of her and ran away at the sound of the charms clinking. She founded the Paul Branch of the Mothers' Union but had no interest in the Women's Institute, which also started in Paul in 1946. In fact, Mrs. Wagner made life very difficult for the W.I. Ladies, not allowing them to meet in the Church Hall, thus they met in Sheffield Sunday School, and inaugurated the Sheffield Branch of the Women's Institute.

Her reasons were that she thought she would lose her Mothers' Union Ladies to the W.I. Although she had a strong personality, she was also very kind and visited people, taking them goodies to help out, and was especially supportive to those in time of trouble. Even a local Clergyman, Revd. Michael Hocking of Madron, found her a very *'difficult lady'*. However, her kindness behind the scenes reminds us that there are always two sides to everyone! She was described as *'one of the old school'*. She also produced many plays and shows in Paul which were thoroughly enjoyed by all.

The Revd. Wagner died in 1953. On 1st June, 1955, as a memorial to this well-respected Vicar, a simple brass processional cross was purchased. Also, at this time, the churchwardens' staves of white painted wood were replaced with two oak staves surmounted by brass crosses.

Revd. Deryck Harry Percival Davey (1953-1960) Paul was his first Parish; he had been Curate

under Revd. Michael Hocking at Madron Church. His wife was called Margaret, and he met her at Durham University where he earned his B.A., and she an M.A. Margaret has been described as *'a dear person'* and also *'her soul was in her lovely face'*. They had four children, two of whom were born in the Vicarage. The Vicarage garden rang to the sound of children's voices, and John and Peter were in the choir. Sadly his wife died, and he married again, another 'Margaret'. He is described as a young, dynamic, modern man, tall, dark and handsome! He was kindly and full of life and his sermons were reputedly short and sweet. Great changes came about in Paul Church under him, he increased number of the congregation, and the Sunday School was packed with children. He was practical, and arranged the removal to the walls of tombstones (Hall Burial Ground) under Faculty dated 7th February, 1955. He was very musical, and took choir practice some times, being a very good singer. The Church would ring with music under him, he took part in quartets, etc. Although some older congregation members were rather put out by his new young ideas. He started the extremely popular Old Tyme Dancing in the Church Hall. Lawrence George was master of ceremonies, and with his gramophone and microphone led the

Revd. Tyrrell

dancing. Revd. Davey was a very kindly man and has been described as *'the best loved of Vicars'*. When he left the Parish it is reported that all the young ladies were sad and went into a decline! He went on to Liskeard and was made a Canon.

Revd. John Herbert Tyrrell (1960-1966). Described as average height, with straight dark hair, a *'sports jacket and corduroy trousers sort of man'*. He was also described as an artistic man who *'didn't look like a Vicar'*. He wasn't very robust looking, although quite broad shouldered. His wife was Barbara, a pretty, bubbly lady who didn't have much time to help in the Church, as she had two children Peter and Sally. He was once an engineer and had trained as a teacher, and was very clever. He also liked to hunt, and was mad on railways and trains. He had an interest in antique guns, which he restored and made parts for them in the Vicarage.

He was a talented artist, and drew the well-known black and white view of Paul Church for the Magazine cover (depicted left). He kept a pony for his children in the Vicarage stables, and pigs and chickens on the little plot behind Hutchens House, which then belonged to the Church. He amused the Sunday School children by tying sweets to trees and bushes in the Vicarage garden, and giving the children free rein to run around and find them.

He was musical, and supported the Choir, but his main attribute was to encourage the youth of the Parish with discussions conducted over coffee at the Vicarage. He was interested in the science of hypnosis and once hypnotised Christopher Carter, brother of Hilary Madron. He was a *'brilliant'* preacher, although he didn't find running the Church very easy. He was also a talented wood carver, and carved a new front on the extension of choir pews to match the others. His beloved dog was sadly killed by a falling grave stone in the School Cemetery. The Revd. Tyrell also had to contend with roof repairs, and the church had to pay £632.3.2d. for repairs in five equal yearly instalments, at this time. He left Paul Church suddenly for personal reasons.

It is rather unusual to mention a retired Priest, who assisted during the interregnum, but this book could not fail to mention the **Revd. Lane-Davies** whom the children Christened: Mr. Magoo! He was reported to be in his eighties. He used to drive all the way from Newquay for 8.30 a.m. Holy Communion, and then have breakfast in the Village with various Parishioners before the next Service. He often went to Rosecott Farm for breakfast with the Harvey family. He was a *'lovely little fellow'* and he adored the farm children, and when he left Paul he took a picture of the Choir sitting on the Church Green (see Chapter 12).

Revd. Lane-Davies

Revd. Reginald Hugh Cadman (1966-1982), Rural Dean of Penwith. He was a gentle man, tall and rather

portly, with receding white hair and often wore dark glasses. His personality was described as having a *'quirky sense of humour hidden by solemn exterior'*. His character was *'good and caring'*. The Revd. Cadman was a Freemasons' Chaplain. He supported bell ringing; when Reg Curtis was Captain of the Tower. His wife Alice, described as *'a slim'* lady, was very community minded and helped with Church cleaning. Alice also worked hard for the Mothers' Union and Women's Institute. They had one son called Hugh. The Revd. Cadman had studied ecclesiastical law before becoming a Vicar. He introduced new responses for which special practices for the congregation were held at 8.30. The main service on Sunday at this time was Matins, and once a month Sung Holy Communion. Both Services took place at 11.00 a.m. using the Book of Common Prayer. When the Revd. Cadman left Paul Church he retired to Drift.

Revd. Geoffrey Harper (1982-1998). He was born in St. Agnes, and is of medium to short stature, with curly hair. He is married to Julie, whom he met during his first incumbency in Birmingham, they have three children; Stephanie, Phillip and Catherine. Julie was always

Revd. G. Harper

happy to help with Church life. Revd. Harper came to Paul from Sheviock Parish, Truro (1973-1980), and had the had the task of introducing the new Rite A Service, taken from the Alternate Service Book, to Paul Church. The pattern of worship was altered at this time, reflecting the changes happening throughout the Church of England. After P.C.C. consultation, Choral Communion Rite A (ASB) was introduced for two Sundays a month, with Matins (BCP 1662) on the remaining Sundays. The main morning service was brought forward to commence at 10.30 a.m. instead of 11.00 a.m. Coffee and tea was served at the end of the Services to facilitate congregational social integration. The Service at 8.30 a.m. remained Holy Communion according to the rites of the Book of Common Prayer, as did Evensong at 6.00 p.m.

The Revd. Harper was Chairman of the Trustees of Hutchens' House, and he worked hard obtaining grants for the greater improvement of the flats for the elderly, with his team of Maurice Smelt, Howard Witt, and Liz Prowse. Geoffrey Harper was very keen on Celtic spirituality and the arts, but was not particularly musical. He had a keen social conscience, and during his ministry encouraged the people of Paul to support those in need locally, as well as those in the third world. Two of the causes he led people to support were "Penwith One-percenters" and "Penzance Breadline".

During his incumbency the Revd. Pat Robson trained as a Lay Reader, who went on to be a one of the first women priests to be Ordained, and was eventually made a Canon of Truro Cathedral. Supported by Revd. Harper, Pat Robson instigated a system (Penwith City Kids Scheme) whereby sixty or so children from (Birmingham) inner city areas came to stay for holidays in Paul. Revd. Harper led the Church through a major restoration programme, which due to dry rot, involved the renewal and replacement of the roof and flooring (see Chapter 3).

Revd. Gordon John Hansford (1999- until the present day).
Revd. Gordon Hansford, his wife, Jean, daughter Joanne, and son David, came to Paul from North Devon in February 1999. There he was Rural Dean of Hartland for three years, and for nine years was Rector of the United Benefice of Landcross, Littleham, Monkleigh, and Weare Giffard. He became Team Vicar when these Parishes joined the Torridge Estuary Team Ministry.

The Revd. Hansford is a tall man, fair, blue-eyed and of slim build. He is an ex-chemistry teacher whose call to full time Christian service came in 1967. He joined the Church Missionary Society, and served for eight years as a teacher in Hong Kong. It was at St. Andrew's Church, Kowloon that Gordon met Jean, and they were married in Wales in 1974. Gordon then trained for the ordained ministry at Trinity Theological College, Bristol, and served curacies in Exeter and Southampton before his appointment to North Devon. The Revd. Hansford supports all Paul Church activities. Jean sings in the Choir and Gordon regularly attends Choir practice, listens and gives encouragement and a concluding prayer at the end of the practice.

During the first three and a half years of Revd. Hansford's incumbency he was assisted by the Revd. Helen Poole, a very popular Honorary Assistant Curate of Paul. In June 2006 the Revd. Yvonne Hobson was licensed as Honorary Assistant Curate of Paul Church, having served her title at Illogan, Portreath and Trevenson. The Revd. Hobson has settled in well, and is playing an active part in the life of Paul Church.

The Revd. Hansford encouraged the development of ecumenical relationships, and the three Villages Youth Project was founded. Common Worship Services were introduced, replacing the Alternate Service Book (1980), which ceased to be authorized on the first Sunday of Advent 2000. The Book of Common Prayer continues in use for Matins, Evensong and 8.30 a.m. Holy Communion.

Revd. Yvonne Hobson

Revd. Helen Poole

THE VICARAGES OF PAUL CHURCH

One could surmise that there may have been four vicarages at Paul over the years, but the truth is Paul had four and a half! Explanations later!

The very first Vicarage of Paul would have been modest, like the Church. Maybe even a tiny thatched cottage built of Cornish granite and situated next to the Church, roughly in the area of the Georgian Vicarage today. As the Church was enlarged, the Vicarage would have kept pace, and the pre-fire (1595) Vicarage number two would probably have been constructed to coincide with the erection of the tower, and one or other or the aisles in the 1400s. In a Glebe

The Vicarage c. 1726

Terrier of 1680, it is described as having had before the fire, *'many rooms'*. As Paul Church owned such valuable plate, it would have had a Vicarage befitting the high status of the Priest. This Vicarage of the Revd. John Tremearne's time (the unfortunate incumbent of 1595), was mainly destroyed by fire during the Spanish Raid. Or was it? See below…!

Documentary evidence in the form of Glebe Terrier demonstrates that the poor chap tried to eke out an existence in the 'western parts, or kitchen area of the Vicarage'. He lived there for a while, in two rooms that he had repaired at his own cost, and also tried to carry on with services in his *'ruinated'* Church, but in the end had to give up. Thus in 1680 after the Church had been rebuilt (1600), the Vicarage was still in ruins. The people of that time were not used to the comfort of today, but even so, the hardship the Vicar and his congregation suffered in the loss of their homes must have been terrible. Who consoled whom? All would turn to the Priest, for consolation as their leader, yet he was struggling with them. So not wishing to desert his Church and home he remained living in the erstwhile kitchen area, at the western end of the Vicarage plot, for as long as he could.

Knowing that the Vicarage was all but ruined by fire, I noticed something very exciting in the old sheds of the old Georgian Vicarage. I happened to be doing some gardening with my husband for the present Vicar, Gordon, and on putting my tools away looked up towards the door where I spied a huge wooden lintel above the door in one of the sheds. Nothing unusual in that, and sheds are constructed solidly of granite, but this beam ***was charred and blackened*** as from a fire! However, I did find out that there was a fire in Mrs. Tyrell's sewing room over the garage, in the 1960s, which *could* discount the garage area. However, huge, charred beams in the sheds, together with the blackened door lintel, gave convincing evidence that I was probably standing in the remains of the pre-1595 Vicarage kitchen area!!! Paul Vicarage number two.

I set about trying to prove this was so, and had read in the Glebe Terrier the fact that the only part of the Vicarage to remain standing was in the western, kitchen end, this just happens to be the location of the sheds today! Another clue was that in one of the sheds is a huge *granite* lintel, such as would be found over the cooking or fireplace area. Well, it was convincing, then I realised that the little 'flower cupboard' was once a passageway (evidence – old map and the door lintel, thought to be a ship's timber, ref: Dr. J. Mattingly) through to the churchyard. Well, the Vicar wouldn't have walked all the way round would he? He would probably have nipped

through, and into the
Church through his Priest's
door in the south aisle.

Thus the burnt Vicarage
remained just about
habitable, for a while, in the
western portion, and it
remained standing until at
least 1680, according to the
Glebe Terrier of that date.
The new Vicarage was
constructed sometime
shortly before 1726, some
forty-six years later. Where
the Vicar lived in between
time is not known. Money
for a new Vicarage would
have been tight, having to
rebuild the Church and the
Village after the Spanish

Vicarage Garden Party 1960 - Mrs. Haughton in dark hat
and coat talking to Zelda Rodda. Mr. Haughton in a suit.

Raid. The Revd. Henry Pendarves, Vicar of
Paul for 58 years (1694-1739), came from a
well known Cornish family, and family wealth may have helped to build the new Vicarage
in 1726.

If one looked at the roof of the 1726 Vicarage before 2005, one could see lions' heads peering
from the guttering, a nice architectural touch. Unfortunately these lions have disappeared with
the advent of new guttering circa 2005. This Vicarage had a large extension on its western side,
now demolished; this may be seen in the Vicarage floor plans, dated 1920s, which are kept in the
Cornwall Record Office. Many of today's congregation fondly recall the Summer Fetes held in
the Vicarage Garden, with its magnificent view of Mount's Bay. To date the Vicarage still has
its old gates at the side entrance, and the double gates at the eastern end of the garden.

The 'half' Vicarage is Trungle House. Trungle House was, in the early 19th century, owned and
lived in by two Clergy of Paul, (the Revds. W.O. Gurney and C.G. Ruddock-Festing), and as
such sometimes was known as 'The
Vicarage', which caused a lot of
confusion, with the real Vicarage (1726).

The Vicarage by the Church is now
known as the 'Old Vicarage' and is in
private occupation. The Rev. Gordon and
Jean Hansford moved to their new
Vicarage, built at the entrance of Paul
Village, in May 2002. This is the fourth
Vicarage house of Paul Church.

Paul Church Vicarage - 2006

CHAPTER 6 - VESTRY MINUTES

The following Vestry Minutes and P.C.C. Notes now in the Cornwall Record Office, both show a fascinating insight into the running of Paul Church in the past. A Church as a body of Christian people is never static: it evolves, and hopefully improves its administration, fellowship and worship over the years. Similar problems were encountered in 1872, over Church restoration, as in the 1980s, and one may read and recognise similar on-going difficulties with finance and administrative situations. The ever present need to keep ecclesiastical buildings up to scratch, fund raising, and the pastoral needs of the parishioners, in essence, do not change; and the human touches in these notes are priceless. They also remind today's congregation that they do not own their Church completely, and that as a building, is merely lent to them for the duration, to be cherished and handed on to the next generation. It seems odd reading of other people managing Paul Church, but of course, in their time it was theirs, and it will naturally pass into the hands of those who follow us. My comments appear in *italics*; their text appears in note form.

1872 - Meeting to consider plans for reseating the Church. Present: Vicar, the Revd. R. Malone Churchwardens Henry Maddern and Simon Hosken. Mr. Seddings' Plans were inspected and:-

1. The doors for the pews were considered too narrow. (*At this point the names William Gage and Charlie Rowe were written on the side of the page and the date - 1918.*)
2. Church floor must remain the same incline.
3. South East entrance will require alteration in one – making the entrance more ? (*illegible*) and not disturbing the children's seats.

Mr. Henry Maddern proposed, Mr. William Curnow seconded, and Committee was elected for NEWLYN – George Dorning, William Tonkin and Stephen Bodinaar. MOUSEHOLE – Captain William Pentreath. and Mrs. Fred Wright. FOR THE COUNTY – William Kneebone (Gwavas), Thomas Edmonds – KEMYELL. William Curnow – TRUNGLE, and H. Gartrell – KEMYELL.

30th November, 1872 - Vicar, the Revd. Malone, Mr. D. P. Le Grice Present.
The amount of £272.14.00 was already promised, and £20.00 more may be expected from the Parish when the fishing turned out more successfully. Tenders from: Messrs. Oliver, Bone, Bodinaar, Maddern and Roberts. Considerations made 17th January, 1873:

1. Joists should go up length of church and should rest on stone blocks, no mention of type of wood.
2. Depth of excavation under floor should be stated.
3. Committee wished joists to be of old oak at 5 x 2½.
4. Roman cement on side walls to join with the present plaster.
5. Chancel door to be raised a foot – new porch to correspond with other work.
6. The Committee thinks that there should be two coats of varnish.
     Reduced estimate resolved – pews should have no doors.
7. Rails of communion to abut against the pillars instead of coming forward as present.
8. Chancel seats to come eastward in a line with side aisle seats.
9. Encaustic tiles within communion rails to be done away with the encaustic tiles in chancel passage to be carried out.
10. Chancel seats to be deal (stained) instead of oak.
11. Depth of excavation under floor 15" instead of 2½ feet.
12. Instead of iron tongues – to be square jointed and dowelled.
13. Concrete bed 3" instead of 6".

Instead of a rail dividing pews in middle aisle – partition to go to the bottom. Consideration by Messrs. Downing, Maddern and Bodinnar for ventilation under the floors (*to prevent direct access of noxious fumes from vaults below to the congregation above*).

5th April, 1873 - William Curnow is to be churchwarden this was moved by Mr. Osborne seconded by Mr. Kneebone, Samson Hosken, to be parish churchwarden resolved that the organist and churchwardens are to be empowered to appoint a competent person to attend to repairing of the church organ.

2nd May, 1873 - The communion rail is to be brought forward to face the wall instead of coming forward as per plan. Stone floor is to be made good to form a step outside communion rail. Floors under the pews to be best yellow deal.

26th May, 1873 – Accepted Oliver's Tender of £345 work to commence by 1st July finished 1st September. (*These definite dates seems very optimistic!*) A temporary licence was obtained from Exeter for Divine Services in School Room Licence cost – 30/-. Work could not be finished in September, extension until 1st November, the Committee are greatly disappointed and another £5 will be needed for the restoration. Restoration Committee met in Vestry room in Church on **11th October** to make arrangements for re-opening of the church on 17th or 24th November. The Vicar Revd. Richard Malone wants this Service to last one hour only, but in event of weather being such as to prevent the fishermen from going to sea, then the Bishop is to be requested to attend the service. A pub luncheon is to be held in the Schoolroom from 1.00 p.m. to be provided by Mr. Hobley of Penzance. The Vicar introduced to the meeting three different specimens of hymn books to be used in re-opened church.

8thNovember, 1873 - A further £60 was needed to complete the restoration of the Church; a Bazaar is to be held at Christmas – the men are to mention suggestions to wives and daughters to canvass funds. Mr. H. Maddern suggested a 'Committee of Women' be formed to canvass the

Parish and endeavour to raise the required sum, but found no seconder. At the re-opening on Monday 17th November, all 'Seats should be Free' in the Church on a first come first served basis.

George Osborne, ploughing Well Meadow Henry (Harry) Osborne, his Father walking beside hands in pockets. Glasshouses of Trungle Vineries in the background.

SEATINGS – Appropriation of Sittings '*All sittings in nave or church will be charged 9d per quarter and all sittings in the aisles 6d per quarter.*' An amendment was passed that all sittings in the Nave - 9d per quarter; all sittings in pews in aisles which join pews in Nave - 8d per quarter. Southern aisle or elsewhere next to the wall = 6d (Mousehole side). Sittings in north aisle of Newlyn side = 6d. per quarter (*note: the north and south aisles were known by the names of Newlyn for north and Mousehole for south*).

25th November, 1873 - The sum of £20 is still outstanding, the Vicar to write to landowners in the Parish for help. List of repairs, altering reading desk – altering pulpit, extra rail on chancel seats – repairing north Gate and door to porch, repairing capitols of arcade and piscina, washing walls and ceiling.

29th March, 1875—New window put in east end of church – it was resolved that in future churchwardens receive 5% of amount of Pew Rents instead of 7/- each. Churchwardens should be changed each year, Joseph Wright elected for the Vicar's Warden, and Will Curnow was re-elected for the Parish.

A Fund was started by the Vicar of £2.10/- for placing two new windows in the western side of the church. It was decided to plant shrubs in churchyard surrounding the church. Mr. Wright mentioned trouble with Pew Rent from George Matthews and Miss Edmonds, although they still occupy pews. Mr. Wright is to notify these two persons that if they did not pay their rental, their seats would be let to other parties. The accounts were duly examined –

resolved on motion of Henry Osborn, seconded by W. Curnow (Penolva) that the Churchwardens Accounts - showing a Balance of £1.1.10½d due to the Parish, should be allowed.

Letter of complaint read – Mr. W. H. Trahair had been deprived of his pew when the Church was restored – he set forth a claim to a pew recently vacated by Philip Tonkin, and hoped the Vestry would let him occupy it. Mr. Charles Wright said he had already let the pew to Mr. Thomas Veale (of Paul Church Town). The Vestry would try and provide Mr. Trahair with a pew a.s.a.p.

On receiving a report that dry rot was in a few pews in the church, inspection by a carpenter was ordered. The Vicar wanted to find a rod and curtain for the south end of the Church in order to serve the purpose of a robing room, owing to the inconvenience of the Vestry room being so far from the Reading Desk. A rod and rail came from St. Paul's Church Penzance.

The Vicar strongly expressed his determination to have order in Church during Divine Service, and in the churchyard during Burials.

A Bill for repairing the organ from Easter 1876 to Easter 1877 - £1.10.00d. The close of **Hutchens' Charity** in 1877 showed a balance of **£11.8.9d.** Miss Carne of Penzance gave the meadow adjoining the Vicarage ground to the Vicar and his successors; it is now part of the glebe lands.

20th March, 1880 – John James Downing of Mousehole put in additional choir seats in the chancel at a cost of 13/6d. The Vicar the Revd. R. Malone, expressed his intent of placing a reredos against the east wall of the chancel behind the altar table in memory of his Father. The Committee said they would be pleased to accept a memorial to the late Vicar of Pendeen, who was well known and universally loved. (*You may just make this reredos out in the interior photo c. 1905/10 Chapter 3.*)

The Vicar had £15 to purchase a warming apparatus for the Church but it was not enough, a warming apparatus could not be purchased for less than £30.00. *I think Revd. Malone must have either returned to Paul for the above, or written a letter, because I eventually found a report in the Cornish Telegraph that he left Paul Church shortly after 16th May, 1876 for the living of Upton in Buckinghamshire. He died in 1908.*

2nd April, 1880 – The Revd. Robert Aitken is now Vicar. (*Although it seems he was Vicar in 1876, it was not reported in the minutes until this date.*)

10th April, 1882 – Parish Clerk decided that the appointment of a permanent Parish Clerk should remain in abeyance as Vicar thinks his duties would be too light in Paul that none should be appointed at a fixed salary. Ask Mr. Wallis, Vestry Clerk, to assist in these duties; an arrangement was to be made between Mr. Wallis and the Vicar.

14th April, 1884 – The Revd. Aitken reported that the church roof was in an unsatisfactory state owing to weakness and was under the necessity of being constantly repaired after every bit of wind. Mr. Joseph Wright suggested that a cargo of slate be brought to Mousehole for a new roof – but the resolution was not passed. The Vicar was on the look-out for a new organist, as Miss Aitken (*Mabel photo—see Chapter 16),* had not been paid for the past two years, so it was decided to pay her off and look for another. There is to be a Notice put up in the porch inviting tenders of washing out of church and cleaning. Also the Sexton was not carrying out his duties to the satisfactory of the Parish - Vicar to speak to Sexton. The Vestry wondered from whom to purchase new Registry Books, the Vicar said the Churchwardens should write to Somerset House for the necessary books. (*These registers, now the **old** books, have recently been taken for preservation to the C.R.O.*)

29th April, 1886 - It was suggested that the removing of heating apparatus to further down the south aisle may mean that heat may be felt in the body of the Church. The Vicar suggested some kind of frame being hung outside the porch door, wherein should be placed certain rules for the guidance of the Constable, so that order may be maintained during Divine Service. James Harvey has been sworn before Magistrates as the legal Officer and was re-appointed to Office of Constable (*truncheons now in a glass case in the Church*). Hat pegs were put in the pews!

A diversion into the near fate of a truncheon or Church Constable's stave. In the late 1970s one truncheon that had belonged to George Robins, the Church Constable, was at his daughter's house, and about to be painted red, to sit by the fire-side as an ornament. Beryl Jackson grand-daughter of George Robins, rescued it and returned it safely to Paul Church, intact! The case for the truncheons was eventually made by Marick (Jim) Carne.

Truncheons dated 1828 and 1838

Paul Church Nativity Play

The tablet commemorating the three Johns was removed from the side of the porch. Church fittings insured for £2,500. In 1894 these were the Caretaker's duties:-
The matting to be taken up and rolled each week – all lamps and chandeliers were to be cleaned and trimmed, he had to attend all Marriages, Christenings and Burials – and keep surplices and table linen clean, and to clean the Stores. The Schoolroom was to be brushed out, all windows were to be cleaned. He was paid £12 for the Church and £1.10.00 for the School.
The Vicar always chose his Churchwarden, and the Parish elected their Churchwarden.

6th April, 1896 - The West Cornwall Infirmary collection totalled - £4.16.1d. A List of vacant pew sittings is to be posted in the Porch.

W.I. 1967, Joyce Osborn centre, Grace George third from back, in the front row, and Marion Harvey peeping through!

11th April, 1898 - Sidesmen were to be appointed to help churchwardens with collections. The window in the chancel facing the pulpit was made to open – to increase ventilation.

24th April, 1905 - Granite base for Lectern – was an anonymous gift to the Church. (*This is now in the churchyard leaning against the wall past the ancient cross, see photo in Chp. 3.*)

11th April, 1908 - Sidesmen Henry Harvey, R. Pentreath, George Laity, Walter Hallo, C. W. Harris, Jas Rodda, and J. H. Osborne. Mr. R. Pentreath raised the question of the correct number of Balls, which should have been shown on that portion of the window by the South door. Whether it was 15 instead of the number now there? Could it be altered without a Faculty? (*This refers to the Cornish shield – number of bezants in the window of St. Paulus of Leon, there are only ten depicted.*)

1913 - £200 needed for work on the Tower.

16th April, 1916 – Sidemen Cecil Aitken, W. Kneebone, W. H. Humphreys, J. H. Osborne, R. Cary, R. Pentreath, James Rodda, C. H. Rowe, W. J. Polglaze, Josiah James.

3rd December, 1917 - Vestry to inspect the drawings of the proposed Memorial window – east end of the Church.
1918 – Organist Mrs. Tregurtha is leaving Cornwall – The new window for Major Bolitho's son is in the Church Tower.

28th March, 1921 – It was proposed by Mrs. F. Ladner, that in case they needed a Faculty for the erection of a Clock in the Tower – they should apply for one. This is to be a War Memorial to the Fallen, of the recent War.

8th April, 1912, Mr. F. Searle – Organist was thanked, and so was the Choir.

That concludes the Vestry Minutes – I now pass on to the Parochial Church Council Minutes commencing in 1922.

Rose Queen - Demelza Stubbings

PAROCHIAL CHURCH COUNCIL

16th January, 1922 - P.C.C. to ascertain whether Church had Coat of Arms for a seal for the P.C.C. *(how very grand).*

30th January, 1922 - The Vicar as Chairman met the lady Organist, and is to appoint a Choirmaster.

11th October 1922 - The purchase of land for Burial Ground put in hands of Solicitor, W. T. J. Chellow. The Official Seal for the P.C.C. is to be authorised as soon as possible. Opinions were expressed that the musical parts of the services are unsatisfactory. After discussion the Vicar requested to consider getting permanent organist instead of the gentleman who was acting in a temporary capacity, and was in poor health.

Sheffield Women's Institute

School Burial Ground Boundary Stone – Mr. Henry Maddern Architect – fixed boundary stone. Prepare ground plan for School Burial Ground. Vicar instructed Mr. Henry Maddern in writing, and now Mr. Maddern wants paying. (*This stone may still be seen in the hedge at the end of the field, a granite stone with 'H' carved upon it.)*

14th November, 1922 - Mr. E. H. Mayne of 7 Greenbanks, Penzance, finished as temporary organist at Paul Church, The Vicar regretted that his interview with Mr. Mayne was of a rather stormy and trying nature, but the organist hoped his nerves would improve.

24th January, 1923 - The Conveyance re: School Burial Ground now completed. Mr. Henry Maddern of Morrab Road said some evil disposed person broke the cross on his Father's grave in the Old Cholera Ground and smashed it beyond repair, he communicated with the Church Constable – and complained about the disgraceful condition of this burial ground. The Urban District Council refused to consecrate a portion of the enlargement of their cemetery. The P.C.C. requested them to consecrate it, and made a complaint.

20th September 1923 - Feast discussed, and the Public Tea on Feast Monday – although it did not pay for itself, it was decided to keep it going as a tradition. Organist Mr. Edwin Smythe was ill causing his temporary absence. The Secretary of P.C.C. had not received Conveyance Deed relating to enlargement of School Burial Ground but had heard it was now ready for signature.

21st December, 1923 - Miss Jarrett paid rent to the Church for a Meeting Room at Mousehole, and objected to it being mentioned at P.C.C. (*Interesting - to find out where the Meeting room was, and who has it today? Was it ever sold?*)
Cholera Ground was closed and handed over to U.D.C. who are responsible for future upkeep – it is no longer to do with Paul Church.

Paul Church c. 1909

15th February, 1924 – The behaviour of certain members of the Choir was *suspect!* Mr. Osborne moved and Mr. North seconded that a letter would be written to the Choir drawing attention to frequent unseemly, and oft times irreverent behaviour, expressing the hope that worship would not be disturbed by such conduct in future.

25th April, 1924 – Mr. Edwin Smythe retired as organist, he appointed Miss Cora Waters Organist with Mr. C. Aitken as Choir-master. Treasurer's Report: Expenses - £211.9.9½d Income - £304.12.8½d - £50 to pay off balance of Mr. Pengelly's purchase of land enlarging School Burial Ground.

2nd May, 1924 - Damage in School Burial Ground by fowls – steps taken to stop their trespass by W. Hocking owner.

25th July, 1924 - A request was made again for the consecration of part of U.D.C. enlarged portion of the Cemetery.

20th February, 1925 - There are 400 signatures on petition to consecrate portion of U.D.C. Cemetery in Paul. The state of the Cholera Ground is disgraceful, the Vicar wrote to the Chairman of the U.D.C. about it.

(*Here is a list of P.C.C. members – I haven't listed them each time they met as they would have filled several volumes.*)
P.C.C. - 31st October, 1925:- Vicar Revd. F. J. Prideaux - present V. Spargo, R. Wallis, Misses F. Jarrett and May Belle Cotton, Messrs John Nicholls, R. Pentreath, W. H. Humphreys, L. North, C. Edmonds, B. Wright, G. Osborne, O. T. Spargo, Arnold Kneebone, James Rodda Snr, James Rodda Jnr, J. Cotton, Churchwardens Jas. Harvey, and C. Aitken.

It was proposed at the P.C.C., passed and women are now admitted! (*Hallelujah!*) Mrs. F. J. Prideaux, Mrs. N. Spargo, The Post Office Church Town, Mrs. Julia Stauffer – The Parade, Mousehole, Miss Potter, Prospect Place, Newlyn. C. Aitken Trungle, Jas Harvey – Rose Cot, Paul. John Nicholls - Raginnis Hill. Piva Wright, Portland Cottage, Mousehole. Richard Pentreath, Duck Street, Mousehole. J. H. Pengelly, Bollowal, Paul. G. Osborne, Paul Church Town. W. H. Humphreys, 'Keigwin' Mousehole. J. Cotton Trevithal Paul. R. Wallis, Sheffield.

Closed Burial Ground 'Cholera Ground', and to repair dilapidated state of lych-gate entrance. There are to be new flue pipes to the church heating stoves if they exist beyond repair (*they went up through the roof, like mini-chimneys see 1910 photo in Chapter 3*). Land was purchased twelve months previously, for purpose of enlarging School Burial Ground. Mr. J. H. Pengelly purchased the land on behalf of the Church for -£200.

25th March, 1926 - The debt was paid off for the enlarged School Burial Ground. The last instalment of £45.2.5d was paid off to Lloyds Banks (a mortgage had been taken to pay off Mr. Pengelly). Church Institute purchased a full sized billiards table – borrowed £20 from P.C.C. for it. U.D.C. says District Council is responsible for cleaning up and the maintenance of the Cholera Burial Ground.

29th March, 1926 - Tenders were invited for enclosing of the new Burial Ground with a new mason built clay mortar hedge 96ft 6 inches long to conform with western boundary.

27th October, 1926 - Bazaar and Garden Fete raised - £43.8.4½d which went into the general Fund.
18th April, 1927 – The churchwardens were considering the possibility of the Church doors opening outwards instead of inwards. (*These were the outer porch doors.*)
11th May, 1927 – Increasing Fire Insurance from £8,000 to £10,000 for church and contents.
16th December, 1922 – New stained glass window in North Aisle in memory of Mrs. Ackerman's late father. Messrs. Powell & Sons, London, made the window.
13th April, 1928 – Window in memory of the Leah family. (*That's all it said!*)
3rd April, 1928 – There was a small fire in the church, which was happily checked, and made good.
31st July, 1928 – There are damp walls in the Parochial School.
11th December, 1929 – The Vicar obtained supply of hymn books no longer required by Truro Cathedral – thanks to Canon Sedgewick.

19th May, 1930 – Mr. Wallis the carpenter hadn't been paid for painting the sun-dial, one window in the roof, and the removal of the collapsed flag pole on the tower. Mr. Aitken said that there was some work that had not been completed, and asked what had become of the flagstaff, and stays, which should have remained on Church property.

14th July, 1930 - The Question of Annual Choir Outing was raised – because of exceptional circumstances – suggested a Social evening in the winter. The Church roof is leaking.
September, 1930 – Choir are satisfied with the Social Evening offer in lieu of their Annual Outing.
The floor in the 'Free Seats' area has collapsed, and was found to be affected with dry rot.
20th October, 1930 – Faculty for Electric Lights in church.
8th January, 1931 – Faculty Granted for removal of existing oil-lamps and the substitution of electric lights by Electric Power Company - £95 - Plus lights over the door, and three lights in the School.

20th February, 1931 – Mrs. Bolitho donated £20 towards the lighting.

24th March, 1931 - £9 received from the sale of old oil lamps.

28th July, 1931 – Purchase of tortoise stove for £3 and Oil warmer 55/-.

12th May, 1933 – Bazaar 7th July, Mrs. Cyril Jarvis to open proceedings and 'Happy Go Lucky' Concert Party to entertain.

7th November, 1933 - In the Men's Club – the Billiards Table – belongs to the Church. The members of the P.C.C. decided the walls etc. were to be whitewashed and repaired. Mr. Osborne was informed that he is quite in order in attending the Club and reporting back to P.C.C. anything he deemed necessary (*a spy – forsooth!*) Paul Bank used a room in the School House too, and Mrs. Tippet cleaned it. (*Paul had its own Bank!*)

1934 – P.C.C. – Present:- C. B. Simons, John Rowe, M. Jordan, Miss M. Cary, R. Pentreath, J. Nicholls, R. Wallis, J. F. Ladner, J. Rowe, R. Drew, L. Spargo, G. Prowse, L. Trenoweth, Churchwardens - L. North, and T. Osborne.

11th May, 1934 – There is a total of £5.8.4d in the Pulpit fund. (*Left over from 1911?*)

16th July, 1934 – Mousehole Male Voice Choir asked permission to give a Musical Service in Church.

19th August, 1934 – After Evensong granted - (*presumably permission for the above, it was not clear*). The Garden Fete mad a profit of £60. Mr. L. North outlined arrangements for the Choir Outing, but no action was taken.

(*The following letter gives the first clue as to the real purpose of the large space called 'the boiler room' - see also Chapter 7.*)

14th November, 1934 – A letter from the Vicar Prideaux to Mr. Harvey re: a vault or crypt, partly completed for a person called Sir Rose Price, more than 100 years ago. Mr. R. Price intended to build a house in Paul Parish for his residence, and oddly enough arranged for a burial vault or crypt, to be made first. Before the house could be built or the vault completed, Trengwainton House, at Madron became vacant, and he went there to live (*incorrect, he lived at Kenegie first*), and is buried in a huge mausoleum in Madron Churchyard. The vault was completed with one exception – places for coffins had not been made, and later on, as it was not going to be used for burial, the door was taken down and the doorway built up between 1810–1820. A Faculty was applied for (*dated 29th October, 1934*), and granted, for a heating apparatus, new flue and new steps into boiler house to be made. The dimensions are 15ft to barrel vaulted roof with 2ft under floor void, which was used for heating pipes.

(*This Faculty is listed later on in the book. The 'door taken down and doorway built up' piece of this letter is very strange; would they mean a slab in the floor, could that be called a 'door', or do they mean the very small entrance that was made from the outside wall of the Church into the vault? This entrance was enlarged and more steps made, as above, to accommodate the new heating apparatus.*)

There was also letter from T. S. Atlee, of Leary Croft, Penzance objecting to the construction of an outside door to the vault (*possibly he meant enlarging the small entrance and making a door*). He states the P.C.C. have to find out if anyone from the family wants to be buried there.

Monday 18th November, 1935 - Burial fees to be same as charged by the Borough of Penzance for Burial in Paul Cemetery. Several members complained of irregularity of Bell ringing, decided to write and ask the bell ringers to adopt a more regular system.

16th July, 1934 – Heating tenders – Garton King, and Visick & Sons. Garton King - £184.18.6d. However this did not including delivery of plant to Penzance Station, whereas Visick =£180 complete.

22nd January, 1937 – Advertisement for new organist at £30 per month was inserted in 'Church Times'. The bell ringing matter was mentioned and Mr. North said he will see them.

29th March, 1937 – The Vicar said there were a total of 107 Communicants on Easter Sunday, and that was the largest number he had seen in 26 years.

23rd February, 1937 - Mr. Curtis from Aberystwyth has been offered the post of Organist.
15th November, 1937 – Improvement seen and heard in the Choir under Miss Oatey.
31st December, 1937 - The donations from Paul Church were shown in the accounts :-

CHURCHWARDENS ACCOUNTS – For December 31st 1937

	£
Bishop's Church School	3.00.00d
Church Missionary Society (Three Johns)	2.10.06d
West Cornwall Hospital	7.10.03d
Newlyn British Legion	1.08.07d
South American Missionary Society (Three Johns)	3.07.08d
Sick & Needy	1.01.10d
Brotherhood	1.05.00d
Society of Jews	1.06.07d
Central Africa	0.10.00d
Sunday School	4.16.00d
British Bible Society	1.13.00d
Printing	47.00.00d
Choir Outing	**17.08.00d**
Church Salaries	69.08.00d

In 1937 the Choir Outing cost £17.8.0d which was the largest outgoing apart from Printing! No mention of Bell Ringers.

8th February, 1938 – School Burial Ground dug over and cleaned – cost £20.
The Sunday School is self supporting – raised £20 for this year's working.
The walls of the Church are to be scraped. A new large safe is to be purchased.
22nd July, 1938 – The organ state is good, mellow and toned.

The Revd. F. J. Prideaux died on **15th September, 1938** – he was a Christian and devoted Vicar, a perfect gentleman in every respect the P.C.C. felt the loss keenly, said John Nicholls. They stood in silence and there was no Feast Dance out of respect.

27th February, 1939 – It was proposed by Mr Nicholls and seconded by Mr. Wallis that the Parish should pay half the cost of a new range in the vicarage kitchen.
18th April, 1939 - The new Vicar, is the Revd. F. E. Eddy. Electoral roll stands at 151, the Vicar asked the P.C.C. to try and get more names on the Electoral Roll as the Parish had a population of 3,000.

The Green (today's car park) is to be closed to the public one day a year, and any stall admitted there has to pay a fee of 6d as the Green is the property of the Church.

A Notice Board indicating times of Divine Service, is to be placed near the Church. The Vicar wishes a box to be placed in the church for the insertion of any communications for him.

A letter is to be sent to the Lord Chancellor expressing the satisfaction of the Parish with Revd. F. E. Eddy their new Vicar. Mr. G. Prowse proposed and Mr. R. Pentreath seconded that the Standing Committee should prepare a Table of fees: for burials etc, based on the Statutory Table issued by the Ecclesiastical Commission for fees charges locally.

10th July, 1939 – Gold leaf is to be used for the lettering of the Notice Board. £30 has been set aside for the organ fund.

22nd August, 1939 – Garden Fete raised £65.

29th January, 1940 – The Electoral Roll - 186 with an increase of 36 during the year.

1st July, 1940 – Buckets to be brought into the church filled with sand or water for fire precautions. Mr. Prowse proposed Mr. Drew seconded, that a Conveyance, (?) was to be supplied to take the choir to St. Ives for the Deanery festival, it was carried unanimously.

4th August, 1940 - Is to be a Thank Offering for the Church. (*This may have been a date for a Service, it was not clear.*) It was Proposed by Mr. Prowse, and seconded by Mr. North that the Vicar should obtain new Tune books and Psalters for the Choir.

A notice is to be placed in the Tower '***NO SMOKING***!' (*Perish the thought!*)

26th January, 1941 – Mr. Nicholls' wife died, the P.C.C. stood in silence, and sent a letter of condolence. Mrs. Nicholls had shown a keen interest in the work of the Church and devotion to its service. There are 197 names on the Electoral Roll an increase of 11.

26th January, 1941 - Revd. F. E. Eddy - Thanks to the Superintendent and Sunday School Teachers for their faithful service.

19th May, 1941 – Vicar outlines provision of War Damage Act 1941 and insurances were to be immediately effected – to cover the themselves (PCC) against Loss to 30th September the amounts proposed were :

	£
CHURCH FURNITURE	150
CHURCH ORGAN	250
Premium=	6

28th October, 1941 - War Damage insurance increased:-

	£
ORGAN	400
BELLS	100
SCHOOL FURNITURE	50
CLOCK	100
CHURCH FURNITURE	150
TOTAL =	**800**

Church Accounts were Audited – Receipts - £89.19.11d Expenses - £231.18.0d signed by the Revd. W. Wagner **9th February, 1942.**

15th April, 1942 – Emergency Meeting in the Vicarage. P.C.C. approved Priest's Stall in memory of Revd. F. J. Prideaux, M.A., who was Vicar of Paul for twenty-seven years. Surplices and cassocks are to be obtained as soon as possible out of church expenses.

(Whether this mean that the choir was not robed until now, or they are just new robes, is not clear. The men used to have black cassocks before the women were robed, then all wore red.)

Rose Queen Float at Mousehole

	£
Sunday School 1942	750.14.7d
Expenses	336.4.9d
Balance	414.9.10
3% War Bonds	100

18th January, 1943 – The Church paths need attention. The P.C.C. was increased from fourteen to twenty members. The alteration of the Choir Vestry – Standing Committee to investigate. Mrs. Wagner (*Vicar's wife*) introduced the Nativity Play *(she used to put on various dramas)*. A box was to be placed in the Church for a fund for altar flowers.

18th January, 1943 – there is a good balance in the Sunday School Funds.

3rd May, 1943 – A 'Permission' Notice Board is placed in the Green (*Paul Car Park - present day*). Attention was drawn to the fact that Paul Local Board Office was to become a dwelling house, and a letter was to be sent to the Borough Council pointing out that the approach to the front of the house was over church property, informing them that The Trustees of that property must ensure that their rights were safeguarded.

It was Proposed by Mr. Carne and Seconded by Mr. Drew to have nothing whatever to do with the allotments in the churchyard, and to see that the churchyards be attended to.

The Mousehole Male Voice Choir was to sing in Paul Church on Feast Sunday. It was decided that a new altar frontal should be placed in the church in memory of the late Mr. Tippett.

Concrete blocks were to be removed from the Green to one of the out-houses. (*There used to be lean-to buildings where the new extension is today*).
There is a box in church for altar flower donations.

30th July, 1943 – Mousehole Male Voice Choir is to give a musical Service on Feast Sunday afternoon, the disposal of the collection would be left with the Standing Committee.

On Feast Monday there would be an evening Social, and a Harvest Home on Harvest Festival Monday night.

7th February, 1944 – Mrs. Simons – reported that the Sunday School had a balance of: 15.12.4d. 1944 – Church Meeting – Numbers to whom Parish Magazine distributed = 160. Clock Repair - £3.10 per annum.

22nd April, 1944 There are several persons who may be willing to ring the bells but are unable to make definite arrangements. The Vicar raised a vote of thanks for the cleaning out, of the out-houses. The Confirmation Service offering went to the Bishop's Special Fund.

5th September, 1944 – Harvest and Thanksgiving proceeds go to Penzance Hospital. There is to be a Social Evening to raise money for Christmas gifts for the Paul service people in the Forces. **29th January, 1945** – 1944 Garden Fete raised £173.13.4d. Offertories, during the year - £304.17.10d. Christmas Gifts were sent to 120 local Service people in H.M. Forces - £60 had been raised for a Welcome Home Fund. Mr. North was thanked for thirty years of loyalty and devotion as Vicar's and People's Churchwarden. The Church School renovation fund stands at £53.

29th January, 1945 – Stone chippings to be put on the Green are to come from the quarry, and the persons using the Green for a car park had to ask the permission of the Church Council. The Church Bells are to be rung on Victory Day. Lord St. Levan is to open the Fete.

10th September, 1945 – Ask Mr. Corfield for advice on the decoration of the Church, and to draw up a specification for the same. The War Memorial names are to be re-painted (*presumably with new names for World War II*). It was decided to ask the Old Cornwall Society for their advice on the re-lettering.

23rd November, 1945 – Tenders invited for re-decoration of the Church are to be put in 'Cornishman' and 'Western Morning News' and 'West Briton' papers.

28th January, 1946 – Sunday School made a loss- £13.16.3d – presented by Mrs. C. B. Simmons. The Jarvis family gave the Church Bible. The bells are to be increased from three to eight in number, and the Vicar decided that the proceeds of the Garden Fete for 1946 will go to the fund for the bells.

6th May, 1946 – The walls of the Church are to be parchment coloured, the outside doors dark oak, and the pipes – dark green. The P.C.C. was to give Mr. P. Drew a wedding present as a token of their esteem and good wishes.

9th July, 1946 – There was to be a tablet placed on the north wall in memory of Ambrose Kerril de Rauffignas and Mary his wife – a Faculty must be raised for same. (*There is no such memorial now.*) Mrs. Malone of Trevayler couldn't open the Fete as she was ill, but Mrs. Edmund Malone stepped in (*possibly another descendant of the Rev Malone, who was Vicar of Paul in 1866-1876*). Dr J. G. Willis consented to judge the Baby Show. A Gate was to be placed at the entrance to the Green. Arrangements were to be made for the Choir Summer Outing.

30th August, 1946 – The Church decorating was postponed as they could not get the materials, after the War.

Fees for Digging a Grave for a Parishioner

	£
Digging	2.10.0d
Filling-in	50/-
Vicar's Fees	6/-
Church Fees	1.1.0d

Fees for non-Parishioner

	£
Digging	2.10.0d
Filling-in	50/-
Vicar's Fees	2.2. 0d
Church Fees	1.2.0d

Total receipts for 1947	£604.0.8d
Expenses	£150
Repairs & Decoration	£671.15.10
Balance at end of year =	£905.18.5d

Children's Corner - once located by the Tonkin window north aisle. The statue of Christ as a boy was give in memory of their son, Frederick John Hosking who died on 3rd August, 1946 age 17 by Matthew and Lizzie Annie Hosking.

Today the Children's Corner is situated at the back of the south aisle and is dedicated to Jessie Ellen Osborne who died 15th February, 1959 age 67, and her daughter Hilda Rose Osborne who died aged 14 on 12th September, 1946.
(See also Chapter 7.)

27th January, 1947 – The fittings and framework of the present three bells have now reached the stage that they cannot be regarded as suitable for further useful service. The bells were cast in 1727 (*a year after the construction of the second Vicarage*) – none have been tuned since. They are badly worn on places of the sound bows where the clappers had been striking. The tenor bell did not have a good tonal quality and should be recast for the note it sounds – the weight should be increased by approximately 1¾ cwts. The stained glass windows are bomb damaged and need repair. The Children's Corner, has been put near the Pulpit in the north aisle, as the children need their own part of the Church (*see previous page*).

27ᵗʰ January, 1947 – There are trees to be cut around the Church, and churchyard wall. The Church ladders are not to be taken out of the Church.
28ᵗʰ April, 1947 – Monday - Revd. W. V. Wagner, R. Drew, L. Spargo, Churchwarden and the Archdeacon – Bishop Holden were present. The Vicar read a letter with reference to the Chancel repairs – concerned with the Tithe Act of 1936.

22ⁿᵈ April, 1947 – The Chancel repair liability devolved upon incumbents of the Benefice and the Benefice of Newlyn, St. Peter. This liability is now accepted by the P.C.C. – they are informing the Tithe Redemption Commission accordingly.

The Vicar read an enquiry from the Town Clerk as to the Church Tithe Records, and arrangements are to be made for their preservation – however their present whereabouts were unknown! The County Moral Welfare Whist Drive to be held in aid of Welfare in the Home at Penzance.

The men responsible for the Whist Drive to invite Colonel Paynter to open the Bazaar, and to hold the Baby Show on 6ᵗʰ August. Bishop Holden informed the PCC regarding 'K' Scheme under which five ecclesiastical Commissions provide, up to a certain limit, an amount equal to the additional stipend contributed from parochial sources. It was unanimously agreed to contribute £75 per annum from Parochial sources for this augmentation.

9ᵗʰ June, 1947 – The Vicar read correspondence from Canon Doble regarding the purchase of books on the ancient History of Paul etc., unanimous decision to purchase same. (*I wonder where they are? Canon Doble wrote Dobles' Saints of Cornwall.*)

The gates for the Green are now complete and are awaiting transport. The Whist Drive in aid of County Moral Welfare raised - £3.5.6d. The K Scheme for augmenting income of the Benefice – add amount required to raise the annual income to £500 – was £80 – Commissioners therefore responsible for a maximum of £40. Paul resolved to send £50 to the Cornish Church Thanksgiving Fund and £4 for the income of the Benefice under the 'K' Scheme.

22ⁿᵈ September, 1947 – Revd. W. Scott-Adams co-opted on to the PCC. The Revd. Crofts of St. Buryan is to preach at Harvest Festival Thanksgiving Evensong. A Table of Fees to be sent to the Ecclesiastical Commissioners.

Revd. Wagner said that the Revd. Michael Hocking of Madron would preach on Feast Sunday morning. 7.45 Mousehole Male Voice Choir Sacred Concert. It was decided to invite the Madron Players to come during Feast Week. Miss Pritchett is to re-letter and renew the Roll of Honour – adding the men who fell in the Second World War.

26ᵗʰ January, 1948 – Sidesmen – John Nicholls, C. B. Simons, W. Polgreen, L. Trenoweth, J. Thomas (Snr), and Junior, James Rowe, A. E. Hunter, E. Lugg, P. Harvey, J. Poppin, G. Prowse, Jack Harvey, Eric Harvey, E. Brown, J. J. McClary, Mr. White, W. Francis, H. Taylor, Desmond McClary, V. Trenoweth, Wilfred McClary, R. J. Cocking, and J. Sampson.

The Vicar was pleased that the Mothers' Union has been formed and hoped it may be a great help to the Church. (*This was spearheaded by Mrs. Wagner his wife!*)

The Old Cornwall Society arranged with Mr. T. Wallis to clean Dolly Pentreath's gravestone and renew the lettering. The churchyard trees are to be lopped.

20th February, 1948 – Heating boiler repaired – It was decided to have a new fire door and to insure the boiler. The Vicar wanted to form a branch of C.E.M.S. in the Parish (Church of England Missionary Society).

14th May, 1948 – Third party insurance on the Church.

MAY QUEEN, Attendants, Scouts and Revd. Wagner

30th August, 1948 – Public Liability Insurance Policy for Church premises – Church Room and Vicarage, compensation not to exceed £1,000. A large part of the Vicarage roof should be renewed at a cost of £200.

31st January, 1949 - Mr. J. Nicholls and Miss Strickland express a wish for the Ten Commandments to be read in their entirety and not in the shortened version. The Vicar agreed to do so. The Vicar had £137 for a Home Coming and Kitchen Fund – he wanted to call a Meeting of Ex-Servicemen on 8th February, 1949. A switch was to be placed in the main entrance, for lighting one, or more lights in the Church.

27th May, 1949 - There was correspondence from the Bell Foundry who intended to commence work in September. The Vicar wanted the PCC to chose someone to open the Bazaar. Either Mrs. Sparrow, or Mrs. Lionel Rogers or Judge Scoble Armstrong. The Proceeds of the Garden Fete are to go to the bell fund. The Electoral Roll stood at 200 and there was £83.0.10d in the Vicar's Account transferred to the PCC. £50 received from the Rural Churches' Repair Fund for renovation of the Church. An electric Blower for the organ was installed thanks to Mr. Bath, - a tablet was to be erected for the same. A Tablet is to placed near the south aisle windows to record replacement of windows damaged during the War.

27th June, 1949 - Mrs. Harvey wanted to know her position as Organist. It was decided to put an advertisement in 'The Cornishman' for her successor. Owing to insufficient accommodation on each side of the central aisle, resolution was carried that Pew holders were asked to be in their seats not later than five minutes before the Service commenced, or the Sidesmen would give their vacant pews to others. The PCC approved the application of a Faculty petition for three bells rehanging with new fittings in new framework made complete for eight bells in total. The recasting of the tenor bell meant it was increased by 1¾ cwts. Addition of three new bells – makes a ring of six.

16th September, 1949 - The Vicar received one application for a new Organist, no appointment was made. Harvest Evensong – a special preacher was to visit, Bishop of Rockhampton, Australia. The post of Caretaker was advertised locally, and a list of duties was drawn up.

18th November, 1949 - The wooden beams of the bell frame were disposed to the highest bidder. Mr. McClary is to remove the trees, which were causing trouble to the woodwork and windows of the church, they are to be cut down to six feet in height.

30th January, 1950 - Mrs. Hosking was appointed Caretaker at £50 per annum. An Entertainments Committee was formed. A letter of thanks from the Mothers' Union was received for the money voted to them for cleaning the church.

11th May, 1950 - Mrs. Simons Memorial was to be an Oak Litany Desk, drawings were to be made by Whippel of Exeter. Flag Day for the Church of England Children's Society – Mrs. Prideaux is to organise the main stem of local activities.

Eight hundred copies of the form of Service to be used for the Dedication of the Bells were printed (*a copy still exists today, more about it in the Chapter 12*). The bells cost £1,224 net, cash received £1,140, and Paul Socials raised £67. The new lightning conductor was not properly clipped to the tower above the clock. The drain pipe from the tower discharges rain directly on to the clock face. A Tablet recording the repairs to the stained glass windows due to bomb damage had been erected and paid for by the Lord Mayor's thanksgiving Fund.
The P.C.C. donated one guinea to this amount.

23rd June, 1950 at 7.30 p.m. – Pastoral Reorganisation Measure. The Vicar explained the far-reaching effects of this on most parishes, there is a Meeting in St. Mary's Parish Church House, on 26th June, to explain the measure.

The Mothers' Union donated £157 – a splendid amount – towards the Mary Bell, which took the P.C.C. by surprise. Total cost of Bells - £1,390 - £1,236.10.0d to Bell Foundry - £153.10.0d to Messrs. Harveys. The PCC was to ask the Bell Foundry what discount they would offer for cash? Improved amenities for the Church Room, with sanitary provisions which, were felt to be a pressing need, to be vigorously worked for. (*I cannot think where this Church Room could be. Somewhere in the Church? I think it must have been in the School, now the Church Hall.*) There was a quote for a Litany Desk with shelf and kneeler, to be fashioned of seasoned English Oak, the design and quote was accepted.

An application was made by Nanclealverne for the loan of white cups and saucers to help at their Fete, but *NO POL DE LEON CHINA* was to be lent. (*Definitely not the good china!*)

15th September, 1950 - The men's collection for the bells came to £250. PCC to send their appreciation to the Secretary of the Men's Society. The crockery was loaned and safely returned all complete. The Fete raised £122.12.6d. The Vicar reported that a children's entertainer, who wished to rent the Church Room, had approached him. As nothing whatever was known of the applicant, the request was declined. Miss Pritchett was to prepare a List of Vicars to hang in the Church.

5th February, 1957 - The Electoral Roll stood at 215-220. The Balance of Accounts - £2,330.15.9d. A letter of appreciation is to be sent to the Captain of the Bell Ringers.
Sympathy is to be sent to the organist, Mrs. Harvey, who is in Redruth Hospital.

8th June, 1951 - It was agreed that £300 Defence Bonds be transferred to the new issue. The tower flag staff and stays to be cleaned and repainted.

Miss Pritchett

Paul Church on the horizon from Sheffield Village

The behaviour of the younger members of the choir, and boys at the back of the Church came under discussion.

10th September, 1951 - Garden Fete – raised £155.1.2d. Town & County Planning Act – under this Act Cornwall County Council was seeking to define the boundaries and areas of Churchyards, Burial Grounds, and Cemeteries on a plan of 25" to the mile. The Living of Paul Church is in the hands of the Lord Chancellor who hopes to visit Paul Church and meet the Vicar and Churchwardens. The Vicar wants a slate War Memorial to be affixed to the Tower.

Two special Services are to be taken by the Vicar at the Mission to Seamen on Trafalgar Day – for the South American Missionary Society (*three Johns*) on a Sunday in December. Service- '*Additional Curates & Society*' – Sunday in November. Cornish Church Thanksgiving Fund – this fund paid for new pipes to be the Vicarage on the mains water Supply – cost £30.

The Deanery Bell Ringing Festival – Bell Ringers of Diocesan Guild of Bell Ringers are to hold their Festival at Paul on Saturday 29th September with tea afterwards. The Church Room wall was damaged through tree felling. May Fete was discussed, no decision being arrived upon.

4th February, 1952 - Electoral Roll – 230. The new Litany Desk is in use, a memorial to C. B. Simons. A chest is needed for the altar frontals, and also the chest in which records are kept is too small. (*Parish Chest?*) Thanks to all who looked after the flowers for the Altar Shrine, Children's Corner. The congregation had been **well maintained.**

Here ends the P.C.C. Minutes, the last comment makes one think of shiny spruced up people neatly sitting in their pews and obediently listening to the Vicar!

CHAPTER 7 – BURIALS, THE CRYPT & SOME OF THOSE INTERRED

If anyone wishes to access Paul Church burial records today, they may do so on the Internet. These may also be found on our own website at www.paulchurch.com. This site is brilliantly executed and is well worth a visit, especially for those wishing to research into local family history. Full details of the headstones in three Paul burial grounds, i.e. the Church Hall Burial Ground (also known as the School Burial Ground), the Cholera Ground, and the immediate Churchyard, may also be accessed from a red book at the back of the Church, also containing sketch maps which are particularly helpful. If the Church for any reason is closed, there is also a copy of these records lodged behind the bar at the Kings Arms, our excellent local public house, across the road from the church. The records have been painstakingly researched by Robert Harrison, a member of our congregation, an admirable task for which we are most grateful. The records are not detailed, just a record of location, Surname, Christian name and date of birth; a great asset nevertheless to family historians.

Skull on Hutchen's Memorial

This chapter is about the various monuments and burials in Paul Church, and tells a little of the lives of those who are laid to rest, often the ancestors of those who worship above. At Newlyn funerals particularly, hymns would be sung to old tunes at the deceased's door, and also on the way up to Paul Church and as the coffin went into the Church.

Any interment inside a church was called intramural. The practice of burying people inside churches came to an end with the passing of the Burial Act of (1880) outlawing this occurrence. People were willing to pay for intramural burial, especially when the interment was in favoured positions near the altar. Underneath the altar in the sanctuary was the most holy and important place, usually only reserved for former Clergy or the Gentry. In Paul Church at least eight people are buried in the sanctuary, or area of the main (or high) altar.

'Here I lie at the Chancel Door
Here I lie because I'm poor
The farther in the more you'll pay
Here I lie as warm as they.'

The above was taken from the epitaph of Robert Phillip at Kingsbridge, Devon, and shows an example of popular thought, which could be interpreted as a sort of 'burial snobbery'. It is a thinking rather out of kilter with the Christian ethos of the body not being of any consequence, the important part of a person being the soul.

People thought that they would be judged in the future on the position of their monuments in church, and that their status would be fixed on where their corpse rested. However, they cannot have realised that restorations of the fabric sometimes necessitated removal of memorials, and they were not always replaced near the actual burial site. This has happened in Paul Church where the plaque for the Rowe family may be seen on the north wall now, moved during alterations to lighting (1991), yet their family vault lies underneath their memorial window today, in the middle of the south aisle.

Alexander Rowe

Alexander Rowe, the son of William Rowe, was a Schoolmaster in Paul who lived at Raginnis. He was a member of the Rowe family as above, and is recorded as being *'buried in the Church'* on 22nd January, 1814. He was an interesting man because he was an annual contributor to 'The Ladies' Diary' and 'The Gentleman's Diary' from 1767 to 1811, to whom he sent calculations of times of solar and lunar eclipses, and transits of stars for the meridian of Penzance. He was a great mathematician, and the majority of his mathematical questions and replies were often printed in the 'Gentleman's Diary'.

Interred in the family vault in the middle of the south aisle with Alexander are other Rowe family members: Elizabeth Rowe, and Johannes Richards Marrick Rowe. Their memorial window is the second in from the South Porch and states that it was erected in memory of John and Elizabeth Rowe of Raginnis by their daughter Joanna Emily Rowe. They died: John aged 63 years on 22nd June, 1845 and Elizabeth 23rd January, 1841 aged 50. Also Joanna's three brothers: John Richard, aged only 6 months died 2nd May, 1822; John Garrison, Surgeon at Hong Kong died 19th October, 1850 aged 28 years, and Richard Marrick Rowe, Fellow of Exeter College Oxford, died 14th December, 1861 aged 32. It then states the remains of four are deposited in the vault beneath the window, presumably it means the four children.

As you can see there is a bit of a conundrum here! Seven people appear to be buried in this vault, yet according to the memorial window, only four were put in! When workmen entered the vault in 1994 only two intact lead coffins were found, with a brass plate on which were the names of Alexandra Rowe, Elizabeth Rowe and Johannes Richards Marrick Rowe. Presumably the workmen couldn't see in the dark, and/or the rest of the coffins had collapsed, and their name plates would have been under the crumbled wood. The only coffins to have survived for over 133 years being those lined with lead.

I think the most reasonable explanation is this: Alexandra Rowe was the first occupant of the Rowe vault middle south aisle, in 1814; followed by the baby, John Richards Rowe 1822; then came Elizabeth Rowe 1841; then her husband John Rowe 1845; then son John G Rowe 1850; last but not least Richard Marrick Rowe 1861. The sister, who erected the memorial window above the vault, is not registered as being buried here and probably is buried in another parish with her husband.

During the 1873 restoration of Paul Church, a man went down a ladder into the vault in the north aisle, describing it as square in shape with shelves for the coffins. The Revd. Harper informed me that human bones found under the floor during restoration, in June-October 1994, were deposited in this vault. Old timbers and coffin lids were seen here. Once again, the nearby memorials bear little relation to those buried in the vault as the memorials have been moved.

In 1924 according to the 'Western Morning News' for the 19th May it was reported that during repairs a vault was opened, and some coffins of the Blewett family were exposed. Whereupon an ancient brass plate was found, probably once attached to one of the coffin lids, and it was taken to Penzance. Presumably this would be the only clue to the vault being of the Blewett family. This is another mystery, as the location of the vault is not disclosed, and there are no Blewett family memorials in Paul Church to assist its location. The only Blewett I have come across in my research is the murdered Martha Blewett, and she is reported to be *'buried in the Church'*, but not necessarily in a vault. So what happened to the brass plate, does someone

Have it on their mantelpiece in Penzance? Would the mystery vault be the unnamed one that is under the font of today?

There was a 'loose burial' of bodies in the area beneath the Vicar's Vestry in the west end of the north aisle. It was approximately the same size as the Vestry but set forward from the west wall by about 9 feet. The Surveyor stated that there could be no idea of the amount of bodies that it had contained, and it was fairly shallow. However within this area a child's coffin lid was found with a brass plate stating in copper alloy studs *'(A)GED 9 1737'* with a very poignant hourglass below with the last grain of sand falling through. This drawing of the coffin lid was made by archaeologist Peter Herring. The original lid is in the Royal Cornwall Museum, at Truro and may be viewed on prior request to the archivist.

Being buried in a church may give one kudos, but adds great peril to those who walk above. A tremendous collapse of the floor, due to water penetration of vaults below, occurred at St. Erth Church, where the floor even today seems very cracked and uneven. Thankfully Paul Church has a brand new floor, and the vaults below have been well shored up. However it wasn't always like that...

'The Cornish Telegraph' of 19th November, 1873 reports on the interior of Paul Church thus:

'Everywhere is ruin and decay. The removal of pews reveals the floor with cracks and crevices everywhere. Underneath lie vaults and graves. They are beneath the organ (in the north aisle) under the pulpit, below the altar, all about the church and imperfectly secured from communication with the air breathed by the congregation are numerous receptacles of the dead. One of these towards the east end of the south aisle has excited much attention. It is a roomy vault, which is estimated could contain, if necessary, 60-80 coffins. The walls are of substantial masonry, the roof well arched with brick, and a drain carries off any damp and ventilates the gloomy abode. The floor is covered with a quantity of loose unworked stones and the explanation is this, the spacious tomb was constructed by Sir Rose Price but was never used. All these voids are to be filled up, and no intramural interments will again take place. Messrs. Oliver & Son will proceed rapidly with the work of repairing and renovating this Church.'

Vault or Crypt of Sir Rose Price
15 ft x 12 ft under south aisle

The danger of infection from fumes emanating from tombs, or vaults beneath the floor in churches could be a serious problem, leading to outbreaks of infectious disease (see Chapter 13). This was encountered when various pews were removed during the 1873 restoration. It was for this reason that intramural burial was outlawed by the 1881 Burial Act; this Act also allowed burials to take place in churchyards for the first time, without the rites of the Church of England.

In St. Neot's Church a total of 548 people were actually intramurally during 1606-1701.

The churchwardens encouraged this practice as they could charge 13/4d for burial in the chancel and 6/8d for burial in the nave! A nice little earner for the church! As it was impossible for this to happen over a number of years, because of space problems, bones were dug up and removed to a charnel house or 'bone hole'.

Towednack Church has a charnel house – and at Helston Church only the skull and thigh bones were stored as they were thought enough to get one through Judgement day! Thus the skull and crossbones idea was first created and adopted by pirates! One chap Thomas Tiddy was so worried about his bones being removed that he had the inscription: *'Tis my desire not to have no person to remove my grave'* on his tomb, which was in the chancel in a Devon church.

A local family of note are the Keigwins of Mousehole. Apart from Jenkin Keigwin, who was killed in the Spanish Raid, James Keigwin was also buried in Paul Church, as stated in his Will, dated 1st February, 1734 and proved on 18th July, 1741. It is written that he was:

Stairs up into Church Entrance No. 1

"to be buried in the same vault as his wife' (Florence Keigwin).

It is likely that he was the son of James, grandson of John Keigwin who died in 1693. It seems strange that we have no Keigwin family memorial as so many of the family rest in Paul Church. Jenkin's eldest son Richard was buried in Paul in 1636, Martin his brother and his wife Thomsine were buried 1616 and 1632, as were many of the succeeding generations of the family. It could be that the Keigwin family vault was under the south aisle, and was hijacked by Sir Rose Price, whose family pew stood over the vault. However the fact that there is a main entrance, plus a side exit to the vault, leads on to conjecture that maybe it was a hiding place for King Charles I. He certainly hid somewhere in Penwith and the Keigwins were great Royalists, mentioned in a letter dated 30th June, 1646. Captain Keigwin, from a ship off Pendennis point, was called a 'knave against Parliament who had the King's Commission!'

Sir Rose Price

Crypt showing lintel of side Entrance No. 2

Although living at Trevaylor Manor, Rose Price thought of himself as a parishioner of Paul, and he wanted to be buried in the church. His Father John Price had a house at Chywoone. Rose was brought up in the Parish of Paul, and no doubt attended the church as a child.

It is presumed that he knew there was a crypt or vault under the east end of the south aisle, already in existence. He constructed his family pew in Paul Church on top of this area, and maybe when this was happening (the floor was definitely made higher at this time by two feet, as the piscina is now too low down to be practical) he could have found the earlier vault. Sir Rose Price proceeded to create a really enormous burial chamber for himself and his family. It is seventeen feet in length and fifteen

Entrance No. 3

feet high with a void space above the brick barrel vaulted roof of two feet. He tunnelled through the east end wall creating a small entrance from the outside with a few steps down. This would have entailed a tremendous amount of earth moving, but Rose Price was used to that, when he created a huge windbreak in Paul (described below); he also had plenty of money to pay for labour.

The whole procedure must have created havoc in the churchyard, and to a certain extent risked the collapse of Paul Church on top! The second flight of steps, or entrance (see photo), which was much steeper and only had half steps, came out by the pillar to the right of the organ console. It is a curious thing that there are two entrances, and, by burrowing through the east wall, Rose Price created a third entrance. The construction of shelves or ledges for the coffins on the walls did not happen, but Sir Rose Price's creation would have housed many more than five, a veritable pavilion for the dead.

Sir Rose Price assumed the right to be buried in the crypt he created (but left unfinished), as he paid pew rent on his family pew (all of 15ft long - the same length as his crypt below!), positioned in the east end of the south aisle directly above the crypt and its entrances from the Church.

A Petition from the Devon Record Office dated 8th February, 1798 pertains to this pew. There was quite an objection to its construction with no less than thirty-six people objecting, one of whom was Abraham Tonkin, my five times Great-Grandfather! Here is an extract:

'Four seats or pews, two continuous in length fifteen feet or thereabouts, breadth five feet eleven inches, or thereabouts. Two others of seven feet eight inches in length, six feet in breadth situated in the south side of the Chancel of the said Church of Paul, two of which have heretofore belonged to Richard Hosking, one to Francis Hitchens Jacko and one to John Barnes, but now to your said petitioner – with the consent of the Minister he is desirous to take down and rebuild for the use of his family, so long as he or they shall be inhabitants of the said Parish, payers of parochial rates there, and member of the Church of England...'
The reply to the above Petition, which must have been in the affirmative, had to be given out at Divine Service on Sunday 18th February, 1798.

As stated earlier, Sir Rose Price wanted to live in Paul Parish, where he had spent his childhood. He began to construct a home for himself and his wife, presumably near the house of his Father at Chywoone, and near the ancient circular enclosure settlement. Latterly also near the mine –Wheal Betsy. He realised that on top of the hill it would be very windy, and he wanted to construct a garden and shelter the house, so he built a huge wall half-encircling the proposed house area and sheltering it from the north and some westerly winds. This is still in existence and is known as 'Price's Folly' or 'The Chinese Wall'. Rose Price was a rich man who was in the sugar trade, and money was no object in his constructions, which always seemed to be of huge proportions.

However, as the story goes, he hadn't though that his wife, Elizabeth, who, when she saw it in 1801, would not take to the proposed building site. Thus she asked her husband if they could go elsewhere. Whereupon, it is said, that he stipulated if she could jump a five-barred gate on a horse, they would move. She being a good rider cleared it, and even though he had gone to a tremendous amount of work laying the house foundations, he abided by his word, and they moved from Trevaylor to Kenegie in 1806. Ten months later he bought Trengwainton, where he built the house, and they had ten children, in quick succession! He was knighted in 1814.

With the house at Trengwainton came a 'Great Seat or Pew' in Madron Church, so he didn't have to build one as in Paul Church! He abandoned his half-finished vault at Paul Church, and built an enormous barn-like family mausoleum at Madron Church, to which he transferred his loyalty, and was buried there when he died in 1834. Curiously this stone mausoleum bears a great resemblance to the stone reservoir by the road in Sheffield Village. What happened to his pews at Paul? Well, they were probably sold to someone else!

While Rose Price was still a member of Paul Church, the war with France continued. Early in 1798 he raised two companies of infantry, which Professor Charles says were based on men of Paul Parish. In July they joined with Penzance Artificers and became The Cornwall Infantry & Engineering Volunteers.

Sir Rose Price inherited money from his family, and their sugar plantations in Jamaica. Lieutenant Francis Price, who was in Oliver Cromwell's expeditionary force to Jamaica in 1655, remained there and founded a sugar-planting dynasty. His unusual name of 'Rose' stems from the custom in Cornwall of naming the son of the family by the maiden surname of his mother, or grandmother. Thus 'Rose' comes from the Rose family of Rose Hall, inherited by Colonel Charles Price, Lieutenant Francis Price's son. Charles' brother John married Margery Badcock and had a son also called John Price. He married Elizabeth Williams on 3rd August, 1764, and they had Rose ('by any other name!').

John Price moved in the Society of Penzance, and in 1774 became High Sheriff, and was Mayor of Penzance in 1779. He and his wife had a house at the top of Chapel Street, the very hub of the town of Penzance. He even had Chapel Street, cleaned regularly (!) at 7/6d per quarter, and he paid for a new town clock and had the cupola built on today's Lloyds' Bank Building in Market Jew Street. His son Rose Price was educated at the 'Latin School', taught by the Curate of St. Mary's Chapel with his brother Charles Godolphin Price and John Vinnicombe from Madron.

It was John Price who wrote an imaginary history of the gold ring, which was found at the site of the 'ring and thimble' in 1781 (see Notes Chapter). These two unusual stone shapes stand by the roadside leading from Sheffield to Newlyn, opposite the Paul turning. The 'thimble' is in the shape of a sugar loaf, from which the Price family fortunes arose.

The sugar plantation of Worthy Park, sold in 1866, is still a plantation to this day. Sir Rose Price lived on the proceeds in luxury for the rest of his life. His Father is reported to have died in sad circumstances, heavily in debt and parted from his wife, on 3rd January, 1797 in his house at Chywoone, owing £1,800. In Elizabeth Sparrow's book on the 'Prices of Penzance' she tells the story that John Price was in so much debt that his creditors wouldn't allow the removal of his body from the house until they were paid. The story goes that his servants then took the coffin by night to the sanctuary of a church. He was buried on 20th January in St. Mary's Chapel, Penzance, so it is likely that he was taken there, although Paul Church is much nearer!

The strange and rather sad fact is, that he must have paid quite a price to erect the elaborate memorial to his friend John Badcock by the altar in Paul Church, yet ended his own life in debt.

To return to the burials, another vault lies in the east end of the north aisle. It was recorded when the new floor was laid in the 1980 restoration, but the extent of it is not known. This vault may not be as large as Sir Rose Price's crypt in the corresponding place in the south aisle, but it is reported to have extended under the former organ area.

There is a vault under the pulpit of today. The earlier pulpit was made of wood, and thus comparatively light. Today it is granite, and extremely heavy, *and* situated on top of a vault or void space. This could be interesting if we have a very well proportioned and energetic Vicar at Paul some day preaching from that pulpit! Also, note the discoloration of the floor tiles in this area, which could be caused by cool damp air rising from below.

The Langford family of Trungle has a vault in the church, but no records have been found to say where it is. The funeral hatchment for the Langfords of Trungle has been moved quite a few times, and was near the organ console, and now it is on the north wall of the north aisle; so it gives no clues to the whereabouts of its family vault. It would originally, of course, been placed above the vault to which it related.

Edward Langford funeral Hatchment - 1781

Under the 'Burials in Church' in the Paul Registers it states that Mrs. Nankwill of Truro was buried in the Langford family vault on 10th August, 1810. More about this lady is recorded in Chapter 18.

Basically there are three vaults for which we do not know the occupants. These are: under the east end north aisle, under the font in the south aisle west end, and, as mentioned, under the pulpit. Apart from the Langfords, there are the Keigwins, Rowes, and Marracks, all who are in family vaults under Paul Church. Also there is William Godolphin, who is probably in a vault under the north aisle, as his memorial is above this area. It would be good to have a map of these underground chambers, stating who rests in them! Some other intramural burials are listed below, taken from a burial Register. Very sadly, one Curate's wife was only 21 when she died in childbirth. '*Written by her most disconsolate widower—once her most beloved husband, 12th March, 1797*':-

'Pure was her mind her manners soft and mild
Religion owned her for her favourite child
Impartial Truth her blameless worth commends
As wife, as daughter and the best of friends
Her countess virtues scarce begin to rise

E're heaven recalled her to her native skies
Where endless pleasures, everlasting peace
And joys celestial that will never cease
Reward her goodness in that blest abode
With Saints, and Angels and th' Eternal God'

This is her sad story:-

'On Thursday 23rd January, 1797, Betsy Oxnam wife of the Rev William Oxnam, Curate of Paul was suddenly seized with premature pains of labour, attended with strong convulsive fits, which, after she was delivered of an infant daughter, put a period to her existence at one o'clock on Friday morning. She felt no previous indisposition but was most unexpectedly spirited away from her distracted husband and afflicted friends in the full enjoyment, a few hours before her confinement, of health and youth. A striking lesson to inconsiderate mortals of the shortness and uncertainty of human life. She was born 8th November 1776, married June 13th 1796 and departed this life 24th February 1797, her remains are deposited in a walled grave directly under the Vicar's seat in the Chancel of Paul Church.'

Unfortunately during the laying of electric cables for the organ console to be connected to the pipes, the floor under the Vicar's desk was disturbed and bones were found, probably those of Mrs. Oxnam. It does seem odd for a Priest to want to sit over his wife's body, and presumably that of their unborn child; although no mention is made of the baby, they were usually buried together when the Mother died in childbirth. It could have been that he wanted them near to him when he was praying.

Brownies, and Maypole Dancing 1950s - to lighten the subject a trifle!

In 1780, a sample total for burials was 31 males 24 females. Further burials in the Church follow, indicating that under the floor is a crowded place:-

8th June, 1793	William Pollard of Newlyn buried in church
7th May, 1791	Mary wife of Bertie Borge b in c
23rd March, 1796	Mrs. Catherine James b in c paid £1.1s Revd. W. Oxenham Curate
25th March, 1796	Mrs Mary Hitchens b in c
4th November, 1796	Penelope Bodinaar b in c
28th February, 1797	Mrs. W. Oxenham (above) probably buried with stillborn baby under Vicar's seat.
21st March, 1797	William Mannack of Castellack b in c
24th July, 1797	John Leggs of Trevenneth b in c
28th October, 1797	Mrs.Elizabeth Hitchens buried in the church
30th April, 1799	Mrs. Charity Marrack
10th January, 1802	Mrs Joan Richards b in c
7th February, 1802	John Alexander Pollard an infant b in c
17th March, 1802	Prudence Matthews was buried in the Church and paid customary fees
3rd April, 1802-5	Elizabeth Matthews
7th April, 1802-5	William Good Badcock (he also paid mortuary fees)
16th August, 1802-5	Jane Matthews
8th September, 1802-5	John Carvosoe
	(the Dates for these five above people show all were buried in the church between 1802-1805)
21st March, 1802-5	Nicholas R. Broad, 1805.
7th January, 1807	Mary Wallace a Lady of London was buried in the Church customary fees £2 12.6d
19th February, 1807	Jane Trewarvas (of Mousehole) was buried in the Church
26th March, 1807	William B. Tregurtha an infant was buried in the church fee £1.11.6d
12th July, 1807	Mrs.Juliana Penneck of Penzance, age 76 widow of the Revd. H. Penneck (under the altar)
24th January, 1808	Mrs. Grace Badcock of Trungle £.3.3.0d—aged 50 died of dropsy
22nd February, 1808	Miss Margery Price Badcock—age 29 'died of decline' b in c
7th March, 1810	Alice Richards Harvey b in c
22nd January, 1810	Grace Marrack of Penzance b in c
10th August, 1810	Mrs. Nankwill of Truro was buried in the Langford family vault

Martha Blewett (who must be buried in the missing Blewett Vault) a murder victim, was buried intramurally on 27th November, 1792:

'This aged person, on Monday 26th November 1792 between 9 and 10 o'clock, as she was journeying on the road from Mousehole to Paul Church Town, was robbed of all her little property, which she had by great industry and parsimony scraped together for the support of declining age; and was most inhumanly murdered. Her throat being cut from ear to ear, for which a William Trewarvas, junior of Mousehole fisherman a young man not exceeding 26 was on the Tuesday apprehended and committed to the County Gaol as the person supposed guilty of this atrocious and bloody deed'.

Here follows an inscription on a cross that erected in the Mousehole road near the place where the body of Martha was found: *'O remember the Almighty the Great King of Kings, and Lord of Lords, hath in the Table of Law commanded "thou shalt do no murder"'.* Subsequently, William Trewarvas was tried at Launceston and found guilty and suffered the punishment due to his offence on Wednesday 28th March, 1793.

In 1793 - 5 males and 22 females were buried at Paul, totalling - 37 for that year. The Vicars of Paul were meticulous in making out burial registers; most of the registers are written in copperplate handwriting. In 1737 Revd. John Allen wrote:

'this book was new bound and twenty leaves were added at a charge of 6 shillings'.

In these registers some of the reasons for death were now reported as: apoplexy, consumption, falling over Newlyn cliff, old age, drowned off Mousehole, mortification of the bowels, nervous fever, croup, dropsy, paralytic stroke, smallpox, decline, sudden death, child bed, colic, asthma, whooping cough, measles, fit, or palsy.

A child of three from Newlyn (this is before St. Peters Parish existed) died from drinking boiling tea from a tea pot (Mary Cattran). One Sarah Sullivan of Newlyn died at age 30 of *'inconvenience of a cold room after childbirth.'* 1799 Miss Grace Wallis - this poor woman was remarkably healthy at 88, but unfortunately fell over Gwavas Quay on Monday evening, and died the following morning.

Sarah Gomer, aged 40 – this woman was on her return from Penzance, where she usually carried some fish to sell, but being unhappily intoxicated, plus the night was cold and dark she fell over Gwavas Quay on Saturday night about 8.00, and broke her thigh. No-one was there to assist her, and she perished from the *badness* of the fracture and the severity of the cold.

William Kneebone, from Raginnis - 1799. This man was returning from Penzance on Saturday evening 22nd June and unfortunately fell over Gwavas quay. By which means he broke all his ribs on one side and survived the fall for about an hour. He was perfectly sober and bore a most excellent character universally. The Vicar then adds a note: *this is the third accidental death by falling over the very same dangerous place within three months. Charles Valentine Le Grice, Officiating Minister.*

Margaret James aged 48 of Street an Nowan; this poor woman had been in a melancholy way for several days previous to Sunday 12th October, 1800. When she left her house about 8 o'clock walked into the sea and was found early on the following morning, lifeless on the beach. Death by 'lunacy' recorded.

There was a Roger (?) – alias Prudence Rouffignac - aged 30 who died 17th November, 1801 of a cold caught a few days after 'lying-in'. William Richards drowned in Gwavas Lake aged 16 on 17th January, 1803.

In1806 Ann Thomas, widow of William Thomas (Commander in His Majesty's Navy) and Aunt to Revd. Warwick Oben Gurney, died in Paul Vicarage (Trungle House – was also known as the Vicarage at this time) on 20th November, and was buried at Tregony, where his Father had retired some years earlier.

21st April, 1808: Edward Kelynack of Trungle was buried in Church aged 74. On 10th March, 1810 John Bodinnar aged 13. This poor child went incautiously near a Water Mill Wheel at Street an Nowan, which turning suddenly crushed him to death. Another sad story - three young boys, two from Paul, one from Madron, took a boat across to St. Michael's Mount. On the way back it turned over, and sank; all died. Two brothers Thomas and Frederick Wright were 10 and 12 respectively, they were buried in the same grave at Paul, on 16th September, 1811. The other chap was buried at Madron.

10th January, 1812. Suzanna Tregurtha buried in Church.

In the next Burial Register from 1813 onwards, yet more intramural burials were recorded:-

Mary Pollard	30th July, 1813
Benjamin Hemy of Mousehole	20th January, 1814
Grace Bodinnar and Alexander Row of Raginnis both buried	22nd January, 1814
John Richard Rowe infant of Raginnis buried in Rowe family vault	22nd January, 1814.
Richard Kelynack – infant	11th March, 1815
Ann Pentreath of Mousehole	9th November, 1816
Catherine Kelynack infant	15th September, 1817
Elizabeth Barnes of Newlyn	16th September, 1817
Lavinia Pollard of Newlyn	1822
Abraham Chirgwin Kelynack	10th October, 1823
Richard Trewarvas	15th February, 1823
James Cobley Marrack	4th November, 1823
Ann Robyns of Trungle	13th February, 1824
Under Vicar Revd. Richard Gurney,	
Churchwardens John Rowe and Thomas Harvey:	29th October, 1817
Ann Cock of Penzance	
Sam Richards of Newlyn	7th October, 1817
James Bodinaar	7th April, 1818
Matthew Wright	1st May, 1818
Joseph Beaden of Mousehole	1827

The Vicar (Revd. Richard Gurney) writes in the Register: *'from the number of persons lately buried in Paul Church, some inconvenience may be apprehended. The Vicar with a view to terminating this inquisorious (sic) practice has thought proper to determine that from 24th May, 1818 no ground in the Church shall be broken.'*

The Burial Register mentions Richard Gurney, Clerk Vicar of Cuby, St. James and of Paul who died 17th May, 1825 aged 77. Vicar of Paul and Father of Revd. W. O. Gurney.

That seems at last to be the end of 'burials in church'. The realisation that there are at least six vaults under the floor, a large *'loose burial'* plus those who would have been placed in their own individual spaces under the floor, adds up to a tremendous amount of bodies, lying beneath the worshippers above!

There are one or two oddities from the Burials Registers: for instance, in 1857 Paul Village is referred to as 'St. Paul'. Also:-

Mary Davy from Union House (this was probably at Madron and not Paul Poor House). On the 20th May, 1854, she was the first to be buried in the New Churchyard consecrated 19th May, 1854.

27th March, 1855 - Thomas Tonkin, aged 35, was crushed between two vessels at Mousehole.

10th July, 1855 – The body of a boy of approximately aged 12 was washed ashore at Mousehole, presumed from the wreck of 'The John' in Grave No. 1.

4th November, 1857 - Richard Pentreath aged 77 of Penzance, Parish Clerk for 30 years, was buried.

28th September, 1860, James Richards of Paul Church town was buried, aged 60, 24 years Parish Clerk (Paul must have had two Parish Clerks at once).

In 1882 on 3rd September, Richard Maddern aged 24, was buried. '*He had been frightened at sea by a narrow escape of his boat in collision with a steamer and he never recovered from the shock, to his nervous system.*' Written by the Revd. Aitken, Vicar.

17th March, 1886 - Susannah Roberts died aged 16; tragically her clothes caught fire while dusting and she expired after several days of great suffering.
Martha Agnes Matthews aged 4 buried 14th March, 1886, fell into a pan of hot milk and died 13 days after. Henry Sampson Harvey aged 8 buried 17th June, 1886, accidentally killed by being ridden over while playing at Buryas Bridge.
Robert Leah Harvey - buried 28th November – this man in going to his work in the dark morning walked over the Quay and was drowned.

15th January, 1887 - Jane Bennetts was buried aged 91; for many years she was Superintendent of Hutchens' House.

William Curnow of Newlyn Cliff was buried 28th January, 1887 aged 77. '*He was an eminent Botanist known, loved and mourned for by a large circle of friends*' (Revd. R. W. Aitken).

William Thomas Tippett died, aged 26, a Sunday School Teacher much loved and respected by a large circle of friends at Paul Church. He was buried 26th March, 1887.

Richard Henry Moncton was buried 22nd January, 1887. He came from Mousehole and was knocked down by a swing boat in the Fair Field Penzance, caught lockjaw and died in a few days, aged 19.

Thomas Henry Kneebone was buried 3rd December, 1887 aged 66. He was many years Chairman of the Highway Board and filled almost every Parochial Office – he was much regarded by a large circle of friends.

Benjamin aged 64 and Mary Batten aged 62, died within a few hours of each other and were buried in the same grave at the same time on 3rd May, 1890.

1891 Elizabeth Trembath of Mousehole buried 25th April, 1891 aged 86; for many years she kept the Post Office at Mousehole.

Albert Charles Heel aged 4 buried 27th July, 1891. He was playing with others near his Father's house at Trevelloe when he was bitten by an adder, and died of the effects of poison in a few hours.

11th July, 1893 – James Harvey aged 83, was buried. For many years he was a respected member of the Parish Church Choir.

30th August, 1893 – Primitive Methodist Minister William Nation, was buried, a long resident of Newlyn.

26th December, 1893 aged 57 was buried Agnes Jane Robins for many years Caretaker of Paul Parish Church (see plaque in Church).

1st August, 1897 was buried Edwin Chirgwin aged 59, from early youth a constant member of the Church and efficient member of the Choir and Band of Ringers.

William Charles Fox, aged 2, was buried on 7th August, 1897, this poor child ate strychnine for rats and died in great suffering within an hour.

18th January, 1898 aged 62 – buried Thomas Tonkin. This man was a school attendance officer and assessor for the Parish of Paul. He stepped inadvertently through a trap hatch of one of the Newlyn sea stores and was killed.

23rd February, 1898 John Trewarvas was buried, he was much respected as one who had a good influence over young people and filled several Parochial Offices with ability.

William and Mary Warren – two aged people who lived together for 60 years – died within hours of each other and were buried at the same time in the School burial ground 23rd December, 1899.

Agnes Jane Tippett – aged 29 buried 1st February, 1901 – Many years Sunday School Teacher. Andrew Harvey – aged 82 an old member of the Choir buried 4th April, 1906.

The Revd. Robert Wesley Aitken, aged 75 buried 17th February, 1910, 35 years Vicar of this Parish, son of Revd. Robert Aitken, great Missionary Preacher, Vicar of Pendeen.

Queen Victoria's Funeral – 22nd January, 1901 – reported in the Burial Register

The news of the Queen's death was received by Telegraph to the Vicar, who instructed the Sexton to toll the bell at one-minute intervals. A Memorial Service was held in the Church on the day of her Funeral, which was attended by Parish Officials and a large number of people. The Choral Service was *'deeply inspirational'*. The hymns were 'Hark Blessed are the Dead', 'Now The Labourer's Task is O'er'; the music for the Service was an Introit composed by the Vicar; the anthem 'The Lamb Shall Lead Them', beautifully rendered by Paul Choir. After the Sermon the Service ended with Handel's Grand Chorus 'Then Round About the Starry Throne' and Chopin's March on the organ.

Present: Vicar, the Revd. Aitken, Churchwardens: R. Wright and Richard Carne. Sidesmen: J. Davies, J. Blewett, Choir:- R.B. McClary, J. Kelynack, C. Aitken, J. F. McClary, J. McClary, M. McClary, W. H. Tregurtha, G. Osborne (Basses). J. R. Wallis, H. Hitchens, E. Trevaskis, and N. Chirgwin (Tenors). Helen B. Aitken, Mary Hodder, J. Kelynack, Ada Spargo, and M. E. Roberts, (Contralto) N. Richards, E. J. Richards, Eva Harvey, Annie Tippett, Winifred Ashborne, Mary Polglaze, J. Pezzack, Gertrude Kelynack, and Susan Chirgwin (Sopranos). Caretaker – Annie Tippett and Daughter. Sexton J. Burase. Beadle – Jas. Harvey.

MOMUMENTS IN CHURCH

I do think that it is necessary to list the burial monuments in the church as a future record. Some of them are rather long, therefore in some cases the important dates and names are taken, in a shortened form. I will start with one of the most poignant – that of the three brave 'Johns'. They have two memorial tablets – one I believe was once inside the south porch, but now is fastened to the eastern outer wall of the Porch.

Three Johns, John Badcock, John Bryant, and John Pearce, young men, became a portion of a Missionary Band led by Captain Alan F. Gardiner, R. N. They left their native land on 7th September, 1850 on perilous enterprise of sowing seeds of Christianity on the barbarous shores of Tierra del Fuego. With their companions they unhappily perished, after a series of unparalleled sufferings endured with exemplary fortitude. Just inside the south door the inside tablet to the three Johns states:

'One by one perished from want and exposure. Their Journal ended by the dying hand of the last survivor bears testimony to unflinching constancy with which they all 'Died in the Faith' – 'God is not ashamed to be called their God' St. Matthew XIX vs 29 Hebrews XI vs 15-16.

In Captain Alan Gardner's Diary John Badcock's death is described *'from scurvy, he had a wonderful spirit and suffered much, and died singing Wesley's hymn 'Before the throne my surety stands, my name is written on His hands'.* The formation of the Anglican South American Missionary Society was a direct result of the self-sacrifice of the three Johns.

Turning to the left through the south door there is the Children's Corner, also known at the 'Osborne Chapel', dedicated to the Glory of God and in loving memory of Jessie Ellen Osborne, who died 15th February, 1959, aged 67, and of her daughter Hilda Rose who died 12th September, 1946 aged 14 (see Window Memorials).

The next tablet on the south wall: *'In thankfulness to God for Walter Stuart Macfarlane (Mac) born 8th March, 1903 died 6th January, 1988, and his wife Betty born 20th February, 1902 died 27th December, 1985.'* Faithful worshippers and generous benefactors of this Church – the south dial of the Clock is also dedicated in their loving memory.

Between the windows south aisle: *'in Memory of Revd. W. Carpenter, D.D., Rector of this Parish, buried in the School Cemetery – he was born in Ireland 1806 and died 24th December, 1865'.*
His sorrowing parishioners erected the tablet as a mark of affectionate remembrance. Royal Cornwall Guardian – 1866 – *'**St. Paul** –During the past week a mural tablet of white marble, gothic design has been erected in the Church to the memory of the late Dr. W. Carpenter, at an expense of £30 raised by subscriptions chiefly from Newlyn.'*

Next is a very large and elaborate memorial, beautifully carved in white marble with cherubs, and at the bottom the tracery and design of an old East Indianman ship. In memory of Captain Stephen Hutchens of this parish who departed this life at Port Royall in Jamaica, 24th August, 1709 and was buried by the Communion Table in Kingston Church, age 44. His death came shortly after winning a single-handed battle with two French ships. A fact that is not on the memorial: he was Commander of HMS 'Portland' Ship of War, ref: draft Bond dated March 1752. He was Captain under what was called 'The John Company' ranking as an Officer of the English Navy. The first line from Virgil follows intimating this fact: *'Arma Virumque cano'.*

He left a fortune of £18,000 (Roughly £9 million in today's money) and out of it:-
'He hath given one hundred pounds towards the repairing and beautifying of this Church; and six hundred pounds for a building a house for six poor men and six poor women in this Parish to live in, and towards their maintenance.'

This is the Hutchens' Charity. Hutchens' House stands by the West Gate of the Churchyard, and still provides homes for elderly Paul villagers (see also Chapter 15). On the memorial:-

'Bounas heb dueth Eu poes Karens wei
tha Pobl Bohodzhak Paull han Egles nei'

'Eternal life be his whose loving care
Gave Paul & almshouse & the Church repair'

'Life without end be thine whose love did fall
On the poor people and our Church at Paul'

'England gave me a body, Jamaica holds my grave
And may God Himself possess my soul'

Hutchens' Memorial

This memorial once had a pointed triangle coming out of the vase at the very top, but the whole memorial was moved to the south aisle from the north aisle, when the walls were refurnished after a storm in December 1828. It is visible in this position in the H. P. Tremenheere watercolours in Chapter 3. The wall plate of the south aisle was too low, so the pointed funerary obelisk had to be removed from the top of the monument, and a rounder carved torch bearing flames substituted to fit the wall. At this time the skull at the bottom was also added to the monument. These alterations may be noticed in the Tremenheere watercolours which show the Hutchens' memorial hanging on the north wall.

Next comes a black marble edged lozenge shaped tablet to Lieutenant Nicholas Millet R.M. who died in 1828 and Jane Painter Millet who died April 1861. Also Francis Hutchens Jacka eldest son who died November 1841, William Smith the second son who drowned off the coast of China in 1854, and George (third son) who also drowned during his homeward voyage from Australia in 1839. Jane Painter Jacka Moyle, the youngest, died in March 1862. Their remains are in the churchyard south of the Church. Emily Jane and Anna Marie Millet, surviving daughters erected the memorial. Emily Jane died in March 1871 and Anna died August 1875, and they are buried in Penzance Cemetery. These are all 'Millets' although their surnames seem to have been left out!

There are three smaller memorial tablets in a line, in the south aisle, to Margaret Ann Tippett born 8th April, 1862 who died 14th June, 1942, *'a faithful worker of this Church'*. The next is to Mary Annie Simons wife of Charles Benjamin Simons and daughter of the above Margaret and William Tippett. Mary Annie died 2nd September, 1949 aged 64 – she *'spared not her life for this Church and Sunday School and was loved by all'*. There is also a small wooden prayer desk that has a dedication to Mary Annie Simons. It is at present near the Children's Corner, there is also a desk dedicated to C. B. Simons.

Over this page is a lovely photo of Mr. and Mrs. Simons in Market Jew Street, Penzance. Charlie was a Dentist and Mary Annie's parents as above, Mr. and Mrs. Tippett, ran a Paul Village shop in Church Street and lived in the house next door. This same shop was later run as an electrical supplies shop by John George's Father, Lawrence Frederick George. A quick mention must be made of Gertie Pezzack, Post Mistress extraordinaire of Paul, a great character, who ran the Post

Mr. and Mrs. Charlie Simons

Office in Trungle with great aplomb, and underneath huge pair of Bison horns on the wall!

The third is a bronze tablet to George Downing born 31st March, 1799 died 27th October, 1873; Catherine Downing born 8th August, 1796 died 2nd July, 1870.

A tablet on the south wall states: *Beneath the Altar are the remains of Revd. Warwick Oben Gurney – of Balliol College Oxford, 47 years Curate of Paul Parish. Died 1st August, 1849 aged 70 years, this tablet is erected by his widow and some of his congregation as a test of respect and affection.*

Also Agnes Gurney his daughter, whose memorial is near the altar and is of white marble surrounded by black marble, she died of consumption at only 13 years of age on 22nd December, 1834, and is buried under the altar next to her sister. She died in Trungle House, which at that time was the residence of Revd. Gurney's wife. Ann Robyn, daughter of Revd. Warwick Oben and Grace Gurney, sister of Agnes above, is also buried under the altar. She has a white marble temple plaque surrounded again by black marble. She died at Poltaire aged 30 on 15th January, 1841 and was the wife of John Richards Robyn.

Next to the altar is fixed a beautiful marble tablet by 'Golden of Holborn, London' a well-known memorial maker. The large tablet memorial is edged in pink marble with a draped urn at its head and a large chubby cherub with wings at its end. It is in memory of John Badcock whose remains are buried under the altar. The memorial was placed there by his relation John Price (father of Sir Rose Price).

A poignant verse follows: *'Hand in hand they trod the paths of infancy unconscious of ills to come or care beyond today; and years improved the union of their friendship… the companion and brother of his youth, for whom he sighs in vain, hath made his bed in the chamber of ashes, where the voice of friendship and kinsman is heard no more.'*

Then follows some names: *John (above) was son of Henry Badcock and Joanna his wife, sole heir of Johannis Goode son of Dorothea daughter of Thomas Penkivel of St. Kew, Henry Badcock married Joanna Keigwin of Penzance daughter of Gulielmi Ince de Lanow of St. Kew daughter of Maria daughter of John Mark of Woodhill. Gulielmi Godolphin de Trewarveneth – Margery daughter of Nicholas Godolphin married Phillipa daughter of Humprey Nicholls de Penvose in St.Tudy. Guilelmi Godolphin, Mother of Johanna Keigwin, Father of Henry Badcock'.* There are a plethora of names on this tablet, it just seems to be some sort of elaborate pedigree, which according to Revd. Aitken is very unusual on memorials in the 1800s.

The north side of the altar has another large memorial to the Revd. Henry Pendarves, made of marble. At the top is a shield on which is the Pendarves Coat of Arms, a golden eagle with three gold stars. The family motto being '*Nec timeo, nec tumeo*' or '*I will not fear, I will not swell*'.

The gist of the Latin is: near this place lies Henry Pendarves, 58 years a Vicar, his Father was Thomas Samuel Pendarves de Roscrow, Mother Margareta Joanna Borlase de Pendeen, he was related to the Godolphin and Keigwin families. He died 14th June, 1739, aged 85, his wife Maria Pendarves 3rd January, 1759, aged 90(!), and Margaret Borlase died 8th April, 1743 aged 42. This memorial tablet is placed on an expansive plaster area, which once supported a very large reredos. The entablature of the tomb was made to echo the top of the reredos which fitted over the plaster. It extols (in what Revd. Aitken calls '*Monks' Latin*') the virtues of Margaret, of the ancient Cornish family of Borlase. I have been lucky enough to find out more about Revd. Henry Pendarves from an expert on the family, David Thomas of the C.R.O.:

His only daughter Margaret married Doctor Walter Borlase Vicar of Madron & Kenwyn Churches. The portrait of Margaret and Walter used to hang in the Borlase collection at Castle Hornick. Henry's wife was Mary daughter of John Borlase of Pendeen, widow of Richard Pearce of Kerris. They were married at Sancreed 8th August, 1701. Henry's Father was a Captain of Foot in the Civil War, his Mother was Margaret daughter of John St. Aubyn of Clowance in Crowan. Henry's siblings were Thomas Pendarves, Valentine, Charles, Margaret, and Grace who all died young. His Grandfather was Samuel Pendarves of Roscrow who died 1643 – Grandma Grace daughter of Josias Roberts of Truro, they married at Constantine 24th June, 1598.

The memorial to the Revd. Henry Penneck, B.A., Vicar of Paul for 32 years (from 1739 to 1771), is a large tablet memorial of greyish marble streaked black. It doesn't sit comfortably in its present place, with edges projecting, therefore it is highly likely that it has been moved from elsewhere in the Church, where it probably sat flush with its mounting. He obviously loved Paul Church enough to insist his body was returned after his death on 23rd August, 1784 (aged 69) and he was buried under the altar, presumably adjacent to his memorial. His wife Juliana died on 7th July, 1807 and is buried near him, also under the altar. Their daughter Frances erected the memorial to her parents.

Captain Elton Memorial

In the choir area of the chancel on the south side of the north arcade is a scroll memorial to Captain Andrew Elton stating: '*Interred near this place lies ye body of Captain Andrew Elton, Commander of the Godfrey Gally. He was killed in an engagement with a French Privateer off Lands End on 4th September, 1710 aged 53*'. This memorial was once on the wall at the next arch (see the Tremenheere paintings Chapter 3).

It then states that nothing more is known of this chap, but luckily Bob Harrison has searched diligently and finally found some very interesting information more about him, and has posted all the details of this fellow, and others, on the Paul Church website, (www.paulchurch.com), which is well worth a visit!

A few details of Captain Elton emanate from his Will in the Public Record Office: that he was a mariner from London, of the Parish of St. Mary, Rotherhithe, and had several houses or tenements in Church Street, Greenwich, plus a 'copyhold' estate in Westerham in Kent. He left £150 to his eldest son, Andrew, and the remainder to his beloved wife and then to his children.

Admiralty records show that four letters of marque (making one a privateer), dating 1692, 1702, 1707 and 1710, were issued to Captain Elton. He was a successful privateer for over 20 years and a man of influence and means. At the year of his burial at Paul on 28th September, 1710; there were on average 18 privateers commissioned to carry out their trade. Captain Andrew Elton lost his life whilst engaged in a battle with a French privateer, and presumably he was buried at Paul because Mousehole would have been the nearest port to Land's End, and Paul the nearest Church. His monument is between two arcades in the choir area, and consists of a handsome white marble scroll unfurled to show the memorial lines in black, with a cherub's head at the bottom and a beautifully coloured coat of arms, no doubt of Captain Elton's family, at the top.

On the opposite side to Captain Elton's elegant scroll memorial is a plainer white marble lozenge-shaped tablet with gothic lettering stating Revd. Charles George Ruddock Festing – 30 years Vicar of this Parish - died in Warminster Wiltshire on 30th August, 1857, and was buried at Witham Priory.

Further down the nave on the south wall near the lectern is a black oval memorial with white relief urn, to the memory of Grace Marrack, who died aged 94 on 18th June, 1810 and was interred in the family vault *'near this place'*. The memorial also mentions Grace Broad her daughter who died 2nd December, 1785 aged 25, and Nicholas Broad her grandson who died 18th March, 1805 aged 21. The memorial was erected by Grace Millett and Wilmot Hitchens, her two surviving granddaughters.

Near the north door there is a memorial to Ida Clare wife of Major C. Sakerman, R.E., and daughter of Vice-Admiral and Mrs. Henry Leah, who died on 8th December, 1959.

There is a black square marble tablet with white marble inset dedicated to Richard Thomas Pentreath who died aged 62 on 17th January, 1869, 'a *good husband, kind Father, and loved by all who knew him'*. This Mr. Richard Pentreath is likely to be the same one who founded a 'School of Navigation' in Paul, and who was Paul Parish Clerk for thirty years.

In the middle of the north aisle is an interesting memorial to Edward Leah, a Surgeon in the Royal Navy who died on 27th December, 1853, and who bore some terrible illness with great fortitude. His memorial floridly describes his appalling suffering, conjuring up images of his dreadful illness and death, probably knowing what he was going to endure being a surgeon. The Royal Cornish Gazette stated on 15th February, 1856:

*'**St. Paul** – a beautiful monument has been erected during the past week in The Parish Church of St. Paul in Memory of Edward Leah, Surgeon R.N. by his widow. It consists of an arched recess in the wall surmounted by a hood mould deeply moulded, having corbels minutely carved with oak and vine leaves, it is divided in to two tablets of marble by three slender shafts supporting trefoiled arches bearing a circle which is quartrefoiled and bearing a circle and fills the head. All is of granite except the shafts which are of polished*

serpentine. The capitals are wreathed with leaves deeply cut in granite in the quatrefoils is a zinc shield bearing the arms of Leah. The whole is the most minute and beautiful workmanship and was worked from the drawings by William Clemens statuary builder of Truro. Whose task and skill are assured need only to be patronage.'

In the north aisle are two swords and some armour; these are fully discussed in Chapter 16. They hang above the white and grey memorial plaque, with two black columns either side, which states: *'Near here lies the body of William Godolphin of Trewarveneth in the Parish of Paul Gent. He died on 9th September, 1689 aged 69. His body being turned to ashes Jesus has taken care of his soul. Also Elizabeth Godolphin, daughter of Thomas Darrell of Trewornan in this County, widow and survivor of the deceased and John Nicholls one of the Clerks in the High Court of Chancery elder son of William Nicholls of Trerife in the Parish of Madron, nephew and co-heir of the said William Godolphin, have erected this memorial to his everlasting memory A.D. 1697.'*

There is a story attached to the above memorial, a shortened form of which follows:

The Godolphin heir William Nicholls had a daughter called Phelipp (Phillipa). As William Godolphin had no children, he arranged for his great-niece to go and live with him as his daughter. This continued for many years and Phelipp was educated and maintained by her great-uncle. William Godolphin then met Thomas Darrell, who had several unmarried daughters. Thomas proposed that William Godolphin (age 50) should marry his daughter Elizabeth (age 15), and this marriage took place.

Phelipp stated that William Godolphin had intended to leave a good portion of his wealth to her, despite his marriage to Elizabeth. It was on this promise of £500 that Francis Lanyon married Phelipp Nicholls. However on William Godolphin's death he had only left her £5. Thus the case of Francis Lanyon v Thomas Darrell related to Francis trying to get his hands on the £500. All sorts of allegations on the mental health of William Godolphin when his Will was drawn up were cited in this legal case. Elizabeth meanwhile took over the estate of Trewarveneth. Unfortunately there are no records on the outcome of the case, thus we do not know if Phelipp and Francis ever received £500. This must have been settled amicably for John Nicholls to join with Elizabeth Godolphin in erecting a memorial to William Godolphin (original research: Catherine Lorigan and Jo Mattingly, V.C.H.).

Under this memorial is another white plaster memorial, with cracks in the tracery representing a window, with two handsome serpentine stone columns on either side, streaked with crimson mottling:*'Memory of Lieut. Gen. Robyns and Wilmot his wife and of Edmund Malone and Marianne wife, parents of Revd. Richard Malone of the Parish of St. Paul and wife Jane Wilmot and their child John Henry Edmund who died in 1861 age 6 years.'*

On visiting Gulval Church I noticed a memorial there to Jane Wilmot Malone, wife of Revd. Richard Malone born 10th August, 1821 died 4th July, 1896. She is therefore remembered in both Churches, as are her parents Lieut Gen. Robyns and Wilmot his wife, Gulval Church being the Parish Church of the Robyns family. The east window of the south aisle is also dedicated to their memory, see below.

At the east end of the north aisle is the marble memorial to William Gwavas:-
'Near this place lyeth the body of William Gwavas Gent (eldest son of William Gwavas Esq and Ann his wife one of the daughters of William Chester of East Haddon in Northamptonshire) Educated in the Practice as well as the Theory of the Law and was of the Soc. of Middle Temple

London having issue by Elizabeth is wife (dau of Christopher Harris of St. Ives, merchant) Elizabeth and Ann his co-heirs. Born 6th December, 1676 at Huntingfield Hall, Suffolk. Buried 9th January, 1741.

'Member of the Church of England Endowed with a virtuous disposition
Was steady in Practice of Fair Dealing, Early Studious in ye Holy Scriptures of the Guide of his Actions Cautious against Evil, Circumspect and Patient.'

Then Bible passages follow in Latin and at the bottom of the memorial 'ADORATE JEHOVA!'

William Gwavas was an assiduous collector of Cornish language information, and kept a correspondence in Cornish with like minded enthusiasts such as John Keigwin, John and Thomas Boson and Thomas Tonkin. The various Cornish language pieces Gwavas collected from a range of people in western Cornwall are a valuable source for examples of Cornish. However within sixty years of his death the language was effectively dead. There is more about William Gwavas, and the Chancery Suit, and a portrait of him, in Chapter 11.

Joseph Trewavas -
Near the above memorials there is a modern slate plaque in the north aisle on the north wall to Joseph Trewavas, V.C., C.G.M., R.N., of Mousehole 1835-1905—Straits of Genitchi (Crimea) 1855. The Memorial was placed in this position by the Mousehole Royal British Legion during a Service in 2002 (see his photo in Chapter 13).

WINDOW MEMORIALS

Osborne Window

Paul Church is very fortunate to have many stained glass windows, alas none of them are of any antiquity, they are mostly Victorian or later.

There is a plaque stating that the windows of the south aisle of the Church were badly damaged by German bombs January 1942, and were restored in May 1949. Revd. W. V. Wagner, Vicar. R. Drew and L. Spargo, Churchwardens.

The stained glass window in the west end of the south aisle was erected in 1903 by John Henry Osborne, the son of Henry and Jane Osborne who died 27th April, 1879 and 2nd March 1892, respectively. This whole area is the Osborne Children's Corner and Chapel, dedicated to Jessie Ellen Osborne who died 15th February, 1959 aged 67 and of her daughter Hilda Rose who died 12th September, 1949 aged 14 (see Chapter 6).

The first window in the south aisle is dedicated to Revd. Robert Wesley Aitken, Vicar of Paul Church for 34 years, erected by the young men of the parish, December 1909.

The next south aisle window is erected by Joanna and Emily Rowe in memory of family members—see the beginning of this chapter for details. Moving along, the next window is dedicated to Richard Pentreath, of H.M. Customs – born in Mousehole 1814, died in London 1880. This was erected by his son Francis Godolphin Pentreath, who died in 1893. There is also a memorial on the south aisle outside wall to the Pentreath family just under this window, and above several vaults which run along this outside wall and probably contain the remains of this family.

Nearest to the north door is a window depicting three Saints: St. Petroc, St. Paulinus, and St. Nicholas. It was erected in memory of Vice Admiral Henry Leah, of the Royal Navy, and of his wife Clara, who after 49 years of happy married life died on 26th and 28th June, 1926. Also of Lieut. Colonel Thomas Coulson Leah D.S.O.R.A., their only son, who died 20th October, 1927. At the bottom of this window in the middle is a little stained glass depiction of St. Paulinus of York baptising King Edwin, just to reinforce that *this* Paulinus, is Paulinus of York and not Paul Aurelian.

The next window in the north aisle is of three more Saints: St. Peter, St. John and St. Andrew. It was erected in memory of Thomas Leah of this Parish who died 30th September and Phyllis his wife who died 26th March, also Revd. Thomas Leah their son who died at St. Keyne where he was Rector for thirty-eight years; he died 15th November aged 58.

Mr. William Tonkin of Newlyn gave the third window along in memory of his sisters Susan Tonkin, who died 30th August, 1874 aged 64, and Jane Chirgwin who died 9th March, 1875 aged 72. William Tonkin himself died 19th October, 1878 aged 81 years.

The fourth window in the north aisle is to the memory of Emily Richards Bath born 26th June, 1842 and died 15th June, 1905. Her husband Richard Richards Bath presented this window to the church.

The main altar window is rather surprising in that it depicts Sir Galahad and not a religious subject. It was erected in memory of William Torquill Macleod Bolitho, Lieutenant of the 19th Hussars, born 13th November, 1892 who fell in action at Chateau Hooge during the second battle of Ypres on 24th May, 1915. The face of Sir Galahad is very distinctive and was probably taken from a likeness of the deceased. It contains the words: '*And you will speed us onward with a cheer, and wave beyond the stars that all is well*' (Maurice Baring). To the left of the window is a black memorial tablet stating that the window is also in memory of his Uncle Lieutenant Torquill Macleod, R.N. of H.M.S. 'Serpent' wrecked off Spain and also his cousin Midshipman Torquill Harry Lionel Mcleod R.N. of H.M.S. 'Goliath' and his Shipmates of the Parish of Paul.

Now the east window south aisle: this is a beautiful window depicting Christ in His Glory and was erected in memory of the Revd. Richard Malone, M.A. born 23rd June, 1820 died 7th June, 1908 Vicar of this Parish 1866-1876 and of Jane Wilmot Malone his wife born 10th August, 1821 died 4th July, 1896, both of whom are buried at Madron, this window is placed by their children.

THE SOLOMON BROWNE MEMORIAL

At the east end of the north aisle is a granite memorial dedicated to the Crew of the 47-foot Watson class Solomon Browne Lifeboat, who all tragically died on 19th December, 1981 attempting a rescue of the crew of the 1,400-ton coaster 'Union Star' in trouble off Boscawen Cliffs, near Tater Du. It was dedicated by the Bishop of Truro on 24th April, 1983 and was designed by Mr. John Phillips, A.R.I.B.A., Church Architect. The idea that the memorial should resemble a light-house was prompted by the beautiful crystal chalice and paten made by B. Jabez Francis of Peterborough.

The chalice is engraved with the initials of all the crew. The tower of the light-house is a granite rock taken from the foreshore of Lamorna Cove, and weighs approximately a ton. This was conveyed to Paul by Mr. George Osborne, with his two sons Chris and Roy assisting. Mr. J. H. Ching, monumental mason of Porthleven, and Mrs. Kitty Prowse carried out the work on the granite rock in the Church. The glazed lantern was made by young men at the Trevenson Industrial Centre, Pool, Redruth and was a Youth Employment Project. Mr. Alan Johns, mason and Mr. John Maddern, carpenter, prepared the corner of the Church. There is also a Memorial to the Lifeboat Crew in St. Clement's Chapel, Mousehole.

This terrible tragedy touched the lives of all those living in Newlyn, Paul and Mousehole, and the bravery of the lifeboat men will never be forgotten. Those who lost their lives on that fateful night were: -

Coxswain – William Trevelyan Richards, Second Coxswain Mechanic—James Stephen Madron, Assistant Mechanic—Nigel Brockman, Emergency Mechanic—John Robert Blewett, Crew members—Charles Thomas Greenhaugh, Kevin Smith, Barry Robertson Torrie, Gary Lee Wallis.

Posthumously a R.N.L.I. gold medal for outstanding gallantry was awarded to William Richards Trevelyan, and R.N.L.I. bronze medals were awarded to each of the crew.

The morning after the tragedy, the Service in Paul Church was taken by a Lay Reader, Mr. Reg Perrott, as the Revd. Cadman was down in Mousehole with the bereaved families. In the middle of the Service, the south door opened, and the Bishop of Truro came in to the Church, on his way down to Mousehole to minister to the families.

On Friday 22nd January, 1982, a Memorial Service for the Lifeboat Crew was held in Paul Church and attended by the Duke and Duchess of Kent. The Duke is the President of the R.N.L.I. A marquee was erected on what was then the Green (car park) to take the over-flow of mourners.

Paul Church Choir under Elizabeth Stubbings, Choir Mistress and George Caunt, Organist, sang Psalm 107 containing the famous words *'They that go down to the sea in ships and occupy their business in great water'*. Among other music, the Choir sang: the *'Russian Contakion of the Departed'*, Richards de Castre's *'Prayers to Jesus'*, *'Adoramus Te, Jesu'* by Palestrina, and the hymns *'Father to Thee we look in our sorrow'*, *'O Sacred head sore wounded'* and *'Ah, Holy Jesu'*. The congregational hymns were *'Abide with me'*, *'In loving-kindness Jesus came'*, *'Jesus, Saviour Pilot me'* and as a Vesper hymn a verse of *'Eternal Father Strong to save —O Trinity of love and power'*. The Choir Recessional was the Nunc Dimittus. The Rev. Cadman addressed the Memorial Service:-

'Brethren, we meet this day to offer Thanks to Almighty God for all who have lived and died in the service of their fellow men: and especially for the Eight Members of the 'Solomon Browne', who gave their lives that others might live. Also remembering with great sadness those who sailing on the 'Union Star' died with them on that fateful night, and giving thanks for the many who searched the coasts and the sea, day and night in an endeavour to recover their comrades from the deep, particularly the Air-Sea Rescue Helicopter from Culdrose.'

H.R.H. The Duke of Kent read the Lesson which was taken from Romans Ch. 8 verses 31-39. The Mousehole Male Voice Choir sang the hymn: *'Sunset & Evening Star'*. The Prayers of Recollection and Remembrance were taken by Revd. T. N. M. Vidamour, Minister of the Mousehole Methodist Chapels, and Superintendent D. C. Cole, Royal National Mission to Deep Sea Fishermen, Newlyn.

Revd. Cadman also wrote movingly in a special edition of 'The Cornishman' - 24th December, 1981:-

'As I moved around the village on Sunday morning, visiting the homes of the crew of the Solomon Browne, the ill-fated lifeboat (for whom I am also honoured to be the Chaplain), I was struck by the fact that the whole village was alive; folk of all ages were moving from one house to another, members of the same families, friends and neighbours offering sympathy and love to each other in the hour of stress, when the elite of the village, the leaders, the initiators, the men who got things done; the young and alive, and happy ones were suddenly and sadly taken away as they answered the call of duty. SOS! Out of their warm homes they came and into a small vessel on an ocean that was menacing and all too demanding. These young men gave of their best to save their fellows. 'Greater love hath no man that he lay down his life for his friends'. We honour them and we weep for their families. They gave their lives in order to save their fellows, even when they were strangers'.

The Predominant feature of Sunday morning amongst those who had lost a Son, a Father, a Brother, was one of complete numbness. Nature in its mercy had anaesthetised them. Truth to tell, the whole village was in shock. It was good to see the Church offering the eternal and never-failing compassion of the Redeemer, as the Bishop of Truro, and myself, three Methodist Ministers, and the Skipper of the Newlyn Mission went about visiting the sad ones and the lonely ones in the name of Christ. May Christmas 1981 mean that the peace of the Christ-child envelopes your home, and may our love and prayers embrace and uphold you as the New Year dawns, God Bless you All; One in Jesus Christ.'

The Mousehole Harbour Christmas Lights had earlier been switched on by one of the lifeboat crew, Mr. Charles Greenhough, Landlord of the 'Ship Inn' Mousehole. They were switched off after the disaster and were not turned on again until the evening of 24th December, after two funerals at Paul Church of William Trevelyan Richards, and Nigel Brockman. Annually, in Paul Church, on the Sunday nearest to 19th December, these brave men are remembered during the Morning Service; and in Mousehole each year on 19th December, the famous Christmas

DEDICATION OF THE MEMORIAL TO THE CREW OF THE SOLOMON BROWNE. 24th April, 1983.
The Revd. G. Harper, Vicar and The Rt. Revd. Peter Mumford, Bishop of Truro. This photo also shows the organ which stood in the south aisle.

harbour lights are dimmed to honour the memory of those who lost their lives.

On Christmas Eve a new centrepiece appeared on the hillside above the village. Shining over Mousehole was a Cross with an angel on either side, with a message of goodwill to the people of West Cornwall.

The Mousehole Lifeboat Station from which the fated boat left on 19th December is now closed and left exactly as it was on that tragic night, as a memorial to the brave crew. There is a memorial garden for quiet contemplation at this spot, on the coast road to Mousehole. The RN.L.I. Flag marks the boat house.

PAUL PARISH CHURCH
(St. Pol-de-Leon)

Friday, 22nd January, 1982

at 2 p.m.

A
**FAMILY SERVICE OF REMEMBRANCE
AND THANKSGIVING
FOR**

WILLIAM TREVELYAN RICHARDS	Coxswain
JAMES STEPHEN MADRON	Second Coxswain Mechanic
NIGEL BROCKMAN	Assistant Mechanic
JOHN ROBERT BLEWETT	Emergency Mechanic
CHARLES THOMAS GREENHAUGH	Crew Member
BARRIE TORRIE	Crew Member
KEVIN SMITH	Crew Member
GARY WALLIS	Crew Member

who gave their lives in the Penlee Lifeboat
"SOLOMON BROWNE"
on 19th December 1981

"We will remember them"

On the plaque below is written words by Sir Winston Churchill:-

'It drives on with a mercy that does not quail in the presence of death, it drives on as a proof, a symbol, a testimony that man is created in the image of God, and that valour and virtue have not perished in the British race'.

PENLEE LIFEBOAT DISASTER MEMORIAL GARDEN
This Memorial Garden was commissioned by the Penzance Town Council and designed by the Architects Department of British Airways.
The site was generously donated by Mrs. M.E. Harvey of Newlyn and the construction work carried out by the Penwith Springboard Youth Training Scheme with materials and donations from a number of local people and organisations.
MARGARET BECKERLEG. J.P.
TOWN MAYOR

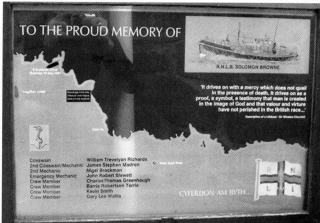

The map shows exactly where the 'Union Star' went down and where the wreckage of the Penlee Lifeboat was found.

Today the Penlee Lifeboat House is by Newlyn Harbour, and the Lifeboat is moored up in the sea, always at the ready to go to the rescue of those in distress.

The Memorial Lifeboat House and Slipway, Mousehole.

A FEW MEMORIAL GIFTS

The wooden parclose screen that used to separate the pipe organ console from the chancel was erected in memory of William E. T. Bolitho and Ethel Grace Bolitho who died 5th March, 1862 and 21st February, 1944. Given by their daughter Brenda Grace Sparrow of Trewelloe – dedicated by the Bishop of Truro, on 12th March, 1964. The painting on this screen is allegorical depicting, as it does, our Church tower with a spire!

The handsome granite pulpit is dedicated to Revd. Robert Wesley Aitken, thirty-five years Vicar of Paul Church, 9th February, 1911. It replaced a similar wooden pulpit. The present Vicar's desk and chair, carved with angels, is dedicated to Revd. Frederick Joseph Prideaux, Vicar of Paul 1911-1938. The stall was placed there by the Parishioners.

An Oak Litany desk was presented in memory of C. B. Simons who died 4th February, 1952. Another desk was given by the congregation in memory of a *'faithful worker of Paul Church'* Mary Annie Symons 2nd September, 1949 (see her photo in this Chapter). A flower stand was given in memory of Sylvia Webber in 1984 by friends in Sheffield. A third Prayer Desk was given in memory of Ellen Lilian Ladner and Joseph Henry Ladner, who died in 1977 and 1979 respectively, *'who faithfully served this Church'*.

In August, 1972 a Silver Chalice and Paten, which are very much in use today, were given to Paul Church engraved with the following: *'To the glory of God and in loving memory of Michelle Louise Beger, June 8th 1954 - November 21st, 1968. Given by her loving Parents, Sister and Grandparents.* The Chalice and Paten were designed by John Phillips, A.R.I.B.A. Church Architect, who also designed the Penlee Lifeboat Memorial.

Offertory salver

Paul Church possesses a really beautifully tooled large brass offertory plate. It is in constant use during services today, but unfortunately nothing is know of the maker or donor as it is not engraved. It is probably dated from before the First World War, and is decorated with the patterns of fish, corn and flowers, possibly representing church tithes. These patterns are used in the decoration of Newlyn Copper ware, and thus it is likely to have been fashioned locally, maybe by a student of Mr. John D. McKenzie, who taught the fishermen the copper beating trade c.1890s, in order to given them an income during winter months when they could not put to sea.

In the north aisle there is a new table of oak, with a slate inlay, made in 2005 by George Robinson, with a bequest from the estate of Philip Hutchens, Church Treasurer and a much-missed Choir member. It is mainly used for signing the register during marriage ceremonies.

Note: these are only a few of the many donations, memorials and bequests given to Paul Church. The Keigwin Silver Tray and some old Will references of bequests are described in Chapter 16. There have been many gifts over the years, some financial as well as practical, and they have been recorded in a leather bound 'Gift Book'. This was itself a gift to Paul Church by the family and friends of Mr. Jack Penrose Williams of Newlyn who died in January 1986 aged 75. This book is in the safe-keeping of the Roger Bond, Churchwarden (2006).

109

CHAPTER 8 - THE CROSSES OF PAUL, THE KING'S LETTER & FACULTY RECORDS

'Grouse' is the Cornish for 'Cross'. Cornwall abounds in Celtic crosses; they were used for sanctifying crossing places, fords, bridges over rivers and streams, entrances to sacred enclosures and property boundaries. They were often sited at crossroads, early signposts showing the way to the nearest church across the county. Or on church town pathways, pointing the way from one to the other nearest church. Or as rallying points similar in a way to the bus stops of today, for passengers travelling through their Christian life. There had to be some sort of marker for Christian gatherings in the early days before churches were constructed, and, as they were wrought out of granite in Cornwall, they have endured down the centuries. They were often found in hedges, maybe thrown there at the time of the Reformation or during the Civil War, or defaced by iconoclasts. As depicted below, many became detached from their shaft. The dedication of early Christians, carving away at the almost impenetrable granite with very basic tools, to depict Christ on the Cross, or other early Christian symbolism, such as the Chi-rho icon or monogram of Christ, cannot but raise admiration and indicate the depth of feeling that the new religion brought to the people.

Chi-Rho

Recently (2006), there has been the fortunate discovery of a Celtic cross shaft in the bottom of the wall of the north east end of the Church. I was looking for the signs of an old window sill with Sennen Church historian, Aidan Hicks (artist extraordinaire, responsible for the amazing front cover drawing), we noticed the tapered end of a long stone in the wall. I looked more closely and saw faint traces of Celtic decoration. The south and north aisle walls were partially re-built in 1864 after a storm rendered the Church too dangerous for worship (see Architecture Chapter). The shaft has been fixed, very low down on the wall; this may indicate that it was used as part of the rebuild of 1600. Tests will be undertaken to ascertain if, indeed, this was the original shaft of the large cross head in the churchyard wall at the front of the Church. It would be satisfying to marry them together. Note the Celtic knotwork decoration, and zig-zag on right towards the base. This zig-zag follows almost exactly the same pattern as the very old back road from Paul to Newlyn!

The Church was re-pointed in 1896 in a rather heavy manner. This pointing work is, at present obliterating the beading at the sides of the cross shaft. It is hoped that this will be removed by experts in the near future to facilitate a closer scrutiny of the shaft. It seems rather incredible that the cross shaft was not observed and recorded at the time of pointing! There is a socket stone with rectangular mortice situated in a hedge by a granite style on the way from Trungle to Gwavas, it is unfortunately too small to be the base of the Paul Church cross head and shaft.

Cross base and mortice

In Paul Church town there are two ancient crosses, the one in the wall, and one at the Vicarage gate.

Ankh Cross

There are also markers that depict other than Christian symbols; for instance at Boscreege farmhouse in Germoe Parish, there is a little Ankh Cross. It is only two feet in height, and each side is filled by a spiral, right handed on one side, and left handed on the other, indicating some form of sun worship (see Early church chapter). At least seven crosses are known to have stood in Paul Parish, mainly of the plain 'Latin' type of cross.

In the age of King Athelstan, A.D. 925-940, Christian churches in Cornwall came under the See of Canterbury. Historical evidence seems to indicate that none of the Cornish crosses are earlier than the fifth century A.D., although the exact time for the introduction of Christianity into Cornwall is lost in the mists of time. Now follows a list of crosses in and around the Parish of Paul (original research—Andrew Langdon).

KERRIS VILLAGE

A Kerris Cross

The Manor of Kerris in Paul Parish is very ancient and has crosses of its own, which are among the earliest relics of human habitation in this area.

A cross was previously situated at Carlanken estate, which adjoins Kerris about one and a half miles west of Paul. This was moved to Kerris Village; the date for this occurrence is not known.

Its shaft tapered more than usual and it was taller than most crosses, being 6ft 9in high by 2ft wide, with the exception of the cross that stood on Paul Down. The shaft became cracked just beneath the horizontal arms; it was also damaged at the base (this cross is no longer in place). The cross pictured on the left is probably the large cross described, minus half its shaft (ref: A. Langdon).

HALWYN, PAUL (Rose-an-beagle)

Halwyn Farm is south of Paul by about half a mile. A cross in this area was built into a hedge to the north of the farm; it may not have been very visible at all. It is reported to have actually formed part of a Cornish stone wall, with only the top being visible (just) the rest of the shaft being buried in the ground. The width is reported across the arms – about 2ft indicating that in its entirety the cross would be pretty large. It was subsequently taken down and re-erected on the road from Penzance to St. Just in Madron Parish.

PAUL DOWN

This cross is estimated to have been 6ft high and 1ft 11ins wide. Some part of its base was still underground, making it a very tall specimen indeed. It stood against a hedge of a narrow lane crossing Paul Down. It was plain and unornamented as are the other two above.

Churchyard cross head

CHURCHYARD WALL, PAUL CHURCH

National Monument Number: 28467 National Grid reference: SW46422707.

This cross is undoubtedly very ancient, and is now situated in the boundary wall of the Churchyard. Maybe this was the first cross to call Christians to worship at this place; before even

a Church of any sort was erected, people were drawn to worship by its powerful Christian symbolism, to listen to a priest making exhortation from its base.

Churchyard crosses were important for defining rights of sanctuary and penance, and it also would figure as a station for prayer in Church Processions, such as that on Palm Sunday. On the side facing the Church, three of the holes fully pierce the head, only the lower hole on the north west side does not. Its five bosses today represent the five wounds of Christ, His pierced hands, pierced feet and side. A large piece has been broken from the boss on the right. On the side facing the road is a figure representing the Christ; the head was once surrounded by a nimbus or type of halo, and the arms are slightly raised in a gesture of welcome. These unusually widely splayed limbs leave little room for the short outer ring. The photo above (approx. circa 1900: Pz Old Cornwall Soc.) depicts the cross head in more detail, with facial features now covered in lichen. The photo was taken some years ago - as one may still see the corner of an

'Engine House' window in the south aisle, and the road looks as if it were still unadopted.

There are two small rods of iron embedded in the cross head immediately below the lower arm on the south west face; the Churchyard wall has then been built up to the boulder. These rods are now rusting and it is intended to renew them shortly.

The head measured some time ago as 2ft 3in high, 1ft 11¼in wide, and more recently in the 1980s modern measurements - 0.6 m high by 0.6 m wide 0.2 m thick.

As the lower parts of the churchyard wall date from after 1595 (evidenced by pre-1595 pillar fragments incorporated in it), the cross and its boulder could have been in this situation since the Spanish raid. Of course, its date of situation also depends on when it was separated from its shaft. Next to the boulder, on the road side, there used to be steps to enable the ease of mounting horses, known as a 'hipping' or mounting block.

The figure of Christ motif is notably found on crosses around St. Buryan. In a study in which Paul Churchyard cross is mentioned, the conclusion is that these date from the late 9th or early 10th century. They provided a major design inspiration for the mid 10th century development of a more highly elaborate series of West Cornish crosses.

PAUL, BESIDE THE ROAD TO MOUSEHOLE

The base of this cross was built into the hedge in 1878, and was situated almost directly across the road from its present location. It has a curve connecting the head to the shaft, which tapers as if pulled in by a belt, and a round head with a cross incised thereon. It is 2ft 9in high, 1ft 10½in wide. Being sited on the old road from Mousehole to Paul, it may have been placed there to indicate to those who disembarked at the port of Porthenys (Mousehole) the Christian nature of both the Villages, and the way to Paul Church.

I have come across a reference to a murder which occurred in Mousehole Lane in the 18th century. Apparently, a cross was erected by John Price as a memorial to the victim of this murder. The murderer's family did not like to be reminded of this dreadful deed, and its removal was announced in the local press as 'Removal of an eyesore!' (the murder of Martha Blewett, is detailed in 'Burials' Chapter).

There was a cross on the coast near Mousehole, as a *'Porth-en-crous juxta Porthenis'* is mentioned in 1341, and a field in Tredarvoe of 12 acres was called *Parken Growz (field of the cross)* in 1631. There was also a *Park en Grouse* at Gwavas (Nos. 562-3 on the tithe map apportionment).

It is interesting to note that Saxon King Athelstan granted a charter of extended sanctuary to St. Buryan enabling miscreants to remain in safety (sanctuary) within a mile or so of the Church, rather than within the normal sanctuary of the Church or Churchyard cross environs only. Thus a cross would also provide a safe haven, an instrument of death becoming a haven of peace.

FACULTY RECORDS

In order to safeguard the church furnishings and fabric a 'Faculty' has to be raised by the Incumbent and the P.C.C. before any changes may be made. Here is a small list of recent Faculty records for Paul Church.

1. Faculty for placing in Church Priest's Stall, in memory of Revd. F. Prideaux - 26th May, 1942.
2. Petition and Faculty for rehanging of Bells and installation of three new Bells – 15th August, 1949 and 13th September, 1949 (tenor Bell recast).
3. Faculty and Petition for the introduction of Churchwardens' Staves and Processional Cross in memory of Revd. Wagner.
4. Petition for works of improvement in closed burial ground (behind Church Hall), removal of tombstones/widening of path – 7th February, 1955.
5. Faculty for widening of pathway to 'new' Churchyard – 24th January, 1956.
6. Faculty for introduction of Oak Chest into Church for Storage of Altar Frontals.
7. Faculty to Install Wrought Iron Gates at entrance of Churchyard (adjacent to Church Hall) on 2nd September, 1977. No. 22/77.
8. Faculty to Place Ancient Holy Water Stoop in Wall of Church – South Porch – 1985.

Faculties Records at Follet Stock & Company – Diocesan Registrar - in note form

3/92 – An old burial ground (the 'Cholera' Ground) was used as a garden until 1971 by Mr. Leslie Davis of 'We-Two' Cottage Paul, in Paul Village. The area was used for at least thirty years but in 1971 Penwith District Council demolished the enclosing hedge. They want to resume the situation standing, up to 1971. (sic)

39/92 - Erection of scaffolding to complete repairs to pinnacles on the Tower, and attention to ironwork: reinstatement of weathervane: renewal of lead deck covering : provision of flag pole on Church tower: repainting and relaying guttering around foot of walling: repairs to north aisle east window: floodlighting of tower: extra clock dial: memorial Tablet to the McFarlanes.

Under Archdeacon's Certificate dated 3rd February, 1975 repairs to walls and porch sealing cracks and repairing plaster – 36A/75.

Cornwall Archaeological Unit Faculty 5th October, 1975 – replacing chairs in Sanctuary 37/75.

1st July, 1979 Conversion of old Churchyard into park and landscaped area. 9/79.

Extensive roof repairs and window mullion restoration 17/80.

1981–8 Archdeacon's Certificate for replacement of wrought iron gates to Churchyard surrounding church, in memory of Mark Stubbings.

1982-8 Memorial to mark the loss of the Penlee Lifeboat–Solomon Browne with all hands on the night of Saturday 19th December, 1981. Memorial to consist of a suitable rock, taken from the sea at the area of the wreck. To be topped with a glazed lantern containing a glass chalice and pattern inscribed with the initials of the crew – bronze plate to be put on the stone listing the names of the men lost.

1986 - Removing twenty pews at the back of the church carpeting and using portable chairs when required.

1987 - To do all necessary work to eradicate and repair the damage caused by the outbreak of dry rot in the church roof.

70 0 - Provision of new lighting made necessary by replacement of the roof and ceiling.

97/91 - Acoustic loop system and sound system installed, position of loud speakers to be determined by experiment. Cornish stone hedge eight feet high to be rebuilt on north side of Churchyard as it is in danger of collapse.

DIOCESCAN FACULTY RECORDS

D/R6/30 - Erection of Stained glass window in North Aisle to, Admiral Leah, Mrs. Leah, Colonel Leah. 15th February, 1928.

D/R8/33 - Removal of Oil Lamps and installation of electric light with plan of Church and correspondence – 6th November, 1930.

D/R12/34 - Installation of new hot water heating apparatus with new chimney stack, correspondence and two plans – 2nd September, 1934.

D/R20/9 - Erection of carved oak memorial Priest Stall to Revd. F. J. Prideaux, correspondence and two copies for design and site plan – 28th April, 1942.

D/R113 - Plans pro Vestry in Base of Tower – 12th November, 1964.

KING'S LETTER

I have decided to include the letter that King Charles I wrote to all the Churches of Penwith – with the exception of St. Ives, who were of Puritan persuasion and Oliver Cromwell sympathisers. The local belief is that the King was concealed in Penwith during his time of trouble (see Chapter 7), and he wanted to thank his loyal subjects.

A copy of this letter used to hang in every Church in West Cornwall, although there is no definite evidence to say that one hung in Paul Church. However, it is very interesting.

The King wrote from Sudeley Castle in 1642 thus:

CAROLUS REX: *'To ye inhabitants of ye county of Cornwall.*

We are so highly sensible of ye extraordinary merits of our County of Cornwall, of their zeal for our Crown and for ye defence of our person, in a time when We could contribute so little to our own defence, or to their assistance: in a time when not only no reward appeared, but great and probable dangers were threatened to obedience and loyalty: of their great and eminent courage and patience in their indefatigable prosecution of their great work, again so potent an enemy, backed with so strong, rich, and populous cities, and so plentifully furnished and supplied with men, arms, money, ammunition, and provisions of all kinds: and of ye wonderful success with which it pleased Almighty God (though with ye loss of some eminent persons, who shall never be forgotten by us) to reward their loyalty and patience by many strange victories over their and our enemies, in despite of all human probability and all imaginable disadvantages: that as We cannot be forgetful of so great desert, so We cannot but desire to publish it to all ye world, and to perpetuate to all time ye memory of their merits, and of our acceptance of ye same; and to that end We do hereby render our Royal thanks to that our County, in ye most public and lasting manner We can devise, commanding copies thereof to be printed and published, and one of them to be read in every Church and Chapel therein, and to be kept for ever as a record of ye same; that as long as ye history of these times and of this Nation shall continue, ye memory of how much that County hath merited from Us and our Crown, may be derived with it to prosperity.

Given at our camp of Sudeley Castle, ye 10th day of September, 1643.'

CHAPTER 9 - MOUSEHOLE CHAPELS, THE LAZAR HOUSE & PARISH BOUNDARIES

Mousehole

'Southwards of the Village of Mousehole at the foot of a hill is a cavern in the cliff commonly known as the Mouse-hole. The entrance to the 'hole' is fifty feet high and thirty feet wide, and depth about one hundred and fifty feet, at about one hundred feet the cavity becomes very small but after passing this strait it enlarges.' An extract from 'History of Cornwall' written by Mr. Gilberts.

This is obviously a place of ancient history as a chap called Raphael Holinshed (1529-1580) when writing in the 16th century (Chronicles of England, Scotland & Ireland) reports that tinners working near Mousehole found spear-heads, battle-axes and copper swords, wrapped in linen, which were very little damaged. No mention is made as to what happened to these artefacts. Richard Carew, a friend of Holinshead, also mentions these finds.

Mousehole & Its Early Chapels

As Paul and Mousehole are very much inter-connected, (Paul being the Church town, and Mousehole being once the chief port (porth) of the area), I am going to write a little of the history of this area, also known as Porth-ennis or Porthenys, Portennis id est Portus Insulae. In Latin it is Portus Insulae i.e. 'an island before it' – in Cornish, 'Porternis'.

Mousehole was once the centre of population in Penwith, being a port much frequented by traders from Spain, and is a very ancient town. It was important enough for King Richard II to erect piers for the preservation of shipping as shelter from storms, in the twelfth year of his reign in 1391.

Mousehole celebrated with fairs at the feasts of St. Barnabas and St. Bartholomew, and contained at least three chapels. The chief of these was the chapel of the Blessed Virgin Mary, which measured thirty-two feet by eighteen feet. A licence for services for a year was granted on 2nd September, 1383, to Benedict Bottesave (or Bossavah) and the inhabitants of Mousehole in the Parish of St. Paulus.

Again in 1387 on 15th April the Mousehole people had licence for service in the Chapel of the Blessed Mary of Mousehole for a year – provided they met the costs themselves, with the proviso that they had to attend the Church of St. Paulus on Sundays. So they still had to climb the hill sometimes! The name of the Chapel of St. Mary at Mousehole occurs many times in the Registers of Paul Church.

W. Boxer Mayne writes: '*The Chapel of St. Mary was probably near the Shipp Inn, as in a nearby cottage is a built-up archway. Another cottage has a stone built into the wall with the date 1261 I.H. with the vestiges of an 'S' above, the Vicar of Paul had license for the Chapel of St. Mary and St. Eda in 1425.*'

Also: '*Washed up on the beach below the Bank at Mousehole was a 'Font' or Holy Water Stoup, probably from the above chapel. It had a drainage hole, and it had stood on a pedestal. The upper part was granite stone square 13" x 13" x 5½"—depth below the square truncated pyramid—length of whole 19". Upper surface of squared top presents a cavity or bowl 9" in diameter 7" in depth terminating in a blunted point rather than a round bottom, one side of the squared top presents a shoulder as if this had been fixed to masonry.*'

This could well have come from the Chapel. The sea around our Penwith shores can be very destructive: as many years later in 1817, a violent storm ruined many fishing boats of Mousehole and Newlyn. They were dashed to pieces even though they were above the high water mark. In 1777, a pig's trough and sty was reported to have been carried off by the sea, and cast back on the shore some 47 years later (ref: John Rhys).

To return to the 15th C - in order to rebuild this Chapel, Bishop Stafford on 17th October, 1414 granted an '*indulgence of 40 days to all those who contributed to the repair of the Chapel of the B.V.M. of Mosal which had been ruinated by the sea*' .

This Chapel had been visible from the sea and had saved many lives, guiding ships entering the narrow harbour. However the Chapel's own revenues were not enough for repairing and rebuilding, so the appeal had to be made for money from the congregation. This appeal was successful and on 15th January, 1420 **John Patry** Vicar of St. Paul (as Paul Church was called then) with Henry Trewyff had licence for the Chapel of St. Mary and St. Eda in the *villula* of Mousehole. This St. Eda is not known as a saint, and the dedication of the Chapel to her remains a mystery.

Meanwhile the Second Blessed Virgin Mary Chapel in Mousehole, (although it must have been desecrated at the Reformation, and presumably burnt in the Spanish Raid of 1595), was still going in 1668, as a rental of the Manor of Alverton in 1668 states '*a Chapple in the middle of Mouseholl town in ye Lord's hand, as allsoe the Land*'.

The other Chapel at Mousehole was dedicated to St. Edmund of Canterbury (who was Edmund Rich born 1180, died 1240). Bishop Lacey issued an indulgence to those from Paul Parish who contributed to the building of the Chapel of St. Edmund on 22nd June, 1440. On 24th September, 1441 he licensed John Power and Agnes his wife for Divine Service in the Chapel of St. Edmund the Confessor, in *Mouseholl*.

It seems therefore, that if the Paul Parishioners of 1420 and 1440 were contributing towards both Chapels in Mousehole, that they also would at that time be refurbishing Paul Church, as the early 15th century was a noted time for embellishing ecclesiastical buildings. If the Chapel of the Blessed Virgin Mary at Mousehole, invaluable as a seamark, had to be repaired, then maybe that was the reason for the construction of Paul Church's high tower – to also be used as a seamark. The tower probably does date from this time, or a little earlier.

In 1266 Roger De Constantino, Vicar of Paul, obtained a charter for a weekly market on Thursdays, and a yearly fair on the Feast of St. Matthias in his manor of Porthenes. The yearly fair did not continue for long, but the weekly market was still operating each Thursday. The Charter for the Thursday Market was then granted to Henry Lord Tyes in 1292, with a Fair for three days on the Feast of St. Barnabas. Then it is reported that John de Arundell certified his claim in 1302, in the reign of Edward I, to a market and fair in his manor of Modishole, inherited from Ralph de Arundell, who bought it from Piers de Ralegh heir of Walter de Ralegh.

Again in 1313, the seventh year of the reign of Edward II, the Thursday market was confirmed to the sister of Henry Lord Tyes, who was Alice de L'Isle; with a Fair for Seven days as above dedicated to the Feast of St. Bartholomew. These fairs and weekly markets contributed greatly to the economy of the area. They encouraged the gathering of people for enjoyment and entertainment, as well as to trading at the markets, where much buying and selling of local fish, produce and animals, would have taken place.

An old Deed of Mousehole exists in the Devon Record Office and states:-
Mousehole: *'Charter of Thomasia widow of Richard Trewothelek in her widowhood, granting the Thomas Trehere of Mowsholl & Agnes his wife, one messuage near the furnace of Thomasia in the Ville of Porthenys to hold for 30 years of the chief lords for service due of right accustomed and after the end of the 30 years at a rent of 3s to the grantor or her heirs or successors. Witnessed by Sir Thomas Mata, Vicar of* **St. Paul**, *Benedict Jackthorna, Richard Kawnte, dated at Porthenys, Monday next after the Feast of St. Luke the Evangelist- 19 year of King Henry VI (1440).'* This ancient deed is interesting merely because, once again, Paul Church is called 'St. Paul'. Presumably a 'furnace' is that of a blacksmith's premises.

Leyland also mentions a *'Chapel yn Newlin'*. On the Tithe maps of 1841 and 1858, a field numbered 928 in the apportionment is called 'Park Chapel'. This is in the area of Trungle Farm, and there were, apparently, quite a large collection of buildings, behind Trungle House of today.

In 1745, and in subsequent years, questionnaires were sent by the Bishop of Exeter to all Vicars about their Parish. Many of them are in the Devon Record Office, and contain really interesting information about each Parish and its Glebe lands. In this year Revd. Henry Penneck Vicar of Paul was asked *'Have you any Chapels in your Parish?'* and he answered *'We have some old walls here and there that ye people call Chapels, and which were so, if at all, before ye Reformation'.*

Just outside *Mousholl* about a quarter of a mile distant there is the little island of St. Clement. Interestingly, from the name Clement comes the Cornish name of Porth-enys. The island was described by Leyland in 1540 as *'a lytle low island with a chaple yn yt. And this lytle islet bereth gresse. It is 1½ furlongs long and 1 furlong in width.'* Leyland, who travelled the country recording what he saw, thus producing a wonderful record of his time, also states that the island had *'a Chapel of St. Clementes in it'*. The dedication of the island may be explained by a story of how St. Clement of Rome, exiled to the Crimeas, was martyred by being tied to an anchor and thrown into the sea. The legend states that when the tide went out his body was found in a marble tomb built by angels!

MOUSEHOLE 'LAZAR' or 'LEPER HOUSE'

In Mousehole there was a community for lepers, containing twenty-seven afflicted people. Leprosy was quite a problem in the 14th C, and the sick had to be cared for in isolation. Cornwall, and Penwith in particular, being peninsulas, were vulnerable to infection from contact with the outside world by sea. Mousehole was a considerable port in the middle ages, when Penzance and Newlyn were only small fishing hamlets, thus diseases were easily carried on shore from the crews of ships from all over the world.

Possible site for the Lazar House, Park Clodgy —lighter grass indicating shallow rooting, and disturbance of soil.

Richard Carew has an interesting take on the cause of leprosy:- *'The much eating of fish, especially newly taken, and therein principally of the livers, is reckoned a great breed of those contagious humours which turn into leprosie'.* Causing: *'pitiful spectacles to Cornishmen's eyes of people visited with this affliction'.*

The Leper House was actually three-quarters of a mile from Mousehole in two fields near Clodgy Moor, west of Sheffield. The word 'Clodgy' is derived from "cla'jy = claf + chy" meaning in Cornish 'Leper House'. The fields are called Higher & Lower Park Clodgy, numbered 1439 and 1440 on the tithe map. Their position is *'under Halwyn, west of the coast road from Penzance to Land's End. On the east bank of a shallow waterlogged valley of Clodgy Moor'.* The footpath from the southern end of Sheffield passes through High Park Clodgy; the spring may be drier, as a ford now shows on the O.S. map, identified as a shallow pool. The road crossing stops short 300 yards before reaching the stream.

The term 'Lazar House' stems from the Knights of St. Lazarus & St. Mary of Jerusalem, a branch of the Knights Hospitallers. In France they were entrusted with the supervision of 'Lazaries', 'Leprosoria' or Leper Houses. These were founded and endowed as religious establishments, and generally placed under the control of an abbey or monastery under Papal Bull. The Church took a most active part in promoting the well-being and care of the lepers, both spiritual and temporal. The Order of St. Lazarus was the outcome of the Church having practical sympathy for the poor sufferers of this dreadful disease. In 1308 Bishop Bytton's executors gave '*13/6d to The Lazar House at Mousehole*'.

Mousehole Leper House was under the jurisdiction and care of the Benedictine Priory of St. Michael's Mount. The Papal Bull also appointed every Leper House to be provided with its own graveyard, so there may well be yet another burial ground of Paul Parish on Clodgy Moor. Leprosy or 'lepra tuberculosa' was a chronic infectious disease caused by the bacillus '*leproe*', which caused formation of growths in the skin, nerves, bones and internal organs, producing horrific deformities and mutations of the human body.

The inmates of the Houses were 'dead to the world', which seems very cruel, but in those times it was the only way they could contain infection. They were allowed to partake in the Mass before going into the Commune, kneeling beneath a black cloth, and earth was thrown on their feet to typify 'death to the world'. Although they were shut away in their houses, they were very well fed and provided for by the local community, with plenty of fresh eggs, milk and butter being donated for their sustenance. Paul Church might once have possessed a 'Leper's Squint' where the infected could watch Mass being celebrated, although they were not allowed inside the Church.

As well as the Church, they were forbidden to enter a mill house, bakery, market or any place of assembly, to wash in running water, to walk in any narrow way, or to give anything to anyone, particularly a child. The male leper was not to have intercourse with anyone except his wife! If anyone spoke to a leper, he was obliged to keep to their leeward, and step off the road if anyone walked towards him; he also had to point with a stick to anything he wished to purchase. The only thing one can comment on this devastating disease, is that the Church and local community cared for the afflicted.

Leprosy peaked in England in 10th century, reached a zenith in the thirteenth century and went into a decline in the fourteenth century. As well as at Clodgy Moor, there were also Leper Houses at Sancreed, and Madron.

MOUSEHOLE METHODIST CHAPEL—ST. CLEMENTS

As at the present time, there is a strong ecumenical link between the Churches of Paul and Mousehole Methodist Chapel. In fact, in the 1830s there was an Annual Bowling match between the men of Paul and the men of Mousehole on Feast Monday; thus a little of Mousehole history is listed here.

In 1932 there were two Methodist Chapels and they became known as 'up' and 'down'. These were not very helpful names in identifying each Chapel, thus, after much thought, the name of: '*St. Clements Methodist Church*' was given to the Wesleyan Church named after the little island of St. Clements just outside Mousehole harbour. It is rather unusual to have a Methodist Chapel named for a Saint, but that is the reason. The other Chapel became 'Mount Zion Methodist Church'. After the little chapel on St. Clements Isle many years ago, the name lives on.

The first meeting for Mousehole Methodists was in the kitchen of a house of a very accommodating John Harvey, a cooper (or barrel maker), who offered the use of his house for services, and also for lodging of preachers. In 1821 there were twenty Methodist societies in the Penzance Circuit, which until 1834 covered Penzance, St. Ives, and Land's End area. In 1730s Methodism was born; John Wesley's conversion was in 1738. The movement has strong clerical roots in the South West, but as dissenters they began to establish their own Churches. They had great success and even supplanted the Church of England, especially in West Cornwall, and in some cases became the majority religion of the populace.

Of course, there were other denominations such as Presbyterian, Congregationalists, Baptists, Quakers and Bible Christians. However the Methodist revival of field preaching was attractive to the Cornish, especially in the time of the great preacher, Wesley.

The first visit of John Wesley to Newlyn was in 1747, when he was forty-three. His visits continued yearly until 1770, and he visited Mousehole in 1766. He travelled from Helston, called at Mousehole and went on to St. Buryan. He wrote in his Journal: '*At eight I preached in Mousehole a large Village south west of Newlyn*'. In 1771 Mousehole Methodists were joined by William Carvosso, then aged 21, his brother Benedict Carvosso, Richard Trewavas snr., and Michael Wright. William Carvosso wrote of some of the people at Mousehole '*John Henry and wife, in whose house class-meetings and preaching happened. Jacob George and wife, Joseph Beaden and wife, John Yeoman and his two daughters.*'

In 1821 the Revd. J. Smith was delighted to observe all four of these preachers sitting in a pew together. Benedict Carvosso was the Methodist Society Steward at Mousehole in 1821; there were then twelve classes, two of which, Benedict led at 77 years of age. Another Leader of two classes was Thomas Matthews; he was number two, his Grandfather being Thomas Matthews number one.

Thomas Matthews II left St. Levan Parish when he was about ten and came to live in the Parish of Paul with his family. He married Jane Victor in Paul on 13th February, 1770 and had two sons Thomas III, and James; both were Baptised at Paul in 1771 and 1775. He moved to St. Buryan but returned to Paul in 1797 and continued as a Class Leader at Buryan, travelling every week from Paul for seventeen years. He died in Mousehole in October 1825, aged 79.

Jacob George was baptised at Paul Church on 1st April, 1804, like his namesake (ref: W. Carvosso) he was a shoemaker. His wife was Lydia nee Barnes, and they had five children - two sons were John George and William James George. He was a Methodist Class Leader and acted as voluntary Caretaker, keeping the oil lamps trimmed. John George wrote '*Memorandum of Old Cornish words still current in Mousehole and Newlyn*' which is now in the British Museum, Egerton Mss. 2331 fol; 397-404.

After 1771 John Harvey's conduct caused the Methodists to seek a new meeting place, and for a while they used Mr. Martin's '*disagreeable and dark salt-house*', where they continued to meet until a large room was fitted up over Peter Willis' fish cellar. This room could contain about 200 people, but unfortunately the first time it was used, the floor gave way and the congregation disappeared into it. No-one was hurt, assured Mr. William Carvosso in his writings; a Mr. Crowle was preaching at the time. The damage was repaired and the room back in use in August, 1782, when John Wesley paid his second visit to Mousehole.

The first small Chapel was built in 1783 opened by Revd. Joseph Taylor in 1784. In 1813 *'the majority of the inhabitants of the Village became members of the Methodist Society'*, thus the small Chapel was enlarged, and opened 1814.

In the early 1800s a Methodist Book Club was instigated to feed the minds of fishermen when storms prevented them from going to sea. There was also a 'tract distributor' who would call every Sunday, leaving a new tract in a brown paper cover and removing the old tract. The older people were pleased with this link from their Chapel.

The first gift of the freehold 1825 of land on which the Chapel stood, at Mousehole, as well as the Methodist Chapel at Kerris, was made by Thomas Matthews III with his brother James (see above).

Methodist Minister
The Revd. Julyan Drew

The Mousehole Deed states *'All that plot of Ground... Formerly called Dog Kennel...containing length north to south – 40' breadth east to west 35', together with the Meeting House or Chapel and all other buildings thereon'* (August 1825). Subsequently the Trustees from the time of Thomas Matthews III always included one of his direct descendants, as in 1954 – Abraham Wright Matthews.

Recently it has come to light that the Keigwin family owned hunting dogs in the 16th century and their dog kennels once occupied the site of the St. Clements Methodist Chapel, hence *'Dog Kennel'* as above.

Although the Chapel was considerably enlarged in 1813, twenty years later the Chapel was *'crowded almost to suffocation'*. The Trustees then decided to pull it down and rebuild on a larger scale. In fact the new Chapel would have been almost built when the lawyers had arrange the title to some of the land on which it stood. By Deeds 15th and 16th February, 1833 for £12 the freehold of some adjoining land south to that already owned, were described as *'belonging to the Common or waste lands of, or called Ragennis Cliff in the Parish of Paul'*.

Sunday 24th March, 1833 was the official opening of the present Methodist Chapel, fifty-six feet by forty feet, with two side galleries and one at the end. The fishermen promised a tithe if they had a *'good catch of mackerel'* which they donated to their *'holy and beautiful house'*. The Chapel cost £700 remaining debt - £450. The pew rental was to bring in £50, there were upwards of three hundred members, and three people *'found peace'* in the Chapel on the day it was opened, and many were *'born there'*. Extensive repairs were found to be needed during the years 1866-67.

In the early 1870s before Sunday Service a Men's Prayer Meeting was held in the parlour of Thomas Mattews IV's thatched farmhouse, where 'Pengarth' now stands. Catherine Elizabeth Harvey (wife of the late Mr. Joseph Harvey), told how her Grandma, Phyllis Matthews, a stately lady in a lacy cap, shook hands with each of the men as they left.
On Friday 8th June, 1877 the laying of the memorial stone – a large granite corner-stone - at the south west of the building took place. The cost of these Vestries was nearly £500. On Saturday and Sunday 15/16th June, 1878, there was a public tea and more money was raised. The School children walked in procession through the streets of Mousehole carrying purses containing contributions to the general fund.

In 1844 the Mount Zion Bible Christian Chapel was built, and in 1846 its Sunday School was added.

Pew Rents: as in Paul Church, there were pew rentals, and in the 1860s all the Trust income derived from this source. The money was paid to the 'Gallery Steward', suggesting that the downstairs pews were 'free'. In the 1950s the removal of the *'offensive'* word 'free' was carried out. In 1863 an *'office of profit'* was held under the Trustees by John McCleary who was paid 5/- quarterly for *'Keeping Peace at Chapel Door'*. In 1871 this was changed to *'one year's Salary as doorkeeper - £1'.*

In November 1883, renovation took place again costing nearly £70, and there seems to be a certain amount of re-seating carried on downstairs by Mr. James F. Rowe, costing £35. On part of the land acquired in 1833, where a shed with a lean-to roof had been built, it was proposed to erect Vestries for the Minister and the Choir. The total cost was £959, and by the time of re-opening on Friday and Sunday 1st and 3rd December, 1899 - £602 had been raised.

After the rebuilding in 1833 musicians known as 'The Teetotal Band' members led the music; the instruments played were violin, viola, bass and the French horn. In those days ladies sat on the 'sea' side of the church and men on the 'hill' side. The minister would announce the hymns verse by verse, as many could not afford their own hymn books.

As in Paul Church, an harmonium was purchased in 1879, and a tea and evening concert entitled 'St. John the Baptist' was held. Mr. Sampson Hosking of Lamorna took over the choir in 1899 and played the harmonium. For twenty-one years he came to practices on horseback and made a stipulation that his horse would be properly stabled during services. On Sundays he drove a gig to Chapel, accompanied by his wife.

In February 1902 the Trustees sanctioned the purchase of a pipe organ (pumped manually), not to exceed £300, and a Tender from Truro was accepted in June 1903. With the organ installed, the opening celebration began on Friday 27th March, 1903 with a public tea and entertainment by Mr. White's Choir. Next evening Mr. Fleming's Choir rendered a Sacred Service of Song. The Trustees then *'unanimously decided that the organ blower be paid £2.20s per annum'.*

The final stage was reached in February 1905 when the Minister reported the wish of the ladies to *'have the outside of the Chapel beautified so as to have it more in keeping with the inside'.* The Chapel was re-opened on Friday 10th November, 1905, and then in May 1924 electric light was installed, and again the Chapel was refurbished with new carpets, lino, and stair rubbers. In 1952 hearing aids were installed in the pews.

On 4th January, 1861 the Chapel was registered as a place for religious worship, but it was not until February 1902 that the Chapel was licensed for Marriages.

St. Clement's Chapel, Mousehole, also contains a memorial in brass to the Three Johns: John Badcock, John Bryant and John Pearce, as the memorials outside and inside Paul Church. Revd. F. J. Prideaux of Paul was involved in the unveiling ceremony 24th February, 1926, and passages from the Bible were read by Mr. Pentreath Johns – a relative of John Pearce.

Again as in Paul Church, there is a memorial to the crew of the 'Solomon Browne' consisting of an octagonal table with the names of the men on each panel; the top of the table bears the insignia of the RNLI. Personal gifts for the memorial area were a piano, a ship's bell, carpet, flower stand, silken rope, copper plaque, a memorial poem and installation of amplification. The memorial was dedicated by the Superintendent of Penzance Circuit, Revd. John P Horner, and the sermon was preached by the Bishop of Truro, Rt. Revd. Peter Mumford, on Sunday 16th May, 1982.

In 2004 the fellowship between congregations of Paul and Mousehole was epitomised in the uplifting joint production for Easter of a religious work, conducted by John Phillips of Mousehole and accompanied by John Harry of Paul. In 2003 Stainer's 'Crucifixion' was sung as part of the service on Passion Sunday, and in 2004, 'Olivet to Calvary' was sung by the combined choirs and members of the congregations.

To conclude with a little Chapel humour, I think would be fun! From R.C.G. 1878:

*'There was an old couple sitting in a Primitive Methodist Chapel. The old man prayed out loud 'O Lord, give us contented minds and thankful hearts. I thank Thee for our daily bread and for the swayt traycle thou has given us ever!' 'Hold tha tongue!' his wife said, 'Thee's ate a poun' an' haaf o' butter **this waik!**'*

Interior– St. Clement's Methodist Chapel, Mousehole

CHAPTER 10 - THE REFORMATION & SPANISH RAID

King Henry VIII

Under Henry VIII, after wars with France, peace at last came in 1525. This time of lull after the storm led to many Cornish Churches being rebuilt and enriched with new screens, etc. Little did they know of the unrest that was to come, and the pride in embellishing their churches, especially for Paul Church, was unfortunately all to be in vain. The shock of Henry VIII proclaiming himself Head of the Church in England in 1534, and the break with Roman Catholicism, caused tremendous unrest and change throughout the land. The Reformation changes took twelve years from 1536 to 1548 to be implemented, with the dissolution of the monasteries. Small monasteries were seized by the Government, followed by friaries, and then the larger monasteries and collegiate churches, such as St. Buryan.

Two Paul men, Henry Chiverton of Kerris, and his neighbour at Trewarveneth, William Godolphin, together with John Grenville, were Commissioners for distribution of monastic wealth and land. They were responsible for the inventory of monastic and church goods, under the Court of Augmentations set up by Henry VIII. Many of those acting as Commissioners took their chances, and added to their own wealth by acquiring monastic lands. Bishops were made to surrender most of their property and became less wealthy and powerful.

However, West Cornwall farmers and fishermen were not worried by Henry VIII (whom they called 'King Harry'), his wives, divorces and beheadings were all too far away. What did bother them very much was the changing of the services in their churches from Latin to English. They were used to the Latin, and mostly spoke Cornish, so that English Services were very alien to them. *'Mee a navidra coza Sawnack'* – or *'I have not learned to talk Saxon!'* (This phrase has also been attributed to Dolly Pentreath!) This was a real problem when the Bishop's Bible was read to the people in English. Years earlier when Bishop Grandisson visited St. Buyran Church in 1336 (when he didn't have time to visit Paul Church), he had to ask the Rector of St. Just to repeat his words in Cornish, so the people could understand him.

This unrest was in the sixteenth century, when even though the Parish Priest rang the same bell to call them to Church, said the same prayers and performed much the same rites as was customary – nevertheless the Cornish rose up against King Harry, and the changes. In 1537 Henry Courtenay Marquise of Exeter tried to raise a rebellion of Cornish people at St. Keverne – when Sir Francis Godolphin heard of this, he managed to crush it before it was started.

Before the Reformation, church walls were often covered with frescoes and paintings of saints and Christian symbols such as:

the Chi-Rho,   the Fish, (Ichthys)   and Alpha & Omega.

          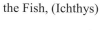

Windows were a blaze of colour with early stained glass. The priests intoned the Service from behind the rood screen, in the Sanctuary – the Holy of Holies. He would arrive for Services through a special door in the south wall – known as the 'Priest's Door'- so as not to mix with the congregation but to go straight into the area beyond the rood screen.

Early medieval worshippers stood or knelt on sanded or rush-strewn floors for the services, only the elderly or infirm would have had stone benches around the walls of the church (see 'Pews', Chapter 3). Some churches did have pews before the Reformation, but in the main they were introduced after the Reformation in the time of Queen Elizabeth I. This was for the ease of the congregation, as the sermons became very long, lasting at least two hours.

Before the Reformation the only time that the congregation would be able to take Communion was Easter Day, when all were allowed through the rood screen to the main altar, where they would kneel on the floor, to receive Communion. There were no Communion rails at that time, just the Priest and his Servers or Acolytes and the altar. (More about pre-Reformation services in Chapter 3.)

In 1549 Parliament enforced the use of English Litany and Cranmer's Book of Common Prayer, replacing Latin liturgy. On 9th June, 1549 Cornish Rebels attacked St. Michael's Mount and Marazion causing *'great decay, ruine and desolation'*, and under the leadership of Humphrey Arundel of Helland they marched to Bodmin demanding Latin Mass and rituals to be re-instated, in a Petition thus:-

'We will nor recyve the new Service because it is like a Christmas game, but we will have our old Services of Matens, Masse, Evensong and Procession in Latten as it was before so we Cornysshe men, where certen of us understand no English utterly refuse thys new Englysh.'

The Petition was refused and 2,000 rebels marched to Exeter, laid siege on 2nd July, and hanged the unfortunate Vicar of St. Thomas' Church from the top of his Tower clad in his vestments. They fought at the bridge of Clyst St. Mary, and marched on to Fenny Bridges under their leaders Arundell and Winslade, who were, eventually, hanged for this uprising. As a punishment to the rebels their largest church bells were supposed to have been removed, but what actually happened was that the smaller bells were left, and only the clappers of the large bells were removed.

The Reformation called for a complete prohibition of images in churches in 1547-8. Paul Church once had a statue over the narthex in the porch, for which the broken empty bracket may still be seen. That would have been removed at this time, together with the statues in the empty niches on the Tower. King 'Harry' died in 1547 and the sweeping changes in the church continued and were ratified under his son King Edward VI.

The Act of Uniformity in 1552 imprisoned any who attended Services other than those of the new Church of England, and attending church became more like going to school with the priest as a teacher, speaking from a high pulpit. Instruction took the form of Bible reading and prayer. The Church had bare whitewashed walls, to replace pre-Reformation colour, only broken by the hanging of texts: The Lord's Prayer, The Creed, and The Ten Commandments (decalogues), as once hung either side of the altar at Paul, and now hang at the back of the Church. These changes were not to the taste of everyone, and for the first time in the South West religious dissenters came into being – the Roman Catholics!

All altars were disallowed in 1550, thus Paul Church would have lost its carved stone altars, and wooden Communion tables were substituted (see Tremenheere photos, in Chapter 3, for wooden altar of Paul Church).

In 1538 Church Registers were beginning to be kept, although these were only on loose sheets of paper. Queen Elizabeth wanted more formal records to be kept, and in 1598 she ordered parchment records to be kept in books.

In 1552 many extra church ceremonies were abolished, and the surplice was the only vestment allowed to be worn by the clergy. Crosses, pyxes, censers, candlesticks and chalices were assessed by Commissions, and confiscated into the ownership of the Crown. Some churches managed to hide their precious pictures with other Catholic icons and artefacts. Together with Fowey Church, Paul had a silver incense boat weighing 10oz (a list of the Church Plate of Paul is in Chapter 5). Colourful vestments used in the Catholic mass often were given away or sold.

In 1552 only a minority of Parishes had crosses, censers or pyxes, and Paul Church had the most valuable plate in West Penwith (for details - see Chapter 5). A Commission collected not less than 6,241oz of precious metal artefacts from Cornish churches; it was all sent to St. Mawes, to be transferred to London and sold for Government funds! They didn't care that the people of the Cornish parishes (Paul included) had worked hard to pay for their beautifully fashioned church artefacts.

The whole process of Reformation took shape under Henry's son Edward VI, and England became officially Protestant. In April, 1559 the Second Act of Uniformity of Common Prayer was passed, which imposed one prayer book of Edward VI to be used for services, which were shortened from eight per Sunday to two. The services became modified from mediaeval rites, and full Communion was only taken three to four times a year. A typical Sunday would have Matins, the Litany, ante-Communion – which is the first part of the Communion Service - (these services ran into each other), and Evensong in the mid-afternoon. Processions, Devotions before images, and Masses at other altars inside churches were abolished.

However in 1553 King Edward died, and Mary Tudor came to the throne, ordering resumption of old Catholic Rites and redistribution of church plate to the Parishes of Cornwall. It is not clear if any church plate had been sold; presumably Mary Tudor came to the throne just in time to save it. The figures and cross were restored to the top of the rood screen, if it still existed after King Henry's rampage.

Queen Mary Tudor

Mary Tudor restored the Latin Mass in 1554 under an appeal to Parliament. She allowed clergy married during the reign of Edward VI the choice of being deprived of their wives, or taking another living elsewhere in the Diocese. Only eighteen of the clergy had married, as prejudice was strong against this sacrament. In St. Keyne in Mary Tudor's time the Rector and his wife were seized as they slept in their beds, and were put in the stocks at Duloe for twelve hours! In Bishop Parker's time there were one hundred and four clergymen in Cornwall, and seventeen had married.

In 1558, under Elizabeth, the Latin Mass became illegal, the Act of Settlement re-established Protestantism, and clergy were again allowed to get married. This must have been very difficult for everyone – no wonder there was unrest. Queen Elizabeth reinstated the Book of Common Prayer in English, and Cornish gradually began to die out as an everyday language, as the people began to get used to the English language through church services. This was a long, slow process, however, and was not easy to implement.

Interestingly, the Parish in 1578-9 became a place of secular as well as ecclesiastical government. For example the Parish would pay for: *'hose and shoes for a poor child –8d; 5/- to fund an orphan girl a place as a servant, 3/4d for a shroud for a pauper's funeral'*.

Apart from all the changes within the Rites of the Church, the people of Paul, Mousehole, Newlyn and Penzance had the most frightening experience, in the form of a sea raid, a reprisal for the defeat in 1588 of the Spanish Armada.

THE SPANISH RAID OF 1595

*Aga syth tyer, war an Meyne Merlyn
Ara ned syth Leskey Paul, Penzance, has Newlyn'*
Translated:
*'There shall land on the stone of Merlyn,
Those who shall burn Paul, Penzance and Newlyn'*

The above verse is a chilling prediction of the invasion by a Spanish force on a misty summer morn at 8.00 a.m. 23rd July, 1595, and it is said that the local people knew of this legend and were frightened by it. It seems a pity that they were not frightened enough to post a look-out, as they did once the Spaniards had departed.

There are two contemporary authentic sources for the true happenings of this terrible raid. The first comes from Richard Carew, historian of the sixteenth century, who obtained his account from his friend, Sir Francis Godolphin, Governor of the Mount's Bay coastline. The second comes from a translation of the original Spanish narrative, written in a letter by the Spanish Commander, Captain Carlos de Amezola, to the King of Spain.

Richard Carew's romantic report states: *'The 23rd of July soon after the sun was risen, and had chased a fogge, which before kept the sea out of sight, four Gallies of the enemy presented themselves upon the coast, over-against Mousehole and there landed about two hundred men, pikes and shot.'*

Once again, the two stories differ; Amezola states that 400 men attacked Penzance, Mousehole and Newlyn, yet Carew states only 200 men landed. Then Amezola reports that 1,200 Cornishmen under Arms met the Spanish at west Penzance Green, and Carew reports only *'something above 100 men'* met the Spanish in combat. I suppose looking at it logically the Spanish would rather exaggerate the numbers they had to fight in order to look brave in their King's eyes!

I will now return to the Spanish report. The four Galleasses (galleons) were called: 'Nuesta Senora de Begona' (the flagship), 'Peregrina', 'Salvador' known as 'Patrona' in this account, and 'Basana'. They originally set sail on St. Anne's Day, knowing that the English fleet lay at anchor at Plymouth. They sighted land, and moved in close to Mousehole harbour, arriving at 8.00 a.m. on a misty summer's morning. Infantrymen were disembarked and made their way up the hill for a reconnoitre.

Meanwhile, the Spanish under Don Leon Dezpeleta, sergeant Juan de Arnica, subaltern Don Gaspar de Perea and Martin Ramirez de Arellano took the rest of their men and marched them around the town of Mousehole. The galleons came in close to shore, and with their bows facing Mousehole they discharged their guns. Shot struck several houses, demolished them, and, it is reported, killed many of the occupants, causing the rest of the inhabitants to flee, leaving the Spaniards to burn the remaining houses.

Strangely, the new burial register commenced after the raid does not include a large number of people, as you would expect after such an invasion. I am not sure that '*many*' were actually killed during this raid. I think, probably, more were able to flee. The four men buried on 24th July, 1595 the day after the raid were: Jenkin Keigwin, John Pearce Peiton, Jacobus de Newlyn, and Similitier T. Cornall (see later on in this Chapter).

Keigwin House, Mousehole

Jenkyn Keigwin, whose house in Mousehole is the only Tudor house to date before 1595 to remain standing today, is reported to have been killed by a 5½ inch bore cannon ball, but the manner of his death is mainly hearsay. A plaque may be seen on his fine Tudor house in Mousehole, recording the death of its owner. He was buried in Paul Church, somewhere in a family vault, together with others killed in this raid. These burials took place even though the church was in ruins.

Apparently there was a spy aboard one of the Spanish ships, a chap called Captain Richard Burley, who was 'esteemed' by the Spanish; he gave inside information to the Captain. This was reported by one of the English prisoners on board called Barnaby Loe, who reported that the English Captain had been sitting next to his Spanish counterpart, and was a renegade.

The Spaniards marched up to Paul burning all houses and hamlets on the way (Carew states '*houses of the countrie, about half a mile compassed or more, by whome were burned*'), and burned the 'mosque' at the top of the hill. The literal translation of 'mesquita' is 'mosque' or church. The report states in Spanish that they found '*un caballo de madera muy labrado y esmaltado*' in the Tower. This translated means a '*horse of wood, very worked (decorated) and enamelled*' serving, as the Spanish presumed, as an idol worshipped by the people.

The enemy report states: '*here was burned a mosque, in which there was a horse fashioned of wood, and greatly enamelled, serving as an idol worshipped by the people, we also set fire to, and burned a good solid tower in the mosque where a lot of people had taken shelter*'.

In the Burial Register commenced in 1595 no mention is made of what happened to the sheltering people; one trusts that they left the church before the fire took hold. This must be the case, as the again, the Burial Register contains only a few names. It is reported that the south porch wooden supporters were '*partially burnt near the Church body*'. This was confirmed years later in a restoration of the porch when blackened timbers were found in the porch roof.

The report that Paul Church had a enamelled wooden horse, maybe even a 'hobby-horse' such as the one at Padstow, is not surprising. The hobby horse legend is probably Celtic, and pagan in

origin, the Spanish were probably right in their reasoning, and presumably the horse was kept in the church tower, as dustpans and brushes are kept in their today! The 'Oss' of Padstow is only a representation of a horse, as is the Minehead 'Hobby-horse'. Paul had a real image. It was probably used in May Day fertility dances to welcome the Spring, and would have hearkened back to the Celtic roots of Paul people, also connected with the Green Man often carved in churches.

The English traitor, Captain Burley, seemed to have imparted local knowledge to the Spaniards, and using it maliciously, resulted in the almost complete destruction of Paul Church.

Richard Carew writes: *'not only the houses as they went by, but also the Parish Church of Paul, the force of the fire being such, as it utterly ruined all the great*

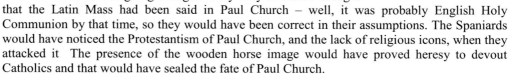
Cannon Balls belonging to Paul Church

stonie pillars thereof: others of them in that time, burned that fisher towne Mowsehole, the rest marched as guard for defence of the firers'. The pillars of soft catacleuse stone virtually exploded in the heat, and those pieces that were left were fashion into the little arch.

The most fascinating possible answer to the reason for the burning of Paul Church, therefore, is the presence of the decorated horse. It also seems likely that our Church at Paul was burned as a direct result of the return under Queen Elizabeth I of Protestantism, as the Spanish, being devout Catholics, would not usually touch a Holy Church – it is an intriguing thought. They may not have thought that the Latin Mass had been said in Paul Church – well, it was probably English Holy Communion by that time, so they would have been correct in their assumptions. The Spaniards would have noticed the Protestantism of Paul Church, and the lack of religious icons, when they attacked it The presence of the wooden horse image would have proved heresy to devout Catholics and that would have sealed the fate of Paul Church.

Apart from Richard Carew's writing, evidence proves that the Paul Church was not entirely demolished as when the porch was being repaired in 1807, a portion of the wood-work was found to be charred. J. T. Blight remarks: *'if the stonework of the tower was injured, it was evidently restored with original materials, but greater probability is that only the woodwork was destroyed, which of course involved the destruction of the Bells'*. Carew also mentions the destruction of the Bells. These Bells had only arrived back into Mousehole harbour, after being re-cast on 30th June, 1595! (See the end of this Chapter.)

Returning to the Spanish account:- Captain Carlos de Amezola was still on board ship, and ordered Captain Juan de Mercado to inspect the headland at Penzance, so off they sailed. They went on to burn Marazion which was protected by a castle, probably St. Michael's Mount. They set fire to houses and a fort (battery) on the coast. Presumably the smoke from all the fires attracted the attention of Sir Francis Godolphin at his house near Breage, and he mustered what men he could to meet the enemy on Penzance western Green.

They eventually met Sir Francis Godolphin and his forces of either 1200 (Spanish) or 100 (Carew), on western Penzance Green. Sir Francis led the men to Penzance, according to Carew, where they were bombarded with shot from the galleys ceaselessly, some men fell down and others ran away. Sir Francis tried to make a stand at the market place Penzance, but found only ten or twelve resolute men with him the rest were *'surprised with fear and fled'*. Poor Sir Francis even threatened them with his rapier drawn, but they fled. He was forced to depart and the Spaniards entered Penzance in three separate *'parts'*, and fired the houses.

One could not blame the Cornish for fleeing before such an awesome enemy, and being unprepared for invasion; but they vowed that if the Spaniards came back they would be ready and waiting! However, they did not return. Carew excuses the Cornish of *'infamouse cowardice'* with these reasons: *'suddenness of the attempt; narrowness of the country, and openness of the towne; advantage of the ships ordinance firing on a people unprepared because of long continuing peace'*.

They burned four hundred houses in Penzance, and outlying hamlets. Three ships were burned as they lay in Penzance harbour. These were 'The John of Mousehole', 'The Angell of Boscastle', and 'The George of Mounts Bay'. They had just arrived from Bristol on 30th June or 1st July, with staves and hoops for barrels, cases of glass, iron and lead bars, grinding stones, and cooking pots. The barrels were probably for pilchards.

Philip II of Spain

The 'mosque' or St. Mary's Chapel – which preceded St. Mary's Church of today in Penzance - was spared burning because Captain Richard Burley, the traitor, informed the Spanish that Mass had been celebrated in it recently! Friar Domingo Martinez who was the principal Chaplain of the Galleys wrote two verses in English declaring the reasons for not burning St. Mary's Chapel, as he was *'trusting that Mass would be said in it again'*. The original Spanish: *'Que esta mesquita habia side primo inglesia'*.

Sir Francis Drake

Meanwhile the Spanish set sail again for Newlyn, set fire again to the houses, killed 50 Englishmen, and then sailed five or six leagues away. The Cornish camped near Marazion with Sir Francis for the night. The next day Sir Francis Godolphin managed to rally the fleeing terrified inhabitants of all three villages, and he sent a letter for help to Plymouth, where the English Fleet lay at anchor. It was addressed to:

'The right worshipful Sir Francis Drake and Sir John Hawkins, Knights General of Her Majesty's Forces now in Plymouth. With all haste post, haste for life. From post to post by the ordinary post, for Her Majesty's Special Service. Signed Francis Godolphin.

'At this instant, four galliasses at ancker before Mousehole, their men landed, that towne fired, and other houses thereabouts, no more of their fleet in sight, 50 or 60 were seen on Monday evening, and yesterday thwart off Falmouth, now consider what is to be done for your own safety and our defence. Written on the greene beyond Penzance this Wednesday, about one of the clock, the 23rd of July, 1595.   Yours Francis Goldolphin and Thomas Chiverton. A post-script: *'There is assembled about 200 naked men (*without armour!*) I attend the coming of more, and so make hed toward the enemy.'*

The next day the enemy returned, landed again, and climbed a hill where they set up a hut with an altar. The Chaplain celebrated Mass within sight of the galleys, and the Cornish, who must have been incredulous at their cheek, watched from a safe distance on other hills around the Bay. The Spanish fired a salvo of harquebuses and muskets triumphantly in the air, and erected a cross on the hillside. They then proceeded to the Penzance battery and captured the artillery, although the Cornish did their best to prevent them, and it was taken to the Spanish flagship.

As they left, they put ashore all English prisoners – well, the Catholic ones anyway, who were supposed to be pleased that the Spanish had come; and were told to inform the other Catholics of Cornwall, so that they would also be exalted that Catholics had raided a Protestant Country. The Catholics saw the whole raid as an extension to their Crusade of driving the Moors from Spain, and the Protestants from power.

In response to the above letter for help, Sir Nicholas Clifford and Sir H. Power and *'certaine other Capitaines, who were sent my the General from Plymouth'* arrived, as did *'some of her Majesties ships were also sent, who being come as farre as the Lizard head, and those Captains to the camp, a plot is layd for intercepting the enemy by ambush, but within one hour of their arrival the winde which was untill then strong South East with mist and rayne, suddenly changed into the North west... but away pack the gallies with all the haste they could'*. As they left Mount's Bay they chased an Irish ship, but it was laden with wine and salt, so they let her go.

After this surprise raid, large numbers of volunteers formed camps on Maker Heights, at Fowey, Pendennis and St. Michael's Mount, but the Spanish did not return. On 25th July help arrived from Plymouth; by that time, however, the Spaniards were beyond reach. This petty invasion of Paul gave rise to the siege and capture of Cadiz in 1596.

Back in Paul, now smouldering and in ruins, the Vicar John Tremearne managed for a while to carry out some services. These were chiefly of Burial of those who died in the raid. Then as time wore on he performed Marriages and Baptisms, in the one part of the Church that still was standing. He also started a new Register for the Parish at this time and wrote in it as below. He was a resourceful chap, and manfully tried to live in what was left of his Vicarage, mainly the kitchens at the western end of the gutted house. However after a while he gave up and left the house (see Chapter 5).

The destruction in the fire of all written records of Paul Church dating from pre-raid is devastating blow for historians, the new Register begins:

'Jesu spes et salus mea' or *'Jesus my Hope and my Salvation'* – *a register of names of all those baptized married and buried in Parish Church of St. Paule in Countie of Cornwall from 23 daie Julie year of Our Lord God 1595 on which daie the Church toure, bells and other things pertaining to same together with houses and goods was burn'd and spoil'd by the Spaniards in sed Parise, being Wensdaie the date aforesed in 37th year of the reign of Soverigne Ladie*

Elizabeth by Grace of God Queen of England and France and Ireland – Defender of the Faith. Per me Johannem Trewearne, Vicarium ejus. First entries record burials of parishoners kild by Spaniards:

- *Jenkin Keigwin of Moussell being killed by Spaniards was buried the 24 July*
- *John Pearce Peiton was buried 24 day of July*
- *Jacobus de Newlyn occisus fuit inimicos et sepultus est 26 July*
- *Similitier T. Cornall et sepultus 26 July.*

Until 1868 (ref: Lakes) there was an inscription in Paul Church recording that:

'The Spaniar byrnt this church, in the year 1595, rebuilt A.D. 1600'.

Thus by 1600 resurrected from the ashes, the rebuilt Paul Church was back in use. At Mousehole, a rock called '*Merlyn Car*' – Merlin's Rock - stands near the pier, with another rock a little to the west named the '*Spaniard*'. Close by a projection in the cliff was once known as '*Point Spaniard*'.

To end, here is an interesting follow-up to the Spanish Raid of 1595:-
In 1980, the roof of the nave and both side aisles, in effect, three large roof areas had to be renewed due to a serious problem of dry rot. Mr. Philip Hutchens, Treasurer of the PCC, wrote to the Spanish Ambassador, Marques de Perinat on 21st April, asking for a financial contribution towards the re-roofing of the Church that they destroyed by fire in 1595. The Spanish Ambassador wrote back and apologised for his forebears' destruction and sent a donation of between £20 - £30 in a token of amelioration!

Philip Hutchens retiring as Treasurer, with Beth and Revd. Harper – May 1999

CHAPTER 11 - SUNDIAL, STATISTICS & THE TITHES

Paul Church is in the Civil Hundred and Ecclesiastical Deanery of Penwith, in the Diocese of Truro, and Province of Canterbury. It is bounded to the west by St. Buryan and Sancreed Parishes, to the north by the Mother Church of Penzance, Madron, and to the east and south by Mount's Bay and the English Channel. The OS Grid reference for Paul is SW 4627. The body of the Church is reported to be thirty yards long by seventeen yards wide.

Paul Church Tower (as reported elsewhere in the Chapter on the Tower) is 89 feet high, with a beacon of 20 feet high – making a total of 109 feet - the second highest Tower in Penwith. The Tower is thirteen feet square inside (ref: V.C.H. 1906).

The Victoria County History of 1801-1901 states: Paul including Newlyn – 3,349 acres, 1,553 arable, 699 permanent grass, 7 acres of woods and plantations. Penlee and Gwavas Quarry employed 50 men, and Penolva quarry had been abandoned. They mined blue elvan stone used for '*metalling*' roads. Sheffield and Lamorna quarries were for mining granite.

Once again, it seems that there is disparity, this time in acreage. Presumably the difference represents the Parish of St. Peter, Newlyn.

Paul Church Sundial

The grid reference for the sundial is: 14640271, and it is situated over the entrance to the South Porch, at Latitude: 50.088 Longitude: 5.545. Slate Wall Bearing 78 Plate Bearing 78.

It is constructed of slate with a splendid gnomon probably cast in brass. Its equation of time is –14 and the time by its dial is *fast* by twenty minutes! When it was visited by an expert in 1992, he said it was an '*east decliner*', and reported that to correct the time error, the bearing had to be checked and a re-calculation of the sub-style may also be necessary.

The Sundial has fine carving of the figure of Winged Time with hourglass and scythe, with decorative fleur de lis in the half-hour marks. The sun has heat rays, which look as if they are interspersed with petals, giving the decoration a floral feel.

Population Statistics

In 1831 Paul Parish contained 3,790 inhabitants; the Church was in the Patronage of the Crown, and is rated in the King's Books a £13.11.0½d.

The Parish contains 2,153 acres, which before 1851 included the ecclesiastical Parish of St. Peter, Newlyn (according to GENUKI 1997).

POPULATION FROM 1801

YEAR	POPULATION	YEAR	POPULATION
1801	2,937	1891	5,997
1811	3,371	1901	5,997 (6,332)
1812	3,790	1911	6,332
1831	4,191	1921	6,014
1841	4,664	1931	5,398
1851	5,408	1951	5,814
1861	5,072	1981	185 (excluding Newlyn
1871	5,748 (inc. Newlyn 3,527)	1991	229 (excluding Newlyn)
1881	2,690 (4,062 inc. 3,638 in Newlyn)		

However in Lysons is stated:

1839 Paul Parish measures =	2,865 acres
Annual Valuation of Real Property 1815 =	£7,464.0.0d
Poor Rate 1831 =	£785.7.0d
Population 1801 =	2,937
Population 1811 =	3,371
Population 1821 =	3,790
Population 1831 =	4,191
An Increase of =	42½% in 30 years

In 1998 it is reported that the Paul Parish Population was only 215 the density was 0.27 people per hectare, and the Parish contained 870 hectares, and 0% of the population had degrees! Does that make it *dense?* That would certainly not be the case in 2004! At least these two different sources of statistics agreed. Which makes a change! Here follow more statistics:-

MEASUREMENTS

Paul = 2,662 acres in 1868. The whole Parish comprises 3.433 acres.
Glebe called 'Churchtown moor' measures – 1 acre 2 rods and 25 perches.
Church and yard – 3 rods 26 perches. School cemetery or higher graveyard - 2 rods 15 perches.

Taken from Lakes Parochial History of Cornwall 1868 - Statistics :

Lands for which tithes are charged for the Parish of Paul – 2662 acres, arable – 1904 acres, gardens – 176 acres, crofts, cliffs and commons – 582 acres.

PARISH MEASUREMENTS

Total measurement	3433 acres 0 rods 16 perches
Glebe Churchtown Moor	1 acre 2 rods 25 perches
Church and Churchyard	3 rods 26 perches
Higher Churchtown School Cemetery	2 rods 15 perches
Roads and Streams	66 acres 2 rods 34 perches

Looking at the total acreage for roads and streams, how on earth did they manage to measure them accurately? 66 acres seems a large area for roads and streams.

Paul was part of the Penzance Union – formed on 10th June, 1837 - for Poor Law Administration. There was a Board of Guardians and Paul had four such Guardians representing the Parish on this Board. There was a Poor House in Paul Village (see Chapter 15).

1831 Victoria County History of Cornwall gives a few facts about Paul Church: Chancel – 101 ft long, 20ft wide, north and south aisles 2ft less in length, 15'3" wide, Tower 13ft square inside. Tower Arch of two splayed orders. Twenty years ago (from 1831) all the windows were 'churchwarden' type with round heads and square wooden frames, displacing older windows, before 1807 now (in 1831) giving way to stone and tracery (*this didn't happen until after 1873*). The arches dated from 1600 the Tower has three stages, west window four lights, but only label and outer order of arch are old. Font – modern square bowl on round stem, with four detached slats. The new font was also put in the Church after 1873; again, the dates are not correct.

PAUL CHURCH TITHES

The word 'tithe' comes from the Anglo-Saxon word meaning 'tenth' - all were supposed to give a tenth of their income to the church as a 'tythe/tithe'. In 900 A.D. tithes became a compulsory levy, and were abolished in 1936.

In a modern day Taxiato Database on the internet, Paul Church comes under Benefice Code: EX.CW.PE.04 taxation = £9.6.8d—Grid Ref: SW465272 to the Cistercian Monks of Hailes Abbey, Gloucester. This was the—*Taxiatio Ecclesiastica Angliae et Walliae auctoritate Pope Nicholai IV A.D. c. 1291.* Thus:-

'*Church of St. Paulinus assesses Tax under Pope Nicholas IV in 1291 - £9.6.8d by Innvisitio monarum in 1340 at the same by Valor Ecclestiastic in 1530 – the Vicarage at £13.11.0½d. Under the Act of 1836 the Rectorial Tithe was commuted for £292, and the Vicar's Tithe for £512*'.

The reason for this tax was that Pope Nicholas IV gave King Edward I the right to collect the taxes normally collected by the Pope, to encourage him to begin a crusade against the Turkish '*infidels*'. Thus a nationwide survey of all churches was instigated, and gives great insight into the wealth - or poverty - of each church. In 1291 the majority of advowsons were in the hands of religious houses. Paul Church was no exception. Edmund, Earl of Cornwall gave Paul Church 'Rectory' (Advowson) as a support to Hailes Abbey in Gloucester, but after the dissolution of the monasteries, this then became known as 'Fee Farm Rent' and it lasted many years, - £2.2s or two guineas (J. T. Blight) payable to the Vicar of Paul (see also Chapter 14). For example, the Abbey had the 'Great Tithes' - usually of grain - and the Vicar was left to subsist on the lesser tithes such as hay, animals and in the case of Paul and such seaside parishes, the tithe of fish.

Paul Church has a Vicar, rather than a Rector. The term 'Rectory' however, in the sense of tithing, '*appertains to the tithes and patronage of the living*', and doesn't mean the house of the vicar. Nevertheless the bundle of rights supporting a rector probably ***included*** his house, and glebe lands, plus the parishioners' 'tithes' i.e. one tenth of all crops, wool, hay, sheaves of wheat, and fish in the instance of Paul Church. As above, the tithes of Paul Church were given to the Abbey by Edmund, in 1277 (see Chapter 2 for details). The Monks of Hailes Abbey then became the 'Rector' (Patron) or owner of the 'Rectory', by virtue of which they owned the right to appoint the Vicar. If a Rector could not service the parish himself he could appoint a 'Vicar'. This happened after the very first Priest of Paul Church, Roger de Sancto Constantino (who was the only Rector in his own right), and continued up to the Reformation and Dissolution of the Monasteries.

In Bishop Stapledon's Register 1307-1326:-

'In Church – Thomas Martyn of Glasney – month August. Father Richard de Gloucestre Procurator Hailes Church, Sancti Pauli in Cornwall – Licence to farm out from Michaelmas 1317 for one year 1st August 1317 again for 2 years from Michaelmas to Richard Trewarveneth Clerk, 3rd August, 1320.'

A SAMPLE OF RECTORIAL TITHES OF PAUL CHURCH DUE LADYDAY 1774

PREMISES	£
House in Newlin Mr John James	6.0.0d
" " Edward Paddy	2.0.0d
House & Cellar in Newlin John Tremethack	7.6d
" " " Henrietta Barnicoal	14.6d.
2/3 of ½ Meadow called Water Meadow – John Matthew	10.6d
House called Stonehouse – Overseers of Paul	1.0.0d
Cellar Called Lower Cellar	in Hand
" " Middle Cellar	"
" " Green "	"
Tithes of Hook, Fish of Newlyn - William Pollard	37.0.0d
House in Mousehole - Nathan Carey	3.10.0d
" Thomas Pentreath	2.5.0d
" Stephen Blewett	1.16.0d
" Robert Yeoman	1.7.0d
House Part " Richard Lanyon	1.16.0d
House in Mousehole Marg Parmenter	10.6d
& Emily Badcock	10.6d
Seine Loft Partly in Mousehole Sean Prop	18.0d
" " Other part Mousehole	18.0d
Tithes of Hook & Fish Mousehole B. Harry & Honor Leah	37.11.0d
Tithes Sheaf of Paul - John Glafson	3.0.0d
Part of New House – John Bodinar	3.0.0d
Other part " - George Glafson	3.0.0d

The following Deed was found in the Cornwall Record Office:-
'In 1291, – the 20th year of Edward I. This Church is valued at £9.6.8d, being then appropriated to the Abbey of Hailes in Gloucester. To this Abbey tithes of corn and fish were appropriated and so became lay fees on the dissolution of the Abbey. Signed Martin James Vicar of Paul, 1536.'

In 1539 the tithes of Paul Church fell into the hands of the Crown, because the Abbey of Hailes was seized by Henry VIII. In the Return made to King Henry VIII in the Court of Augmentations is listed:

Cornubia St. Paulyn	***- £41.0.0***
St. Breac (Breage)	***- £47.0.0***

A Deed from the Cornwall Record Office states:-

'Leonard Yeo (described as from 'Pawlyn') has the right from the Queen of selling the Leasehold of the Parsonage and tithes to Leonard Loveis, for 21 years, at £30 per annum a half to be paid at Michaelmas, and at Lady Day March 25th. John Speccott – 1573'.

Ten years into the Reign of King James I, the King granted the Rectory and Church of Paul to Francis Phillips and Francis Morice, who sold them to the family Cockayne.

In 1629 Charles Cockayne his wife Mary and presumably his Mother Mary Cockayne, a widow, Matt Cradock, Thomas Henchman and James Price, all levied a fine to S. H. R. Haton (farmer) and William Allen, in respect of the Rectory of Paul – all tithes etc.

In 1642 Charles Cockayne and Jacob Price sold the Rectory of grain, hay, wool and tithes of fish to William Gwavas (1638-1684) who was a Receiver under King Charles I.

William Gwavas © Royal Institute of Cornwall

The tithes descended to his son. *'Impropriation of the Sheaf and Tithes of Fish – William Gwavas'*. He returned from London to Penzance shortly before he married Elizabeth. The tithes were heavily mortgaged, and his Cornish property was heavily in debt at his death in 1684, owing to a law suit between him and his nephews the cost of which amounted to £800. Grandfather, Father and Son on the Gwavas side of the family were all barristers of the Middle Temple in London.

His Father had been involved with thirteen lawsuits, and his son William Gwavas (1676-1741) paid off the creditors and redeemed the mortgage on the Rectory (tithes) of Paul Church.

He spent much time involved in a Chancery Suit over the right of the Rector (owner of the tithes) of Paul to the tithes of fish landed at Mousehole and Newlyn in the parish. The suit started in 1680, with victory going to William Gwavas over Jenkin Teague, and twinety-nine other fishermen.

Later in 1724-30 the dispute was revived and went before the House of Lords in 1730, between William and Phillip Kelynack and one hundred and sixteen fishermen and parishioners of Paul. William Gwavas died and was buried in Paul Church in 1752.

After his death the fishermen resisted the tithe and the dispute continued. The tithes continued with his heirs (see below), until 1830 when the tithe of fish was abolished.

Another Deed from the C.R.O. states:-

'In 1774 – the yearly rental Tithes of Hook and Fish went to William Pollard - £37. Undated – Tithes of Sheaf of Paul to John Glafson - £10.5.6d. A house called 'The Stonehouse, Walton Meadow' – Overseers of Paul (Churchwardens) @ £1. per annum'.

As an aside: there is a Collection of Verses, Songs and Proverbs in Cornish made by William Gwavas in the British Museum, which includes an epigram by him of the eight lines verdict in the suit Gwavas v Kelynack respecting the fish tithes. His Common Place book of 1710 embraces a short autobiography printed by the Royal Institute of Cornwall.

After William Gwavas died, the tithes passed to his daughters. One was Elizabeth, wife of William Veale of Trevayler, and the other was Anne, wife of Revd., Thomas Carlyon which passed to their Uncle Revd. John Gwavas. (*The records are a little unclear!*) Elizabeth Veale's Will of 9th October, 1789 gave her moiety to her Grandson William Veale, and the remainder to her three Grand-daughters – who decided to sell.

Lysons, in 1814 states that not only were William Carlyon and Mrs. Elizabeth Veale, co-heirs, but a portion went to the Revd. William Veale.

'Paul 'Rectory' was valued in the King's Book at £13.11.6d. Patronage – The Crown.' This was written in a questionnaire to the Bishop by Paul Church Incumbent, the Reverend Henry Pendarves (early 18th C).

After Revd. Veale, Richard Hitchens of St. Ives bought the 'Rectorial Tithes', and left them in his Will on 8th October, 1851 to John Luke Peter of Redruth, who sold the 'Rectory' on in 1887 to the Ecclesiastical Commissioners for the purpose of **'*endowing a Vicarage for Newlyn Church*'**.

At that time it was split into two half shares worth £398 each, the Vicar's share being £512.12s (*ref Lake*). Anne Carylon's share was inherited by her Great-Grandson Thomas Tristram Spry Carlyon of Tregrehan on the death of his Father in 1854, then to nephew Arthur Spry Gwavas Carlyon.

'Tithes are commuted at £910.12s to the Vicar - £512.12s to the owners of advowson T. T. S. Carlyon and J.T. Peters, in equal divisions - £398.'

Paul lay in the Manor of Alverton, and on 15th December, 1869 parts of the Manor was sold, including the Island of Mousehole, Lots at Kerris, some buildings at Paul Church Town, and the Barton of Raginnis, and the Manor high rents went to Edward Bolitho.

As you can see, many people could purchase, or could be given, the 'Rectory' or tithes of Paul Church and receive their benefits.

The above gives a fairly clear picture of what happened to the Rectorial Tithes of Paul down the ages. The interesting bit is the fact that the Tithes went to endow the Vicarage of Newlyn St. Peters, from one old Church of Paul to the new one of Newlyn.

Tithe Map - 1853

CHAPTER 12 - CHOIR & MUSIC, BELLS & TOWER

'Wherefore with my utmost art I will sing thee' - Revd. George Herbert

PAUL CHURCH CHOIR– c. 1966 Revd. Lane-Davies centre, back row right -Eric Harvey Churchwarden, Tony Burroughs, George Prowse, Roy Osborne, Clive Ellis, Chris Carter, Michael Bennetts, Greg Williams, Tom Penaluna. Joe Ladner Churchwarden left. Jack Harvey, organist second row, Hilary Madron left end of middle row, Chris Osborne, second right second row. Sue Snell third from right ladies row.

The Quire, or Choir, was originally the area where the Clergy sat – the word Choir derives from Corona or circle of Clergy – or singers who surrounded the altar. The choir was once kept low so as not to obscure the sacred main altar. The choir, as a body of people and not an architectural term, are usually placed on either side of the Chancel (Sanctuary), imitating the shape of the cross it was stated that the choir was in position so that it can be heard without consideration for its visibility! A question of being heard and not seen! Although today in Paul Church the Choir is seated one level up on the Chancel step, and is completely visible, but in that position with the pre-Reformation rood screen in place, the choir would have been almost invisible. Before 1873, Paul Church Choir used to sit out of sight in the corner, at the east end of the north aisle. There was no organ at that time and the area was covered in pews; the choir sat beside the small robing area. Once the choir had moved into the chancel, the north east aisle corner then became a much larger panelled robing room.

There have always been those who assisted the Priest by singing and leading Services. Singers were known to accompany a small band of musicians up to the rood loft, and sing with the Priest from a lofty height. Many churches had galleries for musicians and singers at the back of the church and, before the advent of an organ or harmonium, Paul Church was no exception and had a 'Music Gallery'. More about the galleries in Chapter 3.

Early English polyphony is among the finest in the world and was, before the Reformation, sung in Latin. The Cornish could not understand English anyway, and accepted Latin and Cornish as Languages of the early Church. Although Henry VIII suppressed Catholicism, in his talent as an accomplished musician, he did not suppress church music. In fact he encouraged its beauty; which added to the solemnity of the services, by uplifting the congregation to God in beautiful anthems, and various sung parts of the service. These would have been sung mainly by the choir, as polyphony is constructed with complicated counter-rhythms, making congregational input impossible.

This music was composed to aid worship, enabling congregations to listen, while their souls were elevated in music to the Divine.

Paul Choir with Mr. L. Haughton, Choirmaster

After the Reformation the services were sung in English, and the various composers of the day just adjusted their librettos accordingly. Some composers were:-

Adrian Batten	1591-1637
Thomas Tomkins	1572-1656
Thomas Morley	1557-1602
Thomas Weelkes	1576-1623
Orlando Gibbons	1583-1625

Paul Choir have a sixteenth century book of Anthems, including Adrian Batten's wonderful early anthems, and the choir sing Orlando Gibbons' 'Drop Drop slow Tears' anthem every Good Friday, as well as using his beautiful hymn tunes. We also sing a setting of 'Amen' by Orlando Gibbons on special occasions such as Feast Sunday Service. The choir sang 'Exultate Juste' on Feast Sunday 2005, and on Easter Sunday 2006, 'This is the Day' by Thomas Morley.

The present (2006) choir members under John George, Choirmaster and John Harry, Organist are:-
Sopranos: Jean Hansford (Vicar's wife) Linda Burton, Christine, Lillian Carter, Joan Moffat, Amy Madron, Francesca Petersen, Joan Williams, Jenna and Morwenna Matthews, Heather Wright and Jill Hogben.
Trebles: Logan & Adam.

Altos: Mary Wooding, Nancy Renfree, Hilary Madron, Kath Matthews, Doris Walsh (retired), Utee Carpenter (retired), Marta Van Emden. Basses: David Carpenter, Mick Hudnott, Robin Young. Tenors: Matthew Mossop, Brian Carne, John Swan.

New robes for the choir are being made at the present time by Pam Jones and helpers, with money for the fabric donated by Mary and Eryl Wooding in memory of Mary's parents, John and Eileen.

Paul Choir 2006

Music is an integral part of all worship, and music in which all can join lifts the spirits to God. Hymns are well loved and sung with m u c h   g u s t o , especially by Chapel congregations and the Salvation Army! Church of England singing tends to be more restrained but that doesn't mean that the old hymns of, for instance, Charles Wesley, and of course the Cornish hymn writers such as Merrit, are not loved and sung with joy. Hymns were largely derived from psalms, and in fact the book of psalms is the oldest book of songs still in use today in the Anglican Church. There are many 'metrical psalms' which are sung as hymns, for instance 'Tell Out My Soul' is a metrical version of the 'Magnificat'. A definition of a psalm is thus: 'a hymn accompanied by stringed instruments'.

The earliest Christian hymns date from the 4/5th centuries A.D. and are associated with St. Ambrose Bishop of Milan in the 4th century, and therefore are still known by their Latin names. Such as:

Conditor alme siderum 'Creator of the Starry height'

Plainsong (Advent) - New English Hymnal

Pange Lingua 'Sing my tongue the glorious battle...' Lent

(Ave Maris Stella)

Te Lucis ante Terminum (Evening) 'Before the ending of the day...'

Iste Confesser (9th Century)

Vexilla Regis written by Bishop Venantius Fortunatus (530-609)

'The Royal Banner forward go...'

The Reformation gave great impetus to singing, and the congregation were allowed to join in, as wider involvement of the laity was introduced at this time. For a period during the eighteenth century the services were no longer sung by a choir, but were often conducted in the form of a duet between the Parish Clerk (from his desk) and the Vicar. Before 1873, Paul Church had such a Parish Clerk's Desk, situated where the Vicar sits today. They would usually intone

Choir going to St. Michael's Mount to sing Evensong in the Chapel

metrical versions of the psalms in an antiphonal, question and answer mode, with no organ, only a set of pitch pipes to keep them in tune!

It seems the case in Penwith Deanery that choirs would visit other churches, and in 1822 Paul choristers were paid 18s, to help out Madron Choir, by travelling over to their Church to sing with them. This was usually in the case of special services, as on Feast Sunday, although there are no records of any choirs coming to help Paul Choir to sing!

Perhaps we didn't need any help, because were, and still are lucky have such a robust Choir. Paul Choir also used to help out at weddings in other churches, such as St. Erth.

On 19th July, 1979, Paul Choir was invited to sing Evensong in the Chapel of St. Michael's Mount. Paul Church has luckily had a good Choir over the years; up to recently (2004) when the Archdeacon of Cornwall congratulated our Church on its

wonderful Choir! Visitors have often complimented the Choir Masters/Mistresses, and are amazed that a village church in a remote part of Cornwall should be able to support such a Choir. As reported in Suffolk (1764) choirs have not always been an asset to the Church. A clergyman describes the all male choir as follows:-

'They face each other in a ring and with their Backs to ye Congregation, where they murder anthems, abuse improper Psalms, leave off in ye middle of a sentence, sing ye Psalms to new jiggish tunes. If ye Minister offers to direct them he may mind his Text - they sing as they list, or not at all. They frequently leave their own parish church in a body to display their Talents in other Churches. I have known them to stroll six or seven miles for this purpose, sometimes with a young female singer or two in their train.'

Then Porteus, the Bishop of London, complained about the monopolising of psalmody in country parishes to sing in the worst manner a *'wretched set of psalm tunes so complex that it cannot be followed by the congregation. They therefore sit absorbed in silent admiration or total inattention.'*

Church choirs have been traditionally composed of men and boys; it is only comparatively

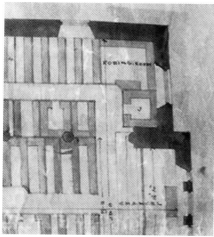

recently that girls and women, have been allowed into this masculine area. In fact, in Paul Church when ladies were first allowed into the Choir, they were not robed, and used to process up to the choir stalls five minutes before the robed male Choir, all decked out in their Sunday best dresses! The ladies would have suits for Easter, spring dresses for Whitsun, and always new outfits for Paul Feast. Men and boys were robed in black cassocks and white surplices.

The Choir seating has been moved around Paul Church, and in the records for the 1873 restoration it states under *'Proposed Reseating of Choir'* *'n.b: it is not proposed to alter this arrangement for singers until the people can be led to wish for, and approve, a change to the Choir seats at the east end of the north aisle.'*

There was a small 'Robing Room' in the north aisle east end, and the Choir sat in pews next to it, because the large ornate pews in the Chancel were for Clergy and the Parish Clerk only. Musical accompaniment in that Victorian period was provided by an harmonium at the back of the Church; situated in the midst of the children's pews that were in front of the Choir Vestry of today. It seems strange to have the Choir up one end, and the music up the other! This would have made it difficult to keep in tune. With an harmonium one has to continually pump with the feet; a long hymn with many verses would have been hard work. No doubt the pews were put into the chancel when a new organ was installed into the north aisle behind the Choir.

When this first pipe organ was put in Paul Church, (19th May, 1865), it was hand pumped by a chap called Joe Llewellyn who came from Mousehole. Another case of labour intensive music! It is reported that if Miss Oatey started to play the organ after the sermon, and there was no sound, the cry *'Joe's gone to sleep!'* went up, and Miss Oatey would rush round and crack Joe on the head with a book! He would then start pumping with gusto! He was reported to say one Christmas, *'you can play what you like, I am going to pump 'While Sheps'!'*

Mr. Leslie Haughton

In living memory the earliest Choir Mistress was Miss Oatey. Mary Barnes well remembered joining under Miss Oatey when she was eleven years old. She had a reputation for being a strict choir mistress who would not stand any nonsense. Her brother was Canon Oatey of Truro Cathedral. He officiated at the marriage of Mary and Billy (William) Barnes, and likened their marriage to *'a pair of scissors; the further you pull them apart – yet still they come together'*. He also married Mary's sister, the widow Ellen, to Thornley Renfree. Ellen was first married to Harold Gruzelier by the Revd. Wagner.

The Revd. Prideaux took a keen interest in the Choir and even chose Choir boys. The late Annie Prowse told me her husband and his brother, George and Charlie Prowse were sent to the Vicarage for a voice test, and the Vicar chose George for a treble, but Charlie was sent home! George eventually had a fine tenor voice. George Prowse was married to Annie in Paul Church, their son Keith sang tenor in Paul Choir for some years. In Paul Church; a much-revered Choirmaster was Mr. F. Leslie Haughton, a Bank Manager, who lived in a house below Mousehole School. He sadly suffered shell shock in the First World War, and subsequently was a rather nervous man, but this did not deter him from being a *wonderful musician and Choir Master'*. He was a strict man, and if the Choir members did not come to practice *'there would be trouble*!' He always sat at the back of the Church during services so he could listen to his Choir, coming forward to conduct anthems and other music.

In 1939 Mrs. Harvey was Organist. She would drive all the way down from Chacewater, even in the blackout, to play for services. She married Fred Harvey and they lived in Devonia House at the top of Paul Hill.

Jack Harvey 1945

The next Organist was Mr. Jack Harvey, Eric Harvey's brother who loved to play with gusto on the pipe organ. He lived in Sheffield with his wife Vera, and he worked as an electrician with the Electricity Board. Eric had previously been in the Choir, but when he was made Churchwarden, he left. This was because Joe Ladner who was also Churchwarden, joined the choir, and they didn't want two Churchwardens in the Choir at the same time, as one had to be about his duties to the congregation. Eric was Churchwarden for twenty-five years until 1960, he died on New Year's Eve 1985. (His photo is in Chapter 3.)

Elizabeth 'Diz' Stubbings

When the choir sang special pieces for Easter, such as 'Stainer's Crucifixion', Mr. Hayes, an Organist of Gulval would play the organ with Mr. Haughton conducting. During the incumbency of the Revd. Davy, the BBC recorded Paul Church Choir singing Evensong, which was broadcast on the Western Region Home Service on 26th January, 1958. A recording was made of this Service. When Jack Harvey, died Mr. Caunt took over as Organist for a while, but had to leave for personal reasons. Next came Mr. Peter Luing, then came our present Organist Mr. John Harry.

Hilary Madron

After Mr. Haughton retired, Mrs. Elizabeth Stubbings (nee Ford) was the next Choir Mistress; during her time the choir was asked to sing Evensong at St. Michael's Mount.
Mrs. Stubbings (Diz) was only twelve when she was asked to train the children to sing carols to take part in the plays produced by Mrs. Wagner, the Vicar's wife. Demelza and Morvah Stubbings, Diz's daughters, were both in the Choir. Next Hilary Madron took over the Choir; she had sung in the Choir since she was a little girl, and worked with Elizabeth Stubbings, taking the Junior Choir Practice, and playing the organ. Hilary is now a Choir Member, as is her daughter, Amy.

John George

The present (2006) Choir Master, John George, joined Paul Choir when he was only seven, although he had a break and attended Chapel. He remembers the musicality of the Vicar the Revd. Davy who often took Choir Practice. John also remembers Valerie Pentreath who was the instigator of new robes for the Choir, still in use today, but soon to be replaced. Valerie was the daughter of Mr. and Mrs. Richard Pentreath who used to run 'The Almshouses or Hutchen's House'. She eventually married David Osborn from Ludgvan.

Choir Secretaries have included: Carol Carne, Yvonne Hoare, Dawn Pentreath, Hilary Madron and today Mr. David Carpenter. The Junior Choir would be paid twice a year for singing, at Christmas and before the

Summer Outing. The rate of pay was: 2p for attending a Service, 5p for a wedding, and if the Choir member was a bell ringer, there would be riches, 10p for ringing! Currently all Choir money goes into a Choir Fund, kept by the Vicar, for new music, robes, etc.

Choir outings were legendary, coach trips to such places as: Plymouth, Lydford Gorge, Torquay or Buckfast Abbey. All were given 10 shillings (50p) towards the slap-up lunch they always had in an hotel. Some of the children would save their Choir pay towards ice-creams on these trips. The Vicar's wife Mrs. Prideaux would bring bags full of gooseberries to distribute on the outings. Mention must be made of Lizzie Annie Hosken (nee Symons), a well-known character of Paul Church. She was married to Matt Hosken, who sang in the Choir, and played the accordion for the maypole dancers at the May Queen Celebrations. Matt and Annie were lively characters and lived in the old Council Offices house in the car park. Lizzie cleaned the Vicarage, and she was very concerned when the Choir children managed to get in a muddle with their psalters and hymn books. Thus she made thick elastic holders for these books which were known universally as '*Lizzie Annie's garters*!'

In Paul Church in the 1970s and 1980s, there used to be a 'Choir Sunday' once a month. At the Services of Matins and Evensong the Choir practised hard to sing special settings of the canticles, responses and anthems. On 28th August, 1977 the Choir and Organist at Paul led the congregation, who joined in with the hymns, with the following:-

MATINS

Organ Voluntary: Vidor – Toccata from 5th Symphony
Introit: 'Praise the Lord ye Heavens Adore Him'
Trumpet Tune in D: Purcell
Processional Hymn: 'Rejoyce today with one accord'
Ein Feste Byrg – Luther 378
Venite: E. J.Hopkins
Psalm 24; Chant W. H. Harris, & L. Dakers
Te Deum Laudamus: Attwood, Cooke, Ouseley
Jubilate Deo: Ayrton
Anthem: 'See Christ was wounded' Brian Foley
Hymn: Angel-voices ever singing' E. G. Monk
Hymn: 'My dear Redeemer, and my Lord': Gonfalon Royal
Offertory: 'Bright the Vision' Laus Deo, Redhead 161
Amen: William Byrd
Recessional Hymn: 'Hail to the Lord's Anointed' Cruger

EVENSONG

Introit: 'O Lord We Trust alone in Thee' Handel
Processional Hymn: 'Hark Hark My Soul' No.223
Psalm 122: Chant from Beethoven
Magnificat: Bayley
Nunc Dimmitis: Heywood
Anthems: 'Living Lord' Patrick Appleford
'Come My Way' A. Brent Smith
Hymn: 'Jesus Shall Reign' Deep Harmony 220
Hymn: 'Sunset and Evening Star' Freshwater, Parry 694
Offertory: 'Come Down O Love Divine' Down Ampney
Amen: Seven-fold: Stainer
Recessional Hymn: 'The Day Thou Gavest' St. Clement
Vesper: 'Holy Spirit, Grant us Thy most blessed Benediction as we leave Thy house of prayer' L. R. Poore

Before Choir notes are closed, mention must be made of the much loved Jackson's 'Te Deum' which was always sung on Feast Sunday morning. The Revd. Davy loved this piece and often Evensong would end with a rousing rendition, even though it was a Matins psalm.

The Choir Vestry, with many cupboards, for books, music and robes, was fashioned in the tower, costing £2,000 and dedicated by the Archdeacon of Cornwall 1968. Today, even that area seems a rather small when the choir are trying to disrobe, and put away their books!

On St. Michael's Mount

In the 1960s it is reported that a certain lady, Mary Thomas, would tell the choir boys off, saying that if they were not Confirmed, they were not to pass a brown line that was painted on the roof of the Chancel! It was set at the Chancel step.

At the bottom of the music list above, it stated: *'Paul Bell ringers will attempt a Quarter Peal before Evensong'*. This statement leads nicely into the next section as ringers and singers united to enlighten Church Services. The Choir, as with the ringers of the present time, are a happy bunch of people, enjoying their music and singing to the Glory of God. Both Choir and Bell Ringers welcome any of those who may like to come and join their ranks! Practices: Wednesday evenings – Choir; and Thursday evenings – Bell Ringers.

TOWER

The lofty Tower of Paul Church is much admired, and is one of its glories, described as *'grandly proportioned'*, and *'a fine specimen of masonry in wrought granite'*. It was constructed early in the 15th century, and is truly magnificent, and at eighty-nine feet tall, said to be among the tallest in Cornwall.

Interior showing the above line 1950s

It is crowned by a beacon turret of twenty feet, which rises above the parapet and is locally known as *'the thumbnail'*. The beacon and Tower total one hundred and nine feet in all! The Tower is constructed with double buttresses, ascending to the summit in three stages of massive granite moor stones. Some stones are very rough and the facings are not dressed, although the rough treatment of the weather over 600 years has added to their uneven surface. Its pinnacles were probably added a little later, and they have supports for decorative pennants, which may have once added to the overall height of the Tower. There is a newel staircase in the north west angle, by which to ascend to the top.

William Williams of Newlyn wrote in his Diary:

'1799 March ye 30.
Wind at ESE a Tempest which Blowd down ye SW pinnackle of Paul Tower'

The West Door in the Tower

The Tower height matches the unusually long main, north and south aisles of the Church making a balanced whole building. It may be seen from miles around, and is the first thing to be spotted on the horizon as one comes down the A30 to Penzance. It always has been useful as a shipping mark for the entry to Mount's Bay. St. Buryan Tower is very similar, and this suggests that they were both constructed as watchtowers, or beacon towers, as they would have been able to signal to each other very quickly in times of danger. During a war with the French, it is reported that the turret was used as a signal beacon, and these beacons were always kept in readiness. Unfortunately during the Spanish raid, as their ships came out of fog and the raid happened very quickly, there was no time for lighting a beacon. Unless, as could have been the case, a beacon *was* lit, and it was used to fire the Church. It is said that a message may be signalled to London, from Paul Church via line of church towers, connecting with other beacon fires, which stretch across England from Cornwall, taking only twenty minutes!

From the top of the Tower it is reported that on a clear day, no less than seventeen Parish churches may be spotted: St. Buryan, Sancreed, Madron, St. Mary's and St. John's Penzance, Gulval, Ludgvan, Towednack, Marazion, St. Michael's Mount, Perranuthnoe, St. Hilary, Germoe, Gwinear, St. Erth, Cury and of course, Paul!

The flag pole on top of the Tower was erected on 24th September, 1994, at a cost of £500. There is also a lightning conductor for further protection of the Tower, erected in May 1950, when the P.C.C. reported that it had not been clipped properly in its place. The weathervane was given in memory of Dennis Laycock Walsh, who was Paul Church Verger from 1983-1988. It was made and erected on top of the Tower by Mr. Fred Alderton in 1979, replacing one bearing the date 1796.

Paul Church Tower is unique in that it is the only Church in West Cornwall to have the 'sheela-na-gig' (a grotesque medieval figure) displayed on three corners of its third stage. It is not easy to spot from the road, and can easily be mistaken for *'a lady holding a pasty'* as a young boy described her. These grotesque figures, along with gargoyles, were meant to frighten evil away from the church, and were often placed over the door of the south porch. It is very unusual to have three such depictions of the same grotesque, one being more usual, and quite sufficient!

The Tower was gutted by fire in the Spanish raid, but luckily, its construction was robust enough to withstand serious damage. The Vicar of Paul at that time was Revd. John Tremearne, who wrote:- *'The church, tower, bells and all things – burned and spoiled'.*

There is an unconfirmed report that the front of the Tower shows traces of fierce Civil War strife, and damage to the hood mould around the west door. This hood-moulding springs from corbel heads; in the

Sheela-na-gig

centre of the moulding is a shield bearing the sacred characters 'I.H.C.' These letters still surviving and enduring in granite, mean, Jesus Saviour of Man – in Greek *'Ieusus Hominum Salvator'*, no political correctness in those days! This includes everyone in a simple statement.

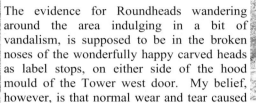

The evidence for Roundheads wandering around the area indulging in a bit of vandalism, is supposed to be in the broken noses of the wonderfully happy carved heads as label stops, on either side of the hood mould of the Tower west door. My belief, however, is that normal wear and tear caused by centuries of battering by westerly winds and rain, is the true culprit for the nasal flattening. Luckily their chubby smiling faces shine through; maybe they were a local married couple of importance way back in the 1400s, well liked enough to be portrayed here by the important west door. They are in stark contrast to the black solemn faces, which can be located on the outside walls of the eastern end of the Church.

This second pair of heads probably date to the same era as the Tower heads, and would not have originally been black. They have been painted black, together with the down pipes, probably to emphasise them, and make sure they are not overlooked. They possess fierce countenances, perhaps that is why they were banished to the east end, moved from elsewhere. One sports a fine wig, and the other either a coif in which case she is female, or it could be a chain mail helmet, so presumably is male! Their gender is not really as apparent as the happy couple! Their features would have been based on local people, who probably were the pillars of the Church of their time.

To add to the Civil War story, local belief is that King Charles was concealed somewhere in the Parish for a long time. Until a few years ago, a huge board was affixed to the interior walls of every Church in the district. This was known as 'The King's Letter' or Royal Order of 'Carolos Rex' conveying thanks to the people of West Cornwall. This is fully reproduced in Chapter 8.

In a Handbook (Murrays) for Devon & Cornwall is a very interesting piece of information. However, Mr. Murray (with suspicious integrity) writes of Paul:-
'here rises a fine granite church tower, a conspicuous land-mark, inscribed with the date 821'
This curious date can have no meaning as far as today's Tower is concerned, being dated from early 15th C. So there is a mystery as to what this 821 means. It could mean 1821, the '1' being lost, although there are no records for anything interesting happening in the Tower in 1821. Maybe a peal was rung of importance or it was just a bit of graffiti.

The Choir Vestry now covers most of the inner Tower walls at ground level, thus, if this inscription existed, it is likely to have been covered by cupboards. At the west end of the nave, the tower arch is described as very grand, of *'superior character and well-proportioned'* (Lake). Outside, the Tower has three empty niches high up on its western side. These empty niches, with their shields below, are remnants of the destruction during the Reformation, when their statues would have been pulled down and destroyed. It is likely that one would have held a statue of the Blessed Virgin Mary in the niche with the 'M' or fleur de lis carved underneath. The top niche would probably have held a representation of God the Father, and the niche with the shield would have held St. Paul (see photo of the west tower window Chapter 3).

There was a lot of wanton destruction to churches, not only at the Reformation but also during the Civil War, when the puritanical roundheads smashed their way around churches, as did the soldiers of the Reformation in Henry VIII's time. All churches have come in for a battering at one time or another, and it is amazing what artefacts of beauty have escaped wanton destruction. Even in later times, although many churches were falling down the Victorians, with passion for high gothic in their lavish restorations, destroyed a lot of earlier beauty.

Margaret Byrne - Tower Captain 2006

DETAILS OF THE BELLS

Treble – E 28" diameter 4-1-24 - MARY
Gift of Paul Mothers' Union

John Taylor & Co., 1950

2ⁿᵈ – D 39" diameter 5-0.22 – ST. POL DE LEON
'God Bless our Parish' W. A. Wagner, Vicar,
R. C. Drew, L Spargo, Churchwardens

John Taylor & Co., 1950

3ʳᵈ - C 33" diameter 7-0-7 – ST. GEORGE
Three new bells added the six hung in new frame in 1950, in memorial to the Men of Paul Parish who fell in the 1939-45 War.

John Taylor & Co., 1950

4ᵗʰ – B flat 35½" diameter 7-1-20 – weighs 8 cwt.
'Prosperity to this Parish'

Abraham Rudhall 1727

5ᵗʰ – G 39" diameter 10-0-27 - weighs 10 cwt.
'Prosperity to the Church of England'

Abraham Rudhall 1727

Tenor – F 43" diameter 14-2-5 - weighs 14¾ cwt.
'I to the Church the living call,
And to the grave do summon all'

Abraham Rudhall 1727
Re-cast by John Taylor & Co., 1950

In another example of a writer, not checking facts, is a reference stating that the Belfry lights retain their original sounding boards. This cannot be true as the Revd. Richard Malone had the windows restored after 1873, with original materials collected from various places. He reported that the tower window mullions and tracery were removed and had been previously *'filled up in a most barbarous manner'*. Therefore the transoms of the belfry windows are not original. On Wednesday, 2ⁿᵈ December, 1987, at 7.30 p.m. the Rt. Revd. Richard Llewellyn – Bishop of St. Germans - Dedicated the New Ringing Chamber in the Tower. During this Service the Captain of the Ringers said *'Bishop, I ask you to dedicate this Ringing Chamber for the Praise of God and for bringing of His joy to the people of Paul'*. In the Ringing Chamber is a brass plaque recording this event, and praising the generous donation of June Waters.

It states: *'the ringing Chamber was dedicated to June Waters who died on 11th December, 1986, and the name of Revd. R. Llewellyn, Bishop of St. Germans, 2nd December, 1987 was added.'*

A copy of the full Order of Service may be seen in the C.R.O.

Revd. Wagner and the Bells

BELLS

'Campana' is the Latin for bell, the tower is a 'campanile' as it contains bells, and the science of bell ringing also comes from this root word 'campanology'. Interestingly, the invention of bells is ascribed to one with a familiar name - Paulinus, Bishop of Nola, Italy in A.D. 400.

The Venerable Bede (672/3-735) brought a bell from Italy to place in his Abbey at Wearmouth. These are very early references for bells being used to call the faithful to worship, and pre-formation Paul Church, as a village Church would only have had a maximum of two or three bells; only Cathedrals and larger churches had more in a peal.

On 18th November, 1935 at a P.C.C. Meeting was stated: *'several members complained of irregularity of bell ringing, and wrote to the P.C.C. to ask if they would adopt a more regular system'.*

Percy Harvey: Mason for Bell frame

When the Evening Service was broadcast from Paul Church in 1958 the Captain of the ringers was Mr. J. Ladner. Today, there is a grand peal of six bells at Paul Church, described in *'The Ringing World'* of 23rd September, 1977 as:- *'being among the heaviest in Cornwall and generally acknowledged to being a very fine ring'.*

The band of ringers at that time was described as possessing: *'erudite experience and enthusiastic endeavour'.* The ringers were: Julian Watson, Eric Harvey Churchwarden, Reginald Curtis Tower Captain, John George, Mark Stubbings, John Waters, Samantha Kitchen, Margaret and Rueben Byrne, the Vicar was the Revd. R. H. Cadman.

On Jubilee Day it was reported that the band rang a quarter peal of Plain Bob Doubles, which was a first for a Sunday Service band for eight years. Today in 2004 we still have a loyal band of ringers, with Margaret Byrne as Tower Captain. They are: Secretary Jenny Ridley, Steeple Keeper Mick Hudnott, John Maddern, John George, John Waters, David Carpenter, John Swan, Mike Cook, Harry Sales, and Andrew Climo-Thompson.

During the Spanish Raid and firing of the Tower and Church, the Vicar, John Tremearne, reported that the bells were also ruined.

They would have come crashing down as their frame burned.

The bells were sent to Gloucester in 1680 for re-casting. In 1727 a brand new set of three bells were made. It seems a coincidence that the dates of 1727 on these bells just happens to be a year after the new Vicarage (1726) was built, and the belfry furnishings were reported as being '*decent*'. It may be that the Parish came into some money at that time; there is no record to state where the Vicars lived for over 130 years, so the Vicarage and the new Bells being of the same date must be telling a story (see Revd. Henry Pendarves).

Lakes' Parochial History of Cornwall does state, that in 1807 there was discovered charred woodwork in the tower, and it was repaired. In 1910 the three bells were described as: '*mellow and pure in sound*'.

On 27th June, 1949, the P.C.C. approved the application of a Faculty Petition for three new bells, to be rehung with new fittings in a new framework made complete for eight Bells in total. The peal is of six bells today, and there is still enough room for two more bells. The recasting of the tenor bell meant it was increased by 1¾ cwts. It is reported that, in 1950, this tenor bell with the added weight, was brought up Paul Hill '*with great difficulty*'! The three new bells were inscribed '*God Bless our Parish*', and the tenor bell was recast as a memorial to the men of the Parish who died in the 1939-45 War. The bell inscribed 'Mary' was the gift of the Mothers' Union; the other two were '*St. George*' and '*St. Pol-de-Leon*'.

Abraham Rudhall of Gloucester cast three Bells for Paul in 1727. He was an active and expert change ringer, and a member of The Ancient Society of College Youths (a society of Bell Ringers) that was founded in 1637.

On Saturday, 19th November, 1994, a Peal of Seven Surprise Minor Changes with 5,040 changes was rung, taking two hours and fifty-three minutes to do so. The ringers were conducted by: Christopher J. Pickford:-

John J. George	Treble
Rosemary J. Pickford	2
Christopher J. Venn	3
Trevor N. J. Bailey	4
Christopher J. Pickford	5
George W. Pipe	Tenor

The P.C.C.'s intention was to provide for a peal of eight bells, and the bell frame was made to accommodate this peal accordingly.

On Saturday 20th May, 1950 at 3.00 p.m. The Venerable, The Archdeacon of Cornwall Canon F. Boreham, conducted the Service for the Dedication of the Bells. The Vicar was the Revd. V.W. Wagner, and Churchwardens were R. C. Drew and L. Spargo. A copy of the

Order of Service is in the C.R.O. At the Service of Dedication of the new bells the hymn was sung:
'And so we pray that God may Bless, Each Churches' ringing band, As in the tower they Praise the Lord, In Cornwall's pleasant land.' The following prayer was read:

'Almighty God who by the mouth of they Servant didst command to make two silver trumpets for the convocation of solemn assemblies. Be pleased to accept these offerings at our hands; hallow we beseech Thee, these Bells and grant that they may call together Thy faithful people to praise and worship They Holy Name; through Jesus Christ our Lord, Amen'.

After the service a band of ringers rang three Grandsire doubles with the six bells, a sound not heard before, and many clergy from neighbouring parishes attended the Service, which was conducted by the Revd. W. V. Wager. They were:-

The Revds: A. S. Roberts (Carbis Bay); W. H. R. Trewhella, (Crantock); the Secretary of the Diocesan Guild of Ringers; R. A. Harvey (Cury); Canon F. Boreham – Archdeacon of Cornwall; and H. M. W. Hocking (Madron).

The new frame incorporated ball bearings on which the bells would move, making a very light action for the ringers. The Vicar Revd. Wagner, stated in 'The Cornishman' that he would like to increase the peal to eight, thus equalling in size the few complete peals in the Duchy of Cornwall.

Clergy at the Bells' Dedication 20th May, 1950

A copy Service sheet for the Dedication Ceremony is still in the Vicar's possession.

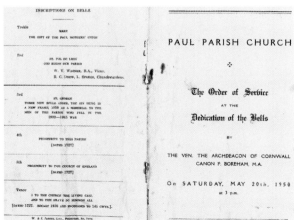

The present Tower Captain, Margaret Byrne, informed me that Paul Church ringers are members of the Truro Diocese Guild of Bell Ringers. They enjoy car outings to bell towers all over the country, such as the Tamar Valley, Calstock, and Pillaton. Margaret stated that ringing is unique in that ringers are always welcomed in all churches with bells. The bell ringers of Paul have good social evenings, at 'The Lugger' in Penzance.

Mr. Reg Curtis was Captain before

Margaret and enjoyed the support of the Revd. Cadman. The ringers were:-
John George, John Waters, Diane Bond, Roger Bond, Julian Watson, Sam Kitchen, Alec Jones, Mark Stubbings, John Maddern, Pat Maddern and Rueben Byrne, Margaret's husband.

On Saturday 20th May, and Sunday 21st May, 2000 there was a '50th Anniversary of Paul Bells' Celebration, with another Service, and many old photos were on view.

Inside the belfry there is a natural curiosity: a large plant of the rare *asplenium marinum* fern thrives, and has been growing there for many years, probably thriving on the moisture percolating through the ancient tower walls!

In the C.R.O. there is a very interesting case of 'Excommunication' at Paul Church. For this, I am indebted to Margaret Byrne and Pam Jones for their research:

Bell ringers on the old Vicarage lawn

Document 1

On 4th January, 1810, a document was written by John Wallis, Registrar, on behalf of William Shore, Archdeacon of Cornwall. This asked that four men from the Parish described as yeomen, named James Murley, John Brownfield, William Ladner and William Hosking, should appear at the Parish Church at Bodmin, on 12th January between 9.00 and 12.00 in the forenoon, to answer charges *'touching and concerning their souls' health and reformation and correction of their manners and excesses'*. This especially related to their breaking up and entering the belfry, and ringing the bells without the permission of the Minister or Churchwardens.

Document 2

This document is dated 9th February, 1810. It states that James Murley and William Ladner had been sought for the purposes of delivering a citation to them, but they had not been found. The instruction to Revd. Warwick Oben Gurney, described as *'The Curate'*, were to affix the citation on the doors of their houses. This required them to appear at Bodmin Parish Church on 23rd February, 1810.

Document 3

The two men still failed to attend, so in a document dated 7th April, 1810, the Archdeaconry Court excommunicated the two men. The Curate was instructed that on *'the Sunday or Festival Day next'* following the receipt of the document he should at Morning Service *'denounce and declare'* James Murley and William Ladner - ***excommunicated!*** Revd. Warwick Oben Gurney wrote back to the Archdeacon to say that he had done this on Good Friday the 20th of April.

Document 4

Another document dated 11th May asks for the same thing to be done and the procedure was repeated on Sunday 20th May.

Document 5

The final document in this set is dated 6th November, 1810. The case against James Murley and William Ladner was still on-going. William Hosking had been cited by the Curate as a necessary witness, but he was refusing to attend the Archdeaconry Court to give his testimony, despite the fact that the Curate had offered to pay his expenses. The Court cited William Hosking to appear at Bodmin Parish Church on 16th November to take the oath and to: *'tell the truth of what he knows on this behalf'.*

The Citation From John Wallis, Registrar: (shortened version)

'We hereby charge you to cite James Murley, John Brownfield, William Ladner and William Hosking of the parish of Paul to appear before us 12th January, 1810, between 9.00 – 12.00 to answer certain articles concerning their breaking open and entering the belfry and ringing the Bells of the Church without the leave of the Minister or Churchwardens.'

This is a very unusual story, which seems to have snowballed, and poses a number of questions, excommunication being a very harsh penalty for ringing bells unlawfully. Perhaps a reader of this book may find it interesting enough to dig further!

BELLS - ANTE-SPANISH RAID

As an important postscript to this chapter there has come to light some information about the pre-1595 bells. Paul suffered badly enough during the Spanish Raid, but one of the worst occurrences was that three Church Bells, weighing 19 cwt., were shipped out with Nicholas Boson on 23rd April, 1595 via Mousehole Harbour to Bristol, and from thence probably by canal to the nearest Bell Foundry at Gloucester to be re-cast. The newly-cast bells were loaded on to the *'John'* at Bristol, on 31st May, 1595, arriving at Mousehole on 30th June, and were presumably re-hung in the Tower.

A mere twenty-three days later the Spaniards arrived, and once the Church was fired, the bells fell from the Tower, and were ruined. The *John* was also fired as it lay in Penzance harbour. This information was researched by Dr. Joanna Mattingly working on *'The Fishing Communities of Mousehole and Newlyn,'* part of the Victoria Country History Project. The author of this book is a volunteer researcher for the V.C.H. - ref: Paul Church.

The Will dated 13th February, 1608 of Nicholas Boson, fisherman, witnessed by Vicar Revd. John Tremearne, states: *'to help make the Belles of Pawle ten shillings if they be made, part of the money that the parishioners of Pawle doth owe me for Ledd that went about the church.'* (Probably lead on the re-built church 1600.)

This Will confirms that the bells being shipped out of Mousehole, were from Paul Church.

The thought may hardly be borne that not only had the bells just been recast in 1595, but the interior of the church, burnt and ruined, may have only recently been the subject of restoration or re-ordering, because of the Reformation. It could be that new bells were placed in the church shortly after the Spanish Raid; however, it seems to me that Paul parishioners would have other things to deal with such as the rebuilding of their homes and lives.

The only clue we have for this is that in 1727 the bells were sent to be ***re-cast*** to Gloucester (ref: Glebe Terrier 1727). The word 'recast' intimates that there were new bells after the 1600 rebuild. Of course, another idea is that these bells to be ***recast*** were actually the ***same bells*** that came crashing down during the fire, and they had to wait a long time to be recast. Keeping large damaged bells from 1595 until 1727 would have been rather an onerous and impossible task. I will leave the readers to make up their own minds about this!

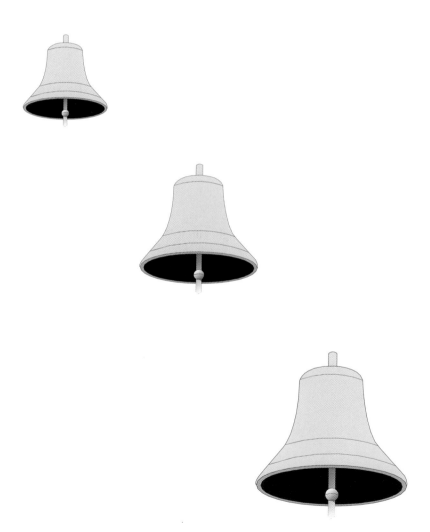

CHAPTER 13 – THE CHURCHYARDS & VARIOUS BURIAL PLACES OF PAUL CHURCH

There are many burial places in Paul: the Penwith Council Cemetery, the Cholera Ground, the School Burial Ground, (today behind the Church Hall), a small plot of land behind Hutchens' House, and of course the main Churchyard which surrounds the Church.

The Immediate Churchyard

Revd. Wagner, other clergy, Chwdns Leonard North & Richard Drew. Note the interesting wrought Iron arch over south east gate.

The churchyard wall is reported to be of 18/19th century construction, of granite rubble with chamfered coping 4'6" high rising to 8' at the north west end. The churchyard wall is Listed Grade II, as are the stone crosses. There are certainly grounds for disagreement on the age of construction, as towards the bottom of the south wall near the gate, is a very interesting piece of stone from the old pre-fire (i.e. pre-1595) decorated pillars. Thus this part of the wall at least must date back to 1600, and could have been damaged as the Spaniards rampaged around the village. There are three entrances constructed of granite. The north west gateway has attractive and unusual semi-circular steps.

Paul Churchyard, surrounding the Church, presents a rather small burial ground (approximately three rods, twenty-six perches in area, this measurement includes the Church); to serve the size of the populations of Newlyn, Mousehole and Paul. Paul Church once was the Mother Church of the Mousehole Anglican Chapels, and of Newlyn. As an interment area, it presents as totally inadequate for the size of the Church, towering above it. It has been raised up over the years due to burials, one on top of the other, for which soil was often imported to provide cover. The Victorians removed the soil from the sides of the Church and inserted a drain and a gap, which prevents the building from being extremely damp. The churchyard wall, a Cornish hedge, is eight foot high in places, again demonstrating the fact that the burials have raised the levels of the ground considerably. The churchyard – along with the old vicarage plot - is triangular in shape, tapering to a point at its west gate. The south and west gates have 'seats' of stone on either side and both have granite 'cattle grids', now filled in with grass, to prevent intrusion by animals. The second south gate is merely an additional entrance, leading to the 'Vicar's door' or south aisle entrance to the Church.

The handsome wrought iron gates incorporating bell motifs were placed at the churchyard entrances in memory of a popular local man, Mark Stubbings, who died in 1980. They certainly make the entrances very attractive. In the centre of the south gate there is a granite stone rest for coffins, awaiting the Vicar who would come out and receive the deceased and the mourners. This was known as a '*corpse stone',* as in 1666 the Woollens Act was passed enforcing the lining of coffins with wool. All shrouds were to be woollen in order to suppress the importation of flax for linen, and encourage the English wool market. The stone resting point allowed the

Vicar to examine the contents of each coffin, checking for wool use, as required by this Act, and if a corpse was found to be wound in a silk or linen shroud a heavy tax was imposed. This Act remained in force until 1814.

There are some old family vaults along the outside wall near the south porch, and elsewhere in the immediate churchyard. These are not large, but would have been brick-lined with shelves for maybe two or three coffins. There is a plaque on the outer Church wall above the vaults to the memory of various members of the Pentreath family. Among them was Francis Godolphin Pentreath who died in 1893. F. G. Pentreath erected a plaque beneath a window in the south aisle to the memory of his Father, Richard Pentreath, born in Mousehole 1814 and who died in London in 1880 (see Chapter 7).

Close to the north corner of the tower, in 1910 was a slate slab depicting a man-of-war from which rubbings could be taken with the words 'Optata Potitus Arena' – 'He has gained wish for shore'- a naval tomb. Lieutenant Millett who fought under Nelson at Trafalgar, and Lieutenants Primrose and Burgess who guarded Mount's Bay during war with the French, are also buried in the immediate churchyard.

There were many broad-leaf trees, and shrubs, surrounding the Church in the 1870s; in fact the Vestry of the time decided to plant even more shrubs. Some of these trees had to be cut down because of Dutch Elm disease, and old postcards show the Church being almost invisible behind many trees. However, the ubiquitous yew is not present in Paul Churchyard.

The Plot behind Hutchens' House

7th January, 1879 - Addition to Glebe – Caroline Carne gave five poles of land adjoining the 'Gift House' to the Vicarage Glebe, marked 919 on the O.S. map. This small plot of land is almost circular, and it was proposed as additional burial ground, but being too small was never used as such. It was however, used by the Revd. Tyrrell for keeping pigs and chickens! (See Chapter 5.)

The First Additional Burial Ground, later known as 'The Cholera Ground'

As a background to the burial grounds belonging to Paul Church, I list here a Settlement, one of many dated 1777-1823 between the Rt. Hon. John late Earl of Bute and Rt. Hon. Mary Wortley late Countess of Bute and Baronet Mount Stuart for £10,000, a large sum of money in 1777!

In effect this was the Manor of Brewinney consisting of: *60 messuages (houses), 2 grist mills, 60 gardens, 1500 acres of land, 350 acres of meadow, 350 acres of pasture, 500 acres of furze, heath and common adjoining pasture with appurtainments in the Parish of Paul Churchtown otherwise Bruenny.*

8th February, 1777 - 172/2/3 - Deed showing a map of the 'Cholera' Burial ground – 32 poles of land were purchased for £32 'The Dry Meadow' and part of 'The Dead Orchard' in occupation of Joseph Branwell Sutherland. Sold to Edward Kelynack and Richard Matthews Churchwardens, as the main churchyard is full. Purchased from James Stuart Wortley McKenzie, James Archibald Stuart Wortley, and Mary Wortley Countess of Bute. People objected to this land being used as a burial ground as follows:- Petition dated 1st October, 1786 by William Hichens, Francis Hutchins Jacka. Churchwardens: *'they have inadvertently* *increased a certain plot of ground in addition to the churchyard of **St. Paul** measuring north west adjoining to the old church yard 54 feet or thereabout, on the north 60 feet or thereabout, on the south west 10 feet of thereabout, for the better and more convenient interment of the dead in the said church yard, the same having been found much too small for that purpose in its former state. Your petitioner therefore humbly pray your Lordship's Licence or Faculty for confirmation of the said plot of ground in its present state to be made use of for the purpose aforesaid until such a time as your Lordship shall be pleased to consecrate the same…'*

The Pretty Committee 2006, an all male band of willing volunteer church and churchyard cleaners, tidy-uppers, mowers, weeders, menders, painters, chatterers and generally happy bunch of chaps; who keep Paul Church and its Churchyards in tip top condition, for which we are all very grateful.

The answer came: from James Carrington, Exeter:- *'Sunday next…publish or cause to be published in the Parish Church of **St. Paul** in the forenoon time of Divine Service…our intimation thereby citing or causing to be cited all manner of persons having or pretending to have any objection to the premises, that they appear…in Cathedral Church of St. Peter in Exeter in the Consistory Court Friday 10th November next…to propound their objections accordingly.'* Faculty granted if no-one showed up!

However the *'objicients'* were many, as follows: William Hitchens, Richard Matthews, Peter Dennis, John Foster, Peter Wills, Joseph Bendon, John Wright, Noy Tregwirtha, Martin Wright, James Nicholls, Charles Francis, John Thomas, Abraham Tonkin (my ancestor! An objicient!), Thomas Tonkin, Richard Wright, John Harvey, John Boase, William Polgreen, Thomas Leah, John Matthews, Michael Dewes, John Tremethack, John Price, John Beard, Francis Hutchens Jacka, Thomas Mattews, Edward Tregwartha, Richard Hichens, George Glasson, William Daveys, and William Pollard. Henry Hoskins was Witness aged 47, as was Richard Gurney – Sexton - aged 49, and William Cattran aged 27 tenant of Promoventin.

This list of names may seem tedious, but the interesting thing about them is that many people reading this book will be able to say 'Ah! My great-great-great-Grandpa was a rebel', as I can!

The objections were published in **St. Paul's Church** 5th November, 1786 by Vicar Revd. G. J. Scobell. Objections were over-ruled and in:- 1790 on 21st October, *a Faculty for Churchyard extension,* was issued. This measured (*note the discrepancies with measurements above*) to the NW adjoining the old church yard 54ft; on the SW 63ft, and on the south east 10ft for better internment of the dead. Later, this area became known as the Cholera Ground, when between September and November 1832 cholera visited the locality, and ninety-one victims were buried there, all from Newlyn.

A Deed of Sale – P172/2/3 for the burial ground later known as 'The Cholera Ground' between 1. Henry Bateman of London, 2. Hon. James Wortly McKenzie, his son John Archibald Wortley, and the Lord Bishop of Exeter plus G. H. Warren. Agreeing to this plot of 32 poles, called The Dry Meadow, taken from a field called the Dead Orchard, (also of 32 poles). This land for an enclosed burial ground was purchased on 29th April, 1817 for £32.

Churchyard extension map 1922

An Abstract of Title of James Archibald Stuart Wortley, and John Stuart Wortley his eldest son, to a piece of ground in Paul Church Town – Bruenny and Paul 1823.

As an historian, I have been driven potty by these purchases of additional burial grounds. Why on earth was the purchase made in 1817, when records state that the proposed first extension burial ground ('Cholera' Dry Meadow) was first mooted in 1777? I can understand that there were objections – but this took a very long time to settle, forty years in total!

William Williams of Newlyn's Diary:-

'1832 Part of the month of August, September and October our Village of Newlyn was visited with a 'dreadful distemper called Cholera morbis' which carried off above one hundred souls. On Paul Feast day no less than six were interred. Nov ye 21 – A Thanksgiving sermon in Paul Church for the Removal of the Cholera, preached by Revd. W. O. Gurney.'

Cholera is an illness caused by a bacterium *'vibria cholerae'*. It causes violent stomach cramps, diarrhoea, vomiting and death. It may be caught through infected food or drink, or fumes emanating from vaults! Churches were a direct source of this disease because churchyards and church floors were crammed with bodies, sometimes with corpses on corpses. The Poor Law Commission of 1834 explored the problems of community health, leading to the Public Health Act 1848, a General Board giving advice on sanitary conditions – and generally churchyards and churches were then closed by law to burials in 1855.

The Cholera Ground Burial area was already closed to burials in 1852, and up to 24th January, 1923, Paul Church had no further responsibility for it, as it was taken over by the Penzance Urban

District Council. This area is totally surrounded by walls and houses, and it once had a lych gate entrance that has now disappeared. It was made, as were the other additional burial grounds, as an overflow for the main churchyard and to contain the victims of the disease cholera. Curiously it is recorded that all the victims of this disease were from Newlyn, one wonders if the vaults under the 'Newlyn' aisle were particularly suspect! Thinking about it, there are two vaults under the floor of the North aisle, and the 'loose' burial' at the west end was just literally under the floor; this area could easily have been a source of disease before the floor was renewed in 1873.

School Burial Area

As an introduction to this burial area, I cite the following Deed No. P172/2/13 in C.R.O. – Revd. Charles Valentine Le Grice, and Revd. W. O. Gurney from Cyprian Richards of Paul (a yeoman who lived at Penolva in 1856), and Henry Pendarves of Tremenheere.

The purchase of land for the erection of a School House, part of a field adjoining the Bowling Green in Paul Church Town, 54 feet x 24 feet wide – 4 Poles of land. Richard Pentreath – Schoolmaster 4th June, 1825.

This area was confusingly known as 'Jack's Tenement' and 'Church Town Field', it also appears on two different maps as field number 1031 and again as field number 949; that reference is the part nearest the Church Hall, and 958 is the extension burial ground. It would have been a lot easier if the whole field known as 'Church Town Field' had been originally purchased, but only the eastern part was acquired.

Under Faculty Petition P172/2/6 dated 21st July, 1817 *'Jack's Tenement'* Revd. Richard Gurney, Edward Kelynack and Nicholas Cornish Churchwardens – from James Stuart Wortley of Wortley Hall in York and his son John Stuart Wortley, *'All said piece of ground lately enclosed in a stone wall, the said piece of ground adjoins the present burying ground – 17 poles' Thomas Turner – Registrar.*

This area of 17 poles was purchased on 20th November, 1823, for £17, under P172/2/5 (C.R.O.), and is the first burial ground immediately behind the present Church Hall, or *'School House'* as it was then known. This area was Consecrated on 1st August, 1825 under Faculty 172/2/6 dated 19th July, 1824 by Revd. John Bull and witnesses by the Principal Registrar for Exeter. The Licence and Sentence of Consecration states:

'Both said pieces and parcels of ground should now be consecrated by us. Pleased by our Episcopal authority to set apart both said pieces or parcels of ground so granted for additional burial ground, ...to consecrate...... and did promise on the parts of future Vicars and Churchwardens that when said parcels should be consecrated ...... should hold and esteem the same for the future and keep the said ground in all respects decent and fit for Sepultre (burial) ......We William Bishop of Exeter...entirely separate from all common and profane uses the said pieces and do dedicate and consecrate...' Revd. Richard Gurney – Edward Kelynack and Nicholas Cornish Churchwardens.

P172/2/6 - The above School Burial Ground Faculty to make the purchase was dated 19th July, 1817, and the Deed for the sale of the Cholera Ground was dated 29th April, 1817, thus both pieces of land were purchased in the same year. However the actual Deed for the **Sale** of 17 poles of land dated 17th November, 1823, states *'17 poles lately hedged off and enclosed part of a tenement owned by James Stuart Wortley called 'Jack's Tenement' bounded on the north by the* *other part of the tenement called 'Jack's Tenement' and on the east by a burial ground* *formerly granted by the said James Archibald Stuart Wortley to the Parish and on the south and* *west by the lands of ……(blank)'.*

Apart from all of the above, the 'Cornish Telegraph' reports that on 6th February, 1877 a body called 'Paul Burial Board' voted against Josiah Wright's one and a half acres of land for a cemetery adjoining the present burial yard. Mr. J. Wright was mentioned as quite a mover and shaker in Paul Village; he lived in Boslandew House.

Moreover, it really is beginning to look as if half of field No 958, (given the number 949) or, on other maps, the half of field numbered 1031, was in fact bought for the Church to use for burials. Somehow one part of the field was used for farming purposes, and bought in 1923 by Mr. Pengelly, who mortgaged the eastern part back to the Church. This is all extremely confusing.

P172/2/7 –21st May, 1832 - Bargain & Sale - £60 – 37 Poles of land in Paul Churchtown, alias *Barton of Brewinney, as additional Churchyard. James Halse, Henry Philpotts Bishop of Exeter* *and Churchwardens Thomas Leah and John Downing. A meadow or enclosure of land situated* *near Paul Church Town, with north and south hedges or fences, 37 poles, more or less bounded* *on the north by the present burying ground, on the south by a high road, on the east and west by* *land of James Halse called Brewinney. Revd. W. O. Gurney and Henry Nicholls were Lessee and* *Tenant.* This Deed also had the date 1st September, 1832.

Having just about put all in order, the above Deed completely threw me! Where *could* there be a burial ground with a road to the south, except the Cholera ground, yet that does not have a burial ground to its north, only Trungle moor! Thirty-seven poles of land is about a quarter of an acre, it is mystifying! I think the answer could be that the Cholera ground was bought in two lots, i.e. 29th April, 1817 and another 37 poles on 21st May, 1832. A 'Dry Meadow' taken from the 'Dead Orchard', and probably ending up with both!
To give some idea of area - 30¼ square yards = 1 pole; 40 poles = 1 rood; and 4 roods = 1 acre.

On 19th May, 1854 in The Sentence of Consecration – Revd. Charles George Ruddock Festing, stated that the last Census recorded Paul's population to be 5,408 and was increasing rapidly. Thus Elizabeth Richards widow of Cyprian Richards sold three roods of land on 18th May, 1852, being *'the eastern part of a field called 'The Churchtown Field' of the Manor of Brewinney No.* *1031 on the Tithe map',* to Paul Church for the use of its parishioners as a burial ground. Revd. W. O. Gurney Solicitor of Trungle (Revd. Gurney was also a Paul Church Curate). So it seems three more roods of land behind the School were purchased in 1854.

P172/2/7 – 11th November, 1920 – Lawyer Mr. C. Aitken's Account of the purchase of land at Paul for enlarging of Sunday School burial ground, once Paul Day School, covering letter to Vicar of Paul Revd. H. Davy. I am not sure if this C. Aitken was Revd. Aitken's son, but he asked Revd. Davy if he may be buried in this area.

10th December, 1920 Field No. 958 on O.S. map (Paul burial ground on east of this field) - one acre, three roods fourteen perches owned by Mr. Joseph Hocking Pengelly, in occupation of William Phillips westernmost part of field 958 plot of land and outbuilding.

A boundary stone was fitted by a Mr. Henry Maddern, Architect of Morrab Road, Penzance on 11th October, 1922. Mr. J.H. Pengelly made the purchase of the final piece of the School Burial

Ground, on behalf of the Church, for a sum of £200. The land was at the bottom eastern side of the above field, No. 958. This debt in the form of a mortgage, taken out by Paul Church, John James Hutchens and George Edward Jenkin (probably Churchwardens), was eventually repaid on 25th March, 1926. On 31st December, 1923, a Conveyance was drawn up for this extension to the School Burial ground. Mr. J. H. Pengelly of Bellowal, farmer, Frederick Charles Jenkins and William Nicholls the younger, and Jane Hutchens. *'For a piece of land for Ecclesiastical Purposes - 3 roods, 21 perches or thereabouts being part of a field No. 958 on OS Map.'*

31st December, 1925 Conveyance of a piece of land near the Churchtown of Paul – J. H. Pengelly to the Diocesan Authority of the Diocese of Truro.

Burial Ground	£98.12.3d
7 months interest @ 5%	£2.17.7d
TOTAL	**£101.9.10d**

Bishop Walter Howard Frere of Truro duly consecrated this land on 19th May, 1926, together with another plot of the Municipal Burial ground as mentioned below. Ref: Diocese of Truro Patent Book in C.R.O.

On 26th October, 1926 a new mortar and clay built Cornish hedge was to enclose the School Burial Ground measuring 96ft 6inches long. On 26th March, 1926 the hedge was built to conform with the western boundary, and on 8th February, 1938 the School Burial Ground was dug over and cleaned up. In 1924 there was damage on 2nd May, in the School Burial Ground by *'fowls'* belonging to W. Hocking.

7th February, 1955 – Faculty under Revd. Davy, for removal of tombstones to walls.

24th January, to 1st August, 1956 Faculty to widen the pathway in the burial ground opposite the Church of Paul by the removal of *one row of graves with curbs and headstones,* and to place the headstones against the nearby wall. Bishop Edmund.

On 2nd September, 1977 under Revd. Cadman there was a Faculty for changing the wrought iron gates to the School Burial Ground to those in honour of Queen Elizabeth II's Silver Jubilee.

Faculty 9/79 An old Burial Ground was used for at least 30 years, but in 1971 Penwith District Council demolished the enclosing hedge – Faculty to resume the situation as Burial Ground up to 1971. *Same Faculty* - 13th July, 1979 Conversion of old churchyard into park and landscaped area. The 'School' (Church Hall) burial ground is a most beautiful and peaceful burial ground, overlooking the sea of Mount's Bay, St. Michael's Mount and the countryside.

On early maps of the School Burial Ground, the building to the right of the entrance is shown as standing inside the Burial Ground area, but today the wall has been moved so that it stands in a garden of a bungalow. This area of garden would once have been the garden of the U.D.C. offices, now a dwelling house, home of Mick Hudnott (choir member and bell ringer), in the Church car park. The bungalow was built on part of the garden of Mick Hudnott's house today.

Joseph Trewavas

As mentioned in Chapter 7, inside the Church on the north aisle wall is a tablet dedicated to the memory of local hero Joseph Trewavas, V.C. The dedication took place on 26th June, 2002. Among the congregation were family members, civil dignitaries and members of the Royal British Legion and ex-service organisations. A tribute was given by Vice-Admiral Sir James Jungius K.B.E. (Vice Lord Lieutenant and President Cornwall Royal British Legion) and a floral tribute on behalf of Her Majesty Queen Elizabeth was laid by Lady Mary Holborow (Lord Lieutenant and Patron Cornwall Royal British Legion).

Joseph was born in Mousehole on 14th December, 1838 and joined the Royal Navy at Devonport at the age of 18. A full description of his deed of valour is on Paul Church website: (www.paulchurch.co.uk).

The above Service took place exactly 145 years after Queen Victoria herself pinned the V.C. on the breast of Able Seaman Joseph Trewavas in Hyde Park. The plaque is erected in the north aisle of Paul Church as, although Joseph Trewavas is buried in Paul Churchyard somewhere, the exact place of his interment is not known, it is just described as 'a quiet corner of the cemetery'. His funeral was fitting for a Cornish hero, and was attended by 2,000 people who lined the route of the cortege from Mousehole to Paul. The procession left the house at 3.00 p.m. and slowly made its way up the hill to Paul Church. It was described as *'nearly a mile long'* of those who had come to pay their respects to this brave local man. Captain Runella with a detachment of Paul & Penzance Artillery Volunteers walked in the procession, and the Church was full to capacity for the *'very impressive'* Service.

William Curnow (1809-1887)

Is buried in the Church Hall Churchyard. He was is described as a 'Gardener and Botanist'. He was an expert on mosses and liverworts, and was recognised as such by leading botanists. He recorded the various species of each that he found. He was baptised at Madron, and his parents were John Curnow and Ann Crewes. He lived at Pembroke Cottage in Newlyn, and his son William lived at Trungle Farm, Paul. He was married three times: to Sophia Ladner, Susan Wright Harvey and Harriet Rogers, and had two sons.

Municipal Burial Area

The Cemetery adjacent to the old Seawallis School was taken over in 1936, when Paul and Newlyn were amalgamated into the Borough of Penzance. There are 5,026 headstones in this burial ground (pre-2004). The Vestry of the Church complained to the District Council that this area had not been consecrated. This eventually happened, on 19th May, 1926, when Bishop Walter Howard Frere of Truro came to Paul and consecrated both this additional burial ground as well as the new part of the School or Church Hall Burial Ground. In 2006, a new portion of land, next to the main plot of Penwith District Council's Paul Cemetery, has been prepared as an extension.

Confusingly Revd. Cadman wrote *'In 1868 the School or Higher Cemetery/Graveyard measured 2 roods 15 perches'*. I am not sure where he got this piece of information; one presumes this is the Municipal Cemetery.

Dolly Pentreath – a renowned local Celebrity

Dolly Pentreath

It is said that the funeral of Dolly Pentreath, who died in 1777, aged 102, was interrupted for a 'whisky break!' A old Cornish newspaper describes her funeral thus:

"At Dorothy's funeral there were eight chosen bearers to take her to her last resting place. Those were Whiskey and Friskey days. They had got the corpse up as far as Watering Lane – near Lynwood from Mousehole where she lived – on the way to Paul Church and there the bearers made a halt, protesting that they would not budge another inch until they had something to drink. A bottle of gin was produced; this having been drunk and discussed, the old lady was marched off with every solemnity."

Dolly used to sell fish in Mousehole, and her fame, when haggling in Cornish, spread before her. It was said that she was a married lady with the name of Jeffery, but she preferred to use her maiden name of Pentreath. However, Mr. W. T. Hoblyn searched the Paul Marriage Records and failed to find any record of her marriage. He thought she may be Dorothy Crankan who married Nicholas Pentreath 1706/7, or Dorothy daughter of Nicholas and Joan Pentreath baptized at Paul 16th May, 1692. A Mr. John Halse also writes:

'Dolly Pentreath never married and died in the house opposite the 'Keigwin Arms' on 27 December 1777, probable age - 90.' He also put Nicholas and Joan Pentreath as Dolly's parents, and apparently a rhyme was about at that time:

'Said Dolly: I can not see why, any curious or quizzing Paul pry, should wish to enquire of my dame or sire—my secret. No use. Let it Lie!'

The monument to her credits her with being the last person to speak (and apparently) swear, in the Cornish language. However Dolly Pentreath was the last ***monoglot speaker*** of Cornish, but not the very last person to speak Cornish.

A chap called John Davy (1812-1893) of Zennor is a strong contender for this title. He was born after Dolly's death, and was the last to possess a considerable knowledge of the Cornish language. Today, 2006, it has been estimated that 3,500 people speak Cornish at a basic level, with 500 fluently; that is more than at any time in the last 25 years. Although Dolly is buried in the immediate churchyard, there is no record of the exact location of her burial. She is entered in the burial register as *'Dolly Jeffery buried 27th December, 1777'*.

Her monument, in the form of an obelisk set in the Churchyard wall, bears a text from Exodus, and a transcription of the fifth Commandment 'Honour thy Father and thy Mother' in old Cornish. It was erected at the expense of Prince Louise Napoleon, in June 1860, who had a keen interest in languages, and was the nephew of Napoleon Bonaparte.

The Revd. J. Garrett (described as 'Vicar of St. Paul') also assisted in the monument's erection. The Cornish Telegraph dated 25th December, 1877 describes the method of her commemoration:-

"An interesting meeting is expected to be held next Wednesday (27.12.1877) at Paul, where the ancient Cornish language died out about one hundred years ago in the town of Mousehole. The funeral of the last person who is believed to have spoken Cornish is known to have taken place on 27th December, 1777 at Paul Churchyard by the record in the Parish registers. The actual day of her death is unknown, but probably December 26th is as near as can be guessed. There proceedings of the centenary will be varied. They will commence with a regular Cornish tea. After this there will be speeches in the ancient language, varied with the old Cornish songs and carols bringing back the times of 'the old men' and giving a popular character to the meeting. By the kind help of friends, the charge of entry will be hardly the cost of the tea, so that rich and poor alike, if interested in the subject, may be able to attend."

The Meeting was addressed by the Revd. Lach-Szyma; W. C. Borlase was in the Chair and thanks were given by Mr. D. P. Le Grice. Apologies were given by Mr. Henry Jenner.

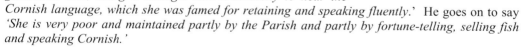

Cornish (Kernewek) shares basic vocabulary – 80% with vocabulary made up of Breton; 75% with Welsh; Irish 35%; and Scots Gaelic, 35%. Apparently, when Dolly Pentreath spoke Cornish, it sounded very much like Welsh according to Hon. Daines Barrington, who researched the ending of the Cornish language in 1768. In a letter to John Lloyd he describes Dolly thus:

'*Dolly Pentreath is short of stature and bends very much with old age, being in her eighty-seventh year, so lusty, however, as to walk hither to Castle Horneck (about three miles) in bad weather in the morning and back again. She is somewhat deaf, but her intellect seemingly is not impaired; has a memory so good that she remembers perfectly well that about four or five years ago at Mousehole, where she lives, she was sent for by a gentleman who, being a stranger had a curiosity to hear the Cornish language, which she was famed for retaining and speaking fluently.*' He goes on to say '*She is very poor and maintained partly by the Parish and partly by fortune-telling, selling fish and speaking Cornish.*'

She is reputed to have been 102 when she died and her last words are supposed to have been '*Me ne vidn cewsel Sawnek*' - '*I don't want to speak English*'. This phrase is very similar to one reported to have been spoken by the Cornish people during the Reformation, when the Latin Mass was taken from them, and English Services were held (see Chapter 10).

M. Tomson of Truro wrote Dolly Pentreath's epitaph, but it was never inscribed on her tomb, for when she was buried no tombstone was set up for her. This was erected later in 1860, as reported above.

The epitaph was:

> *'Old Doll Pentreath, one hundred aged and two,*
> *Deceased and buried in Paul Parish too,*
> *Not in the Church with people great and high,*
> *But in the Churchyard doth old Dolly lie.'*

This epitaph echoes the comments I made in Chapter 8 on Burials, that those interred in the church had, in death, the appearance of a higher social status than those buried outside.

The following is a comment on the Cornish tongue, from a letter written by the Revd. Lach-Szyrma, Vicar of St. Peters, Newlyn:

'John Keigwin was the last educated man at that time able to speak Cornish and the first to translate his County's literary relics. Edward Lluyd, the keeper of the Ashmolean Museum, a zealous Celtic scholar utilised his labours. Paul Parish and St. Just were the last two strongholds of the Cornish language. The reason is manifest for both were remote from the rest of England. The Fishing Industry of Paul and the mining of St. Just kept together the last speakers of the language. It at last narrowed down to Newlyn and Mousehole, where a few old people still chattered in their old Celtic tongue. Maybe the enthusiasm of John Keigwin for his native tongue inspired a few people of Mousehole to keep up their dying language when it had been silenced elsewhere. Without him, the old Cornish language would have been hopelessly lost, up until his time no interest was taken in the dying tongue.'

Cut into the stone on this memorial is the fifth Commandment:

'Honour thy Father and thy Mother that thy days may be long upon the land which the Lord thy God giveth thee.' Exodus XX 12.

In Cornish:-

> *' Gwra Perthi de Taz Ha de Mam Mal de Dythiow*
> *Bethenz Hyr War An Tyr Neb An Arleth de Dew Ryes*
> *Dees.'*

Dolly Pentreath Memorial—
Paul Churchyard wall
Photo reproduced by kind permission of
Mr. Richard Pentreath

CHAPTER 14 - GLEBE TERRIERS OF PAUL CHURCH & PARISH BOUNDARIES

Glebe Terriers were inventories of Church property; the word 'glebe' comes from the Latin word 'gleba' meaning literally clod of earth. The Glebe lands were plots of land belonging or yielding profit to a Parish Church or Ecclesiastical Office. These for Paul Church are set out exactly as they were written:

Glebe Terrier – 25th March, 1680

House: The Antient house belonging to sayd vicarage consistinge of many rooms was wholely burnt and demolished by Certaine Spanish Invaders about yeare 1595 of which sayd house some parte was Reedifyed and some part left ever since in the Ruines. 'In the late troubles' the then Vicar 'being sequestred and Removed' it became wholly Ruinous and dilapidated and soe remain to the present Incumbent. At present he has repaired at his own charge only 2 ground roomes covered with thatch, the kitchen and adjoining room at the West end.

Glebe: Three gardens and a little court *'with waste places to make fuell on'*, which with the old wales (walls) and Ruines contain ½ acre bounded on the West by the Churchyard and on the South by the Highway to Mousehole on the North by lands of John Keigwin, the whole being in the form of a triangle narrowing towards the East.

Payments: £2.2s formerly due from the Monastery of Hayles now due from 'his Majesties Revenues' to the vicarage. Signed Vicar John Smith, John Harry and John Tonkin, Churchwardens, 25th March, 1680.

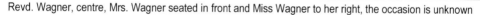

Revd. Wagner, centre, Mrs. Wagner seated in front and Miss Wagner to her right, the occasion is unknown

Author's Note: I have seen the following Glebe Terrier, it is very fragile, and not very legible. It is virtually the same as the 1727 Terrier; one was probably based on the other, as they are not usually produced at one year intervals:

Glebe Terrier - dated 1726 in C.R.O. ref: X.573/260

Vicarage House lately built consists of five ground floor rooms about 14 ft square and some of deal board and the rest of earth. Six chambers 4 x 14ft square. Two somewhat less. Bounded by the North and South by the lands of James Keigwin and on the South by the Highway and West Churchyard (sic). There are 14 Ash trees of no great value.

> Marrying – 2/6d Burying – 1/- Churching 1/- Mortuaries scrupled.

Furnishings decent there is no Clock.

Signed: Henry Pendarves   Richard Marrack and Richard Pearce
          Vicar   Churchwardens

James Keigwin, Phil Tywarthedreath, William Hopkin, William Kelynack, Oliver Hoskin, Bernard Yoome. At the bottom it states: '*A new Terrier was delivered in 1746, however this should be preserved and lodged with the Vicar, a copy of the 1680 Terrier, the same*'.

Glebe Terrier – dated April 1727

House: Lately built – 5 Ground rooms each 14ft square, one deal floored, remainder earth floored – 6 chambers of which 4 are about 14ft square other 2 somewhat less. A Study – no rooms wainscoted or ceiled – roofed with heling stones. Stables reed thatched.

Glebe: 2 Gardens and small orchard about ½ acre without commons, bounded on East and North by land of James Keigwin, Esq., On the South by the highway, and on the West by the Churchyard in which stands about 14 ash trees of no great value.

Payments: A pension of £2.2s Fee Farm Rents in Devon and Cornwall, when and by how is not known to us, and no deed or memorial being found among us, paid to the present Incumbent for the last 45 years.

Tithes: All small tithes except fish, which goes to the impropriator paid in kind or composition.
Fees: Marriages – 2/6d Burials – 1/-, Churchings – 1/-, 'Mortuaries Scrupled'.
Furnishings: 'Decent' – No Clock, '*The Bells are now sent to Gloucester to be new cast*' a silver flagon inset 'the gift of Mrs. P. Hutchens, widow', of about 3 quarts weight, weighing 5 lbs ¼oz – a silver cup of 1 quart, and 2 silver salvers each about the same weight; also 2 old pewter flagons.

Church: No money or stock for its repair. Church and Churchyard repaired by the Parish.
Signatories: Vicar Henry Pendarves, Richard Marrack and Richard Pearce Churchwardens, James Keigwin, Phillip Tregurther, William Hoskin, Martin Bodinar, Oliver Hosken, Bernard Heamon, Will Kelynack, April, 1727.

I located a further Glebe Terrier in 2004, the original being placed by unknown hands in Bangor University Archives, in Wales. Ref: Mss. 26929, in 1977. It seems very odd that an original document of Paul Church dating from 1746 should be in a Welsh University archive. Bangor University staff were very helpful, and once I had located the Terrier they agreed to let me have a copy which is now in the C.R.O. Being a curious person, I tried to find out how this document, belonging to Paul Church, was in Wales; however when I asked those in the University, I was informed that they could tell me the date of deposit, but the depositor was protected by the Data Protection Act. It all remains a mystery! Here is the copied document:-

A Terrier of the Vicarage House, the Glebe, the Church and Churchyard

Of the Parish of Paul in the Hundred of Penwith in the County of Cornwall: made and taken at the Command of the Right Reverent Father in God, Nicholas, Lord Bishop of Exon, 26th April, 1746.

1953   The Induction of the Revd. D. Davey - Richard Drew and Lionel Spargo, Churchwardens

The Vicarage House (the Walls whereof are Built with Stone) consists of six ground rooms, four of which are about 14 feet square, the other two somewhat less; one Roome is floor'd with Deal, one with Lime Ashes, the rest with Earth; and of six Chambers; four whereof are about 14 feet square the other two somewhat less, neither of which Ground Rooms or Chambers is Wainscotted. There is likewise a Small Closett. The whole house is covered with Healing Stones. There is a small Stable covered with Reed.

The Glebe; consists of two Gardens and a Court Adjoining to the Stable. The whole (house and all) containing half an acre, with right of Commons. It is bounded on the West by the Church Yard on the south by the Highway that leads to Mousehole, and on the East and North by the lands of Mrs. Joan Hutchens (or her daughter(s)) growing narrower towards the East. The whole being somewhat in the form of a Triangle. On the Church Yard and Glebe there are a few ash and sycamore trees of no great value.

There is a pension of £2.2.0d., yearly paid to the Vicar by the *Receiver Generall* of his Majesty's rents in the County of Devon and Cornwall; when or by whom given is not known to us, no Deed or Memorial being to be found among us. ALL small *Tyths* (except fish which is said to be Impropriated to the Rectory) paid in kind or by composition. (Tithes - see Chapter 11.)

The Surplice fees are for Marrying – 5/- , for Burying – 1/-, for Churching of Women – 1/- and *Mortuarys* payable.

The furniture of the Church and Chancell is decent. There are three good Bells, but no Clock. The Communion Plate consists of one silver flagon or Chalice with this Inscription:-
'*Paul, the Gift of Mrs. Penelope Hutchens widow of this Parish 1712*'. It holds about three quarts, and weighs 60 oz and 15 pennyweights. And two silver Salvers the largest of which weighs 10 oz and 18 pennyweights. The smallest 7 oz and 18 pennyweights. The Cup and Salvers have this inscription: viz: '*Ex don Maria Pearce uxoris Ricardi Pearce de Kerris given 24th December, Anno Domini 1696*'. There are also two old useless Pewter Flaggons.

There is no money or Stock for the reparation of the Church, which (Except the Chancell) is with the fences of the Church Yard repaired at the Expense of the Parish. The Clerk is appointed by the Vicar, the Sexton by the Vicar, and the Parish jointly; their wages respectively paid by the Parish; the former hath four pounds, the other three pounds a year.

Signed by Henry Penneck Vicar, Abraham Chirgwin and Thomas Bodinnar Churchwardens, George Keigwin, Richard Marrain, John Harry, William Hopkins. *Copyright of University of Bangor, Wales MSS 26929.*
In addition the above: 1695 - Silver Flagon weighing 60 oz – valued by W. B. Mitchell, Jewellers in January 1971 - £1,000 – (taken from a note found in the Vestry).

It is interesting that although Edmund Earl of Cornwall gave the 'Rectory' or advowson of Paul to Hailes Abbey', out of this they gave the Vicar of Paul financial gain, maybe in time of need. This fact was incomprehensible to the two Vicars, the Revds. Henry Pendarves and Henry Penneck. The two guineas were paid to them by the Crown (because the Abbey of Hailes became Crown property, at the Reformation); the Crown continued paying this 'fee farm rent' to the Vicar of Paul (see Chapter 11 - 'Tithes').

Although, in the past at Paul Church there was such an amazing array of church plate, and seemingly Paul was a rich Parish, there did not seem to be any money left for repairs, and the people were left to find the money as best they could, so really nothing changes! Often if the advowson of the church belonged to a local Lord of the Manor, he was held responsible for repairing the chancel but, in the case of Paul Church, it was the people who had to repair their chancel and church.

PARISH BOUNDARIES – founded A.D. 500-1200

Paul Church and Parish first belonged to the Earl of Cornwall, as did eight other Cornish Parishes. Parish size was based on the length of time it took the Priest to circumnavigate on horse-back, or foot, to visit and administer to the newly born or the dying. A medium Parish would be approximately three miles across. There was no helpful information on Parish size or shape in the Glebe Terriers in the early 1600s.

The Parish of Paul once included part of Newlyn, and before the creation of the Parish of Newlyn St. Peter in 1851, Paul Parish bordered that of Madron, the Mother Church of Penzance. The new Church of St. Peter, was built on Newlyn Coombe, and its boundaries stretched up Chywoone Hill to the North of Tredarvoe Lane.

Description of the Boundary - (ref: C. Aitken 1910)

The Boundary of Paul extends north east from the Tolcarne Stream following the coast to Mousehole, then along to Pyzarra Point, from thence goes south to Carn Dhu (black rock) then down a steep drop to Lamorna stream which separates the Parishes of Paul and St. Buryan. Thence up the valley to the wood below Bijowans (this marks the western point of the Parish), and follow the highway to Stable Hobba and down into Newlyn – this is the general limit of the Parish of Paul.

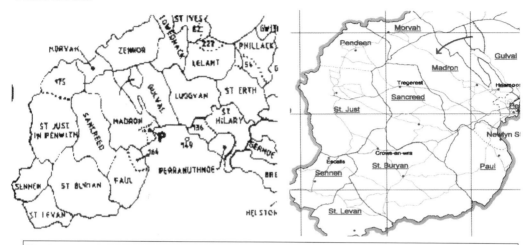

The Map above left is copyright Cornwall Record Office, taken from the Cornish Parish map (note the new Parish of St. Peters - 366 - taken out of old Paul Parish) and the Map on the right is copyright West Penwith Resources (www.west-penwith.org.uk/wpenmap.html)

CHAPTER 15-THE POOR HOUSE OF PAUL, CHURCH HALL, HUTCHENS' HOUSE

Removal Order

From the Middle Ages there were strict laws about aid for the poor. The wandering poor were seen as a threat and a financial burden. There were repeated Acts which tried to control them, and ensure that they were sent back to their home Parish if they became financially dependent through age, or infirmity, or unemployment in another.

Settlement and removal entries in the quarter session papers are found in C.R.O. archives. During research, I was lucky enough to encounter a Removal Order in the Dorset Record Office, which relates to a poor family of Piddletown in Dorset who arrived in Paul, in 1819, but had to be removed and transported back, to be supported by their Dorset Parish. The family consisted of:

> 'Richard Riggs, Elizabeth his wife, and Elizabeth aged about five years,
> and Susanna aged about two years, their children'.

The family were accused of arriving at Paul, with no legal right of settlement in the Village. They did not produce any Certificate owning them to be settled elsewhere. The document states that two Justices of the Peace required:

'The said Churchwardens and overseers of the Poor of the said Parish of Piddletown, to receive and provide for them as Inhabitants of your said Parish according to the Statutes in such case made and provided' This Order dated 7th May, 1819.

Paul came under the Penzance District called a 'Union' – and poor local people were sent to a small workhouse in Penzance, until the Madron Workhouse opened in 1839. However, there is a Deed for some land for a Poor House of Paul; an exciting recent find, it still exists being now called 'Trungle Moor Cottages'. The Deed is dated 28th December, 1844, in the reign of King William IV re an Indenture of a Lease dated 1st September, 1832 – and names Joseph Carne, James Halse, Robert Matthews and Cyprian Richards who did:-

 'grant, demise and Lease unto Thomas Leah & John Downing the then Churchwardens and Richard Davey Chirgwin, William Matthews, William Harvey and Thomas Wallis the then Overseers of the Parish of Paul...... for the purpose of Building a Poor House and other conveniences for the reception, habitation and residence of the Poor of the said Parish of Paul.........in all that piece or plot of ground situate in the Parish of Paul near the Church Town thereof ....parcel of the waste or unenclosed Lands commonly called Brewinney Common belonging to the Manor & Lordship of Brewinney containing Sixty Poles or thereabout bounded on the East by the enclosed Lands of the said Joseph Carne ...by another part of the Common on the South by the enclosed Lands of the said James Halse...West – by the Common and on the north by a carriage road or Highway then marked out and ...agreed to be formed and made by Thomas Leah, John Downing, Richard Davey Chirgwin William Matthews, William Harvey and Thomas Wallis, leading from the said Church Town over the Common of Brewinney.'

It continues stating that these people, the Churchwardens and Overseers of the Poor of Paul Parish from the date above, for the term of 999 years be subject to payment of annual rent of five shillings. It then states: 'the said Poor House with other erections have been duly erected

Trungle Moor Cottages once Paul Parish Poor House

and built on the said piece or plot of ground...the guardians (as above) plus James Richards and Thomas Edmonds the Churchwardens, John Rowe, John Boase and Peter Harvey Overseers of the Poor in Paul Parish do grant and lease all that Dwelling House and Premises with the Garden or plot of Ground attached thereto situate in or near the Church Town of Paul...

The above Deed definitely sets the position of the Poor House. This building was actually divided into cottages all in a row, each with its own wash house and privy in outbuildings in a line behind, together with an allotment of land stretching out in front. The terrace was divided into two, back to back, with one room up and one down for each occupant with a corridor from the end house leading through all the others, provided for the Overseer.

Each of the occupants had a long narrow stretch of land on which to grow fruit and vegetables and keep chickens or a pig. Today Chris and Jane Osborne's bungalow is actually sitting on part of the Poor House allotments site. The Highway mentioned in the Deed is the unmade path leading to Sheffield from the road through Paul, up through Trungle Moor. The Poor House appears on the Tithe Map of 1844, and is named in the Apportionment.

In the burial registers there are references to people who died '*in the Poor House*', and before I knew of the existence of the above I thought they meant Hutchens' House; however that was always known as '*the Gift House*', '*Almshouse*' or '*Hutchen's Clift*'. The Poor House was not probably used for very long, as once Madron workhouse was constructed many families would have moved there; in fact, as early as 1880, it appears on an O.S. map as 'Trungle Moor Cottages'.

Old Deeds are very confusing: in the narrative of this one, the Churchwardens changed from Thomas Leah and John Downing (1832) to James Richards and Thomas Edmonds, who were probably Churchwardens in 1844! '*The Churchwardens were the Overseers of the Poor in St. Paul.*'

Linked to the above is yet another Deed dated 21st March, 1845, a year after the Poor House was built, for 1¼ acres, part of Brewinney, '*a parcel of the Charity lands*' drawn up by Edward

Kelynack, Thomas Carvosoe, *'remaining Trustees of the Paul Charity Lands for the maintenance of certain poor people in the Parish of St. Paul'* and William Tonkin and William Lanyon (labourer) who occupied this land. Then the lengthy jargon citing the land follows, which is near the Poor House and is a Deed for mining rights *' to dig and search for tin, copper, lead ores, or stone'* on the land after yearly rent of one pound to the Poor of Paul.

The Poor Law Act of 1834 attempted to prevent paupers and their families from suffering deprivation, although the life in the workhouse as illustrated by Charles Dickens left a lot to be desired.

On 9th April, 1922, the Poor House premises were converted into ordinary dwelling houses - *'all that dwellinghouse and premises with garden lately used for the reception and habitation of the Poor'*.

Formerly they were six (and once seven), dwelling houses, gardens, stables, (outhouses) and then they were known as nos. 1, 2, 3, 4, 5, and 6 Trungle Moor, Paul.

The poor and aged folk were well catered for in Paul, thanks to Captain Stephen Hutchens, who provided Hutchens' House almshouses, standing next to the Church. There is a slate panel to this effect on the south east side of Hutchens' House which states:

'Ex Dono Ducis Stephani Hutchens- Anno Domini 1709 –Arma Virumque cano' The first words of The Aeneid by Virgil (70-19 BC): – *'Arms I sing, and the man, who first from the shores of Troy came Fate-exiled, to Italy and Lavinian strand, Much Buffeted he on flood and field by constraint Of heaven and fell Juno's slumbering ire.'*

The parallels may now be seen. Stephen Hutchens was embroiled in wars not of his own choosing, in a far off sea longing for his homeland, yet died aged only 40, before he could return to see his beloved Cornwall.

In 1854 these were the inhabitants of 'Hutchens' Clift –another name in 1841 Census for the Almshouses:-

Sally Rosewarren was the Matron, and the residents were: Nicholas Hosking 79, Joseph Pollard 72, William Richards 72, William Cattran 72, Thomas Matthews 82, Catherine Murrish 72, Leah Roberts 68, Alice Richards 73, Jane Dennis 52 and Mary J. Tippet age 43.

PAUL SCHOOL, WHICH BECAME THE CHURCH HALL

Paul Church Hall is used for all Church and Village activities. It is situated across the road from the Church on the 'Manor of Brewinney'. It was built in or around 1825 as one of the village schools, and used to be called the 'School Hall', or 'Paul Day School', as well as the rather grand 'Paul National Academy'; and it also doubled as Paul Church 'Sunday School' (c. 11th November, 1920).

PAUL SCHOOL - 1900 - pupils sitting outside the Council Office

Here follows the reference for the Deed of purchase of the land on which to build Paul School; interestingly, two Clergymen of Paul, the Revds. C. Valentine le Grice, and Warwick Oben Gurney, were involved. One was Vicar and the other Curate. The Revd. Gurney was probably acting as the Solicitor in this case, as he did in other deeds. The other interesting person surprisingly involved is H. P. Tremenheere, the painter of the watercolours in Chapter 3:-

2/13 £4 demise for 1000 years 1. Cyprian Richards, Paul yeoman 2. Henry Pendarves Tremenheere. Revd., Charles Valentine Le Grice, Revd. Warwick Oben Gurney. The Purchase of land for erection of School House. Part of field adjoining Bowling Green in Paul Church Town 54 feet x 24 feet wide – 4 Poles of land with School House erected on land. Richard Pentreath Schoolmaster 4th June 1825.

Victory Celebrations — 8th May, 1945

In 1828 when there was a terrific storm, the Church roof and walls were so badly damaged that the School Hall was temporarily licensed for 'Divine Service', as the church was considered too dangerous to use. (More details are in Chapter 3.) The licence cost 30/- and came from Exeter. As you can see in the above photo of the Victory (VJ) Celebrations in 1945, the car park area in front of the Village Hall was once just grass, and had been, in the past, a Bowling Green.

There were some lean-to areas, described as 'sheds', before the extension was erected. The Hall was the subject of a painting by an artist called Elizabeth Forbes (Armstrong), who was married to the painter Stanhope Forbes. Both were members of the 'Newlyn School' of artists.

On 31st July, 1928 'damp walls' were recorded. In 1912 the Hall supported a Girls' Club on Fridays, and in 1912 there was a Men's Club that met nightly until 10.00 p.m. in the Hall, with a billiards table that belonged to the Church. Mr. Osborne attended the Club and reported back to the P.C.C. making sure everything that went on was correct!

The P.C.C. of that year (1933) whitewashed the Hall walls and made repairs. Also in 1933 there existed 'Paul Bank' which used a room in the Hall, and Mrs. Tippet was its cleaner. On 8th January, 1931 the Hall was given three new electric lights. In 1920 it was reported as '*once*' being a Day School, as gradually all the children had been transferred to '*Seawallis School*', or the Paul Board School, constructed in 1883 at a cost of £800 next to the Municipal Burial Ground.

Paul Church is very lucky to have such a magnificent Hall for all activities, including the provision of lavatories for the ease of those attending Church Services; plus a well-equipped kitchen, in the extension. The Hall was restored and re-opened by Rt. Revd. Bill Ind, Bishop of Truro on 10th December, 2000. The restoration was funded by Bequests kindly given by Josephine Passfield, Margaret Baliol Beagley and Sydney A. Kneebone, together with a Grant from Penwith District Council and Church Funds 'For Church and Community'.

Paul Church Hall 2006

HUTCHENS' HOUSE

Mention must also be made of the 'Gift House' or 'Hutchens' House' that stands by the Church.

It was erected in 1709 by means of £600 bequeathed by Captain Stephen Hutchens (see Chapter 7 for memorial details), for the purpose of building an Alms House for the Poor of the Parish.

In 1961, under the Revd. Tyrrell, Hutchens' House was re-opened after extensive modernisation, being re-named 'Hutchens' House' instead of 'Hutchens' Alms Houses'. The bedrooms previously only had wooden screens between them with latch doors to each one, and the accommodation was definitely more primitive.

In the photo below, to the right by the door, is the tail section of a 550 lb. German bomb which fell on open ground in Paul, and thankfully failed to explode. Inverted, it was in use as a flower-pot!

Hutchens' House was again modernised, re-constructed and re-opened in 1995 under the Revd. G. Harper, and today, in 2006, yet further accommodation for the elderly of Paul is being constructed.

The Re-Opening in October 1961 by Mrs. Charles Williams, with Mr. Wright, Mr. H. Tonkin Vice Chairman, Mr. G. B. Drewitt Architect, Mrs. Mavis Lawry Mayoress, Mrs. Lilian Garston Lady Mayor, Mr. L. Tonkin Secretary, and the Revd. Tyrrell.

At this time Mr. & Mrs. Richard Pentreath were Caretaker and Matron of Hutchens' House, respectively. Mr. R. Pentreath was also Paul Church Verger.

Photos taken before the 1960 re-furbishment.

Note the above chimneys are of similar construction to those of Kerris Manor.

CHAPTER 16 – NOTES

In this chapter I am going to place all the interesting pieces of information that I have come across, and which do not really fit under any other headings, for instance:-
Just by the south door, on the left, there is a really lovely painting which surrounds the alms box. This was beautifully executed by Mrs. Ann Smelt in 1986.

Not everyone was well behaved in Paul Church as in the 18th century the following Citation was raised: *William Carey of Paul to appear at Bodmin Church on Friday 9th January, 1789, "touching and concerning his soul's health and the reformation and correction of his manners and excesses, and more especially for profanity entering the Parish Church of Paul aforesaid and behaving impiously, irreverently and profanely therein".*

Paul Church was unusual, in that there was once a Church Constable to keep order; the truncheons now hang on the back of one of the pillars in a glass case (photo, see Chapter 6). James Harvey had been sworn in before the Magistrate as the Church Legal Officer, and obviously made a good job of it as he was re-appointed to the Office of Constable, on 26th April, 1886.

An interesting fact - the Baptisms in Paul Church from 1595 (date of Spanish raid) to 1812 - total **8,423**.

Arthur Mee, the famous author of '*The Children's Encyclopaedia*', was poking about the outside of Paul Church in the 1930s, and wrote that he '*found ancient carvings on the exterior still visible, birds and flowers, over the door a rising sun with a face!*' Finding no signs today of what he saw, one can but wonder if he had the correct Church!

The three magnificent embroidered panels were made by Margrit Winkler and helpers, and were given to the church on 23rd July, 1995 before Margrit went to Switzerland.

In 1930 on 6th November oil-lamps were removed from the church, and electric light came to Paul Church. Before electricity, people had to take their own 'dips' to Evensong, to light their way.

Paul Church had a Girl Guide troop, led by the Vicar's daughter Miss Merelle Wagner; she also started a Brownies group in 1949. Pat Maddern was pack leader and Pauline Rhodda was Tawny Owl; other guides were Diane Carter (Bond) and Eileen Carne.

A note about Church services in the 1930s. As a rule, Evensong was the most well attended Sunday

Service, because most of the local farmers and their wives were working in the morning, so the morning services were mainly attended by the older folk. In the 1960s and 70s, Matins was the main service every Sunday, which was followed by a shortened Holy Communion at 12.00. On Christmas Day and Easter Day Holy Communion was at 7.30 a.m. and again at 8.30, the main Service being at 11.00 a.m.

Rogation-tide always included a procession to bless the fields; the choir and congregation processed to the river, through the fields to the Rhodda family Farm at Trevithal, and to Trungle. It was in 1969 during such a Rogation procession that a romance started, our Churchwarden, Mr. Roger Bond met Miss Diane Carter, and are happily married, and are now grand-parents.

The Harvest Evensong was a celebration for crops being safely gathered in, and was very popular with all, especially the local farming and fishing families. In the 1950s the church was often draped with fishing nets across the many iron bars present at that time. Fruit and flowers decorated the church in abundance; these were distributed to the older members of the parish, or to the sick. At the beginning of December there was a Service during which all children brought Christmas gifts to give to children in orphanages. The Service of Nine Lessons and

Carols was always held on the Sunday evening before Christmas, and marked the beginning of the Christmas festivities.

George Osborne and Eric Harvey were practical Churchwardens, and when a leak was discovered under the south entrance, they dug the stone steps out, and replaced them after the leak was repaired. Eric Harvey was very upset about the rattle of the latch of the door into the Church, so that when he died in 1986, new cast iron hangings were fitted, purchased from his memorial money, and what was left started the loop system for deaf people, as he had been hard of hearing.

George Osborne

Eric Harvey

Early in the 1970s two separate Missions from the Church Army came to Paul Church and stayed in the village. They wore uniforms and evangelised, inviting the congregation to come up to the altar after the Service, in the style of Billy Graham, the American Evangelist.

THE QUEEN'S SILVER JUBILEE 1977

Maypole dancing

Paul parishioners celebrated the Jubilee in style with a special Service at Truro Cathedral, Choir and congregations went to Truro in buses, and the Choir had special Jubilee badges to wear on their robes. There was a Jubilee Party in the car park, children decorated their bicycles in red white and blue, trestle tables were erected, and, as usual, Paul people brought mountains of food to share. Miss Morvah Stubbings was the Paul Jubilee Queen, and wore a

Maude Cotton Crowned Demelza Stubbings

green velvet gown – her attendants wore white and pink dresses. In 1990 on Feast Monday evening, there was a torchlight procession to celebrate many years of worship in Paul. The road was closed and the Service of Thanksgiving took place in the middle of the village. Hundreds of people came, and the Mousehole Male voice choir sang, followed by a hog roast in the car park.

Paul Feast Monday was a day that was always held in great affection by the children, as they were given sweets, and took part in races, with prizes. Different stalls were open and were very popular. The local West Penwith Hunt always met at the Kings Arms on Feast Monday; hundreds of people would turn up to watch this event ('Feast' see Chapter 4).

Ruth Glasson 1948

MAY QUEEN/ROSE QUEEN

Each year in Paul Village a Rose Queen is chosen. She used to be chosen in May as the May Queen but as the air temperature in May can be very cold, the celebration of Spring is moved to June and became the Rose Queen. The first remembered May Queen was Ruth Glasson (see photo) surrounded by her attendants in 1948.

There is a Procession of the Queen and attendants through the village to the Car Park where the crowning ceremony takes place, together with maypole dancing and a pasty supper. Today it starts at the Post Office, but this Procession used to commence at the gates of the Municipal Cemetery. As you can see above, girls and boys were paired together wearing their best clothes.

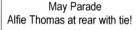
May Parade
Alfie Thomas at rear with tie!

Front couple: Paul Strick and Nicholette Thomas

PAUL CHURCH SUNDAY SCHOOL

Living memories of the 1920s Sunday School recall that it was run by Mr. Charlie Symons and Mr. Freddie Phillips, who took it in turns to be Superintendent. Among the first remembered voluntary teachers were Gertie Thomas, Iris Thomas and Gwennie Richards.
On 8th February, 1938 it was reported as being 'self-

Everyone dance!

supporting' and raised £20 for the year's work. Classes took place in the Church Hall in Paul Village and the children sat on forms, which were placed opposite each other, with an adjoining form at the

Sunday School

end for the teacher. The girls sat all the way down on one side of the room, and the boys on the other, in the sets governed by age.

In the 1920s there were more than one hundred children attending Sunday School, which was held at 2.00 p.m. on Sunday afternoons. In those days young children were not allowed into the Church Services; in fact, the first age that children were welcomed was seven or eight. The children attended Sunday School until they were fifteen, and then the youth of the church took part in organised concerts, plays, social evenings, pasty suppers, dances with live music bands, and they often had Magic Lantern shows in the School Room. There were huge Sunday School Christmas Parties, at which Eric Harvey wearing his big farming boots would play 'Father Christmas' and holler and somewhat scare the children!

There were actually two Sunday Schools attached to Paul Church, one as above, and one held in a Cadet's Hut at Gwavas in the playing field, which was run by

Sunday School, Christmas 1946

Mrs. King. The children of Gwavas Sunday School were marched up to Paul Church for Services.

In the 1950s to early 1960s, Mary Llewellyn ran the Sunday School with a Mr. Trimmer, who lived at Trevithal; Pat Maddern and Diana Carter (Bond) were his assistants. Mr. Trimmer was an older chap whose in-depth religious teaching sometimes was a little difficult for the children to understand. Mary was much loved as a teacher, and when she went to Australia in the late 1950s, there was a farewell party for her.

Paul Fete Baby Show in old Vicarage garden. Marian Harvey & Susan (Snell) back row end right. Mary Barnes & Margaret middle front row

At this time the children received stamps depicting religious figures for attending, which were pasted on a card. The child with the most stamps collected during the year received the prize of a book. The Revd. Tyrell set up a model railway upstairs in the Church Hall, in a Sunday School room; this was very popular. Sunday School Outings were much anticipated with glee; up to two coaches were filled with eighty or so children off to St. Ives Beach for the day.

Next, Mr. Alfie Thomas took over as Superintendent. Alfie lived in Lynwood Cottage on the Mousehole Road. He worked in an office at Newlyn harbour and ran the Sunday School for many years. Alfie Thomas' speciality was making figures out of shells, to sell and raise funds; some of these survive today. He always gave a box to the local hospital for the children. He was also famous for his puppets, and even used 'Sooty' and 'Sweep' puppets from behind the piano, to tell Bible stories. He is remembered as being a very kind man who often had sweets for the children. Mr. Thomas was assisted by Gwen Sleeman who took the little ones: Ethel Jones, Tom Penaluna, Leota Pearce, Annie – wife of Charlie Symons, Sue Snell, Betty Pitchers (Johns), Elizabeth Stubbings, and Margaret Spargo daughter of Lionel Spargo. Margaret used 'fuzzy felt' pictures to illustrate the stories of Jesus, much to the children's delight. Alfie died in the 1980s, during the Revd. Harper's incumbency.

Paul Church Sunday School attracted children from large local families, such as the Stevens of Trevithal, the Bodinaars, the Rogers, and many more who came from Paul Village. Among the many Sunday School children were:- Adrian Nicholas, William Matthews, Tony Burroughs, Tony Bennets, Reg Bennets, Reg Jefferies (he was killed in the Yemen, and is on the Roll of Honour in Church), Keith Gruzelier, Raymond Rule, Eileen Carne, Carol Carne, Gwyneth Williams, Maureen Phillips, Decima Carne, Margaret Spargo, Myra Phillips, Anne Kelynack, Marlene Ladner, John Waters, Jennie Cornish, Paul Strich, Roy and Chris Osborne, Hilda Osborne, John George, Keith Prowse, Denise Edie, Gregory Williams and Valerie Pentreath, to name but a few. These names that will be familiar to a lot of people, and will surely bring back memories.

In 1856 the Sexton of Paul Church was Joseph Penrose, and he lived in No.1 Mousehole Lane. Later the Sexton was Walter Carne, Brian Carne's Grandfather; he served Paul Church for forty years and lived in a wooden bungalow at Trevithal, but moved to the Kings Arms when Emily Harding was there to save himself from having to walk two miles to Paul.

The Car Park in front of the Church Hall was once the Bowling Green, and is mentioned as such on a Deed of 1825 for the School, now the Church Hall:- '*5th June, 1825 - Ground part of a field adjoining Bowling Green in Paul Church Town, 54 feet x 24 feet in width containing 4 poles of land together with School House erected on land'.*

In 1781, there was reputedly found an ancient gold ring, ½ inches in diameter, bearing the motto: '*In hac spe vivo'*, meaning: '*In this hope I live'* which is the motto of Pericles. This place is purported to be marked by the 'Ring & Thimble' a conical granite stone in the grass by the road from Sheffield to Penzance (more about the Ring and Thimble under Sir Rose Price in Chapter 10).

'Ring & Thimble'

Here follows an extract from a letter re: The Revd. W. O. Gurney, Curate of Paul Church 1802-1849, written by his nephew:-

'*Our holidays were spent at Paul, near Penzance with our Uncle Warwick, our Father's elder brother. He was perpetual Curate of the Parish of Paul with the fishing villages of Mouse-hole and Newlyn. He was also Vicar or Rector of a Parish near Bridgenorth besides. Here let me mention, lest **I should be thought irreverent, that***

Revd., Mrs. & Miss M Wagner, Churchwardens Lionel Spargo and Richard Drew and others

MOTHERS' UNION 1950—L-R Mrs. Wagner, Miss Pritchett, Ven. F. W. Bonham, Mrs. Phillips, Revd. Wagner, Mrs. Vickery, Miss M. Wagner

nobody called the Parish of Paul, St. Paul in those days whatever may be done now. We were happy at Paul, our Uncle was a kind but melancholy man, deeply inbred with Calvinism, and one who took his terrible creed to heart. Of right our Uncle should have been a cheerful man, for his life was blameless. Dear Uncle! How was it that he lived and died a believer? As we sat, my brother and I, in Paul Church listening to his eloquence – for that it was though he harped mainly on one string – and receiving his soul-appalling teaching, one of us at least shook in childish shoes. Many a time have we seen our Uncle pacing his garden whilst meditating, as we understood, the discourse which he was to preach without a book on the following Sunday. The garden abounded in the Spring with sweet peas, and yellow lupins, and sweet-briar, and sweet leaved tree verbenas. Our Uncle was fond of his eldest nephew taking pleasure in the boy's marked literary taste and would talk about books, though generally given to silence. He had foresworn literature on his own account, apprehending God's curse to be on it. Naturally his taste was that of a gentleman and scholar. I could tell more about him that I think would be interesting, but I forbear. The view from Paul garden over St. Michael's Bay was never eclipsed for us by any later scenes.

We had our cousins for companions at Paul, all older than us, and all, all passed away. Big Oben, the eldest son, was hearty and genial: John seemed to us to have low tastes for a De Gournay; and William was ever solemn and friendly. We got on well with our Aunt, whose own house, Trungle, was close at hand, and now for the girls. Nanny was bright and merry, and not a little pretty. Agnes was very sweet; she died early of consumption, in the spring.'
Here, unfortunately the letter ends, the last page is missing.

Faculty Causes for Paul Church - from the Devon Record Office - Pew Disputes

Exhibit A in the following Pew Dispute:
'No person erects seats or puts on locks in Paul Church who are not honest to keep their word.'
Paul – 26th July, 1790

From **28th August, 1790 to 6th May, 1791** – there raged a pew dispute between William Nicholls, Esquire of Trereife in Madron, and William Hitchens of Paul, Shopkeeper and Churchwarden. This was a lengthy and involved case. Apparently Nicholls obtained permission of the Incumbent and other Churchwarden to build a pew for himself and his tenants on a 'vacant plot of ground' in Paul Church. The pew was built by Henry Hosking of the Parish of Paul – a joiner, assisted by his son of twelve or thirteen.

According to Hosking, it stood in the south east corner in the north aisle of the Parish Church (other witnesses say south east corner, which is very vague and not helpful), and its construction began in May 1789. The pew door was not hung until the beginning of October when a lock was provided, and the key was given to Nicholls.

In the account by Hugh Murley who was the Sexton, the door had been locked in the tower on Hitchens' instruction to prevent the pew being completed. Hosking had only been able to complete the pew, and receive his payment for the work, because the Sexton's wife let him have the tower key. Hitchens, took matters into his own hands by tearing out the lock.

In his defence, Hitchens stated that William Nicholls had promised to give the parish permission 'to take down a certain piece of hedge belonging to the said William Nicholls…which projected into the road leading from the Village of Newlyn in the said Parish to the Parish Church of Paul, in order to widen and enlarge such Church Road for the better accommodation of the inhabitants of the said Parish, in their going to, and returning from, their said Church.'

However Nicholls had failed to keep his word or to apply for a Faculty for his pew. William Hitchens – Church Warden.

Exhibit B: William Nicholls Esquire, Trereife. – The outcome: Nicholls was found to be at fault.

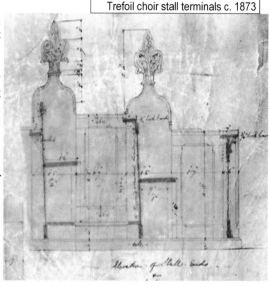

Trefoil choir stall terminals c. 1873

The Nicholls family of Trerife had previously owned a large portion of Paul Parish including Tredarvoe, Bollogas, Trewarveneth, Chywoone, Paul Downs, Trevelloe and Kerris Vean.

William Nicholls Senior ran into difficulties, whether because he supported the lost cause of the Stuarts, or simply over '*aggrandisement*' of life style is not clear, but in 1742 he was forced, by order of the Court of Chancery, to sell most of his lands at Paul. His son William re-purchased some of the other property, and with it Trewarveneth, however he sadly ended his days in prison, in Marshalsea London, due to a committal order for debt by the Court of the King's Bench. His wrangling over a Church pew seems to have cost him dearly, possibly with his life.

9th February – 28th July, 1791:

Another Faculty cause concerning the Nicholls pew was brought via William Hitchens by the tenants of William Nicholls' Barton of Trewarveneth. The tenants were John Hocken, William Lawes, John Selivan, William Roskilly, Melchisideck Bosence & William Cattran, the younger. There seems to have been a lot of people who would have occupied this pew, and if their families came too, they must have all been sitting on top of each other. It probably was a double pew where the occupants sat facing each other as in a train carriage. The pew measured 6 feet square and was four feet, nine inches high, and these tenants should have occupied it on Sundays, probably very squashed! No sooner had they become comfortable, when along came Sir Rose Price (more about him in the Chapter on Burials), and wanted to begin building in this same area of the Church.

8th February, 1798:

Sir Rose Price, of the Parish of Paul lodged a Petition to remove four seats, or pews, two of which were 15 feet in length and five feet eleven inches in breadth. The other two were seven feet eight inches in length by six feet in breadth. These were sited on the south side of the chancel and previously belonged to Richard Hosking (2), Frances Hitchens Jacka, and John Barnes. Sir Rose was '*desirous*' to take (these) down and rebuild (a new pew) for the use of himself and his family. This family pew would have then stood on top of his family vault, which is the custom, those living worshipped above their dead ancestors below.

There were bound to be other domestic squabbles about pews other than those reported and almost brought to litigation above, therefore at the 1873 restoration of Paul Church, on a proposed drawing was written:

'The entire West end and all the North Aisle seats will be declared to be free and appropriated'
However people continued to pay for the privilege of their own pews until at least the 1930s. Many of our older parishioners today remember paying for pews and in Chapter 3, I have reproduce a Receipt for Paul Church Pew Rents. The free seating area was at the back of the Church – some paid ones were in the south aisle, the first pews that were removed were those behind the font, when the altar and chapel was made in memory of Hilda Osborne.

People like to sit in Church where they feel comfortable in their 'own' pews, and one indomitable lady, Mabel Thomas, objected to being moved on Paul Feast Sunday and stated:
'I am not moving from my seat for no Councillors, this is my seat and I am staying here!'

Feet of Fines

The term "Fines" has its origin in the middle ages. After the Norman conquest, William the Conqueror took possession of all English property and all landowners became his tenants. If a knight wished to sell or transfer property to someone outside his family, he was required to pay a fine to the king, and later to the Royal County Court. Thus the term "fines" came to mean a registered deed of property. The parchment on which the Fines were recorded was split into three separate sections, and the details of the property ownership were inscribed on each section. The three sections were cut apart with a wavy cut, to discourage forgers. The upper two thirds were divided between the old owner and the new owner, while the bottom third ("foot") was kept by the court. All that was meant by the possession of land "in the Feet of Fines" was that property was owned for which a registered deed existed.

Feet of Fines for a Paul Manor – Raginnis and the Vicar:

No. 445, Feet of Fines – 12th November, 1315 between John de Kelenneu (of Callenno in Camborne) and his wife Gilda claimants, and John de Bosvuragh Chaplain (Vicar of Paul - 1317), two messuages and a moiety of one acre at Kelenneu (Callenno in Camborne) and Gonelgy (there follows lengthy legal jargon).

No. 583 – 13th October, 1348 at Westminster between Drogo de Trebuer, claimant, and Hugh de Trewoef and Nicola his wife, deforciants, a quarter part of the Manor of Reghenys (Ragennis) in Paul. Drogo gave Hugh and Nicola – 20 marks of silver (one mark = 6/8d).

The Ancient Sport of 'Hurling'

In 1705 a hurling ball inscription was composed by Thomas Boson son of Nicholas Boson:
'This silver bale was given with many hurlers stronge & greet to William Gwavas Gent. The first day of Sept. was the times in the Parish of Paule in Cornwall in the year of our sweete fair Lorde Christe 1705.'

A Mr. Pearce of Penzance had two silver hurling balls, won by his ancestors in the 18th century belonging to this Parish of Paul. They were 2¾ inches in diameter and bore the inscription in Cornish:

'Paul tuz – whek Gware tek heb ate buz, Henvis, 1704'
'Paul men – fair play, without hatred, is sweet play 1704'

These are reported as being in 1868 in the possession of Mrs. Jago, Mr. Pearce's daughter. Later they went to the Natural History & Antiquarian Museum, in Penzance.

Hurling dates from A.D. 1100 and it is said that the game of 'Rugby Football' evolved from hurling in Penzance. It was a popular sport in Paul, and in Cornwall generally: Richard Carew historian of the sixteenth century writes at length on this sport thus:
'Hurling to goales 15, 20 or 30 players chosen on each side, stripped to the lightest apparell joined hands in ranke against one another. Out of the ranks they match into a pair embracing and moving apart, each to watch each other during play.'

The rules are explained at length but the gist is: it seems that two *'bushes'* are pitched 8 or 10 feet apart, presumably at one end of the pitch and then two more at *'ten or twelve score'* another two are placed. About 80 yards apart then, and as in football, there seems to be each couple opposing, with *'guards'* for the goals *'their best stopping'*. The ball is thrown up, and is carried to the adversaries' goal (carried or *'carved'*) by the best hurlers. If a man should obtain the ball, the other *'thrusteth him in the brest, with closed fist to keep him off'* which is termed *'Butting'*, and apparently one's manhood rests on how well one *'Butts!'* If the chap's opposite partner misses – they all jump upon him and he either touches the ground with one part of his body, or cries *'Hold!'* , which is the word for yielding. He then must throw (*cast*) the ball to his fellows (*Dealing*) who *'maketh away'*, to outrun to the goal. Apparently these hurling matches were most commonly vied at weddings where it was quite the thing for the guests to undertake to encounter all comers!

Hurling to the Country: this is a different game altogether, less rules apply and it usually happened on a *'holy day'*. Goals were towns, villages or a Gentleman's residence about three to four miles apart. A silver ball is cast up, and those who catch it, seize it, and take it by force to his goal. He is usually pursued by the *'adverse party'* who will not leave until the owner of the ball be *'layd flat'* – whereupon this chap jumps up and *'does the same to the next receiver'*.

It is not surprising therefore that this game is commended for manhood and exercise making bodies, strong, hard, and nimble putting courage into their hearts *'to meet an enemie in the face'*. At the end of the game they go home *'as from a pitched battle with bloody pates, bones broken and out of joints, and such bruises as to shorten their days!'* All this took part in the Parish of Paul in 1704 and in earlier times.

Ancient gold necklace

In 1783 a gold lunula or gorget, a type of ancient neck adornment of the early bronze age, circa 2000-2250 B.C. was purported to have been found near one of the Paul Parish earthworks, weighing 2oz. 4 dwts. 6 grams. It was slightly engraved with chevron ornamentation, terminating in lozenges.

These ornaments are never found in graves, and therefore very little understanding exists as to who would have worn or owned such splendid artefacts of adornment. They certainly would have been highly prestigious items

Photo copyright British Museum
GOLD LUNULA

for an individual or community, and may have had a specialised role in ceremonies. It was said to be in the possession of Sir Rose Price, possibly being found on his land when he was constructing 'Price's Folly', and is now in the British Museum. Well, - that is what is written – however, the British Museum have informed me that this has been a matter of debate since the nineteenth century. Their Register records: *'found about 1783, in the hundred of Penwith'* and subsequently their records have favoured the view that it was purchased from the Revd. E. Trafford Leigh and was from Trevarnon Round, Gwithian. The registration number for this lunula is 1838, 519, I.

So there is another mystery! The British Museum entry date 1783 matches the date the Paul Lunula was found. I have managed to get a photo of this ornament, and have permission from the British Museum to print it in this book. So was it from Paul or Gwithian?

Here are a few interesting Will references for Paul Church:

1608 – 13th February – Nicholas Boson, Fisherman, left 10/- *'to help make the belles in Pawle… if they may be made, parte of the money that the parishioners of Pawle doth owe me for Ledd that went about the church'* (ref: TNA, PRO – PROB/11, 119 fo. 74v). Nicholas Boson also leaves *'to Jane my wife, a cowe, twenty shillings a year'* to the poor *'ten shillings'* and *'to the poore mans boxe of Pawle five shillings'*. He then had a conscience and *'in primis for my forgotten tithes - ten shillings'*. This Will is discussed again in Chapter 12.

Many people left but a few shillings to Paul Church, as evidenced in the Wills registered in the Archdeaconry of Cornwall, however livestock was a popular bequest:- *15th February, 1610 – John Hacke left one sheepe to parish church. 17th March, 1631 – John Richard, husbandman left a ewe sheep or 5s in money to 'the church stock of Pawle'. 19th October, 1643 – Jenken Bodenar left one ewe sheep to the church.*

These gifts of animals were considered valuable in those days; perhaps the Vicar grazed them on glebe land, and the sale of wool or lambs probably went into Paul Church coffers. These gifts usually were one tenth of a man's belongings, offered as a tithe upon death.

ARMOUR

Hanging above William Godolphin's Memorial in the east end of the north aisle, there is armour – a breastplate, and two swords. Under Revd. G. Harper someone called 'D.W.D.' removed the armour from the Church, presumably to examine and record it all. The findings are as follows:-

Notes on Militaria removed from Paul Church, Penwith on 11th October, 1989

A Cromwellian type (c1649-1660) Lobster tail helmet with iron face guard; the ear flaps missing, and lobster tail badly damaged at extremities. The guard is bent into a U form where it had been riveted to the Church wall. As with all items, the helmet seems to have been dipped in tar, perhaps in an effort at preservation. Where the tar is missing heavy rust is apparent. 'Arms and Amour' 1979 states that Cromwellian type is a single piece skull. This is in two sections, so is possibly early – 1630.

A Cromwellian style back and breastplate, a cuirass, the leather straps are missing apart from the pin ends, and the two sections crudely riveted together. The condition is as for the helmet. A swept hilt rapier in 'relicky' condition, the blade approximately two thirds of its original length; the grip is missing, guards and counterguards are bent and flattened. Most unusual pommel, being of an open eye appearance rather as a stubby manilla – perhaps to balance its appearance, with the typical Spanish pierced end knuckle bows. Tar covered. Spanish circa 1580, with Moorish influence.

A rare mid-seventeenth century cavalry sword (Cromwell?), possibly 1630; in better overall condition than the other rapier, but still missing the grip, the knuckle bow broken and pierced shells crushed somewhat. Tar covered overall. It is not clear which sword was meant but a footnote states: German blade, made in Augsburg area, the hilt made in England. Inlaid in the blade is a copper wolf, the sign of the maker.

THE 'KEIGWIN' SILVER TRAY

In 1994 a benefactress, Mrs. D. E. Keigwin Ledbury, left a beautiful 'pie crust' silver tray to Paul Church. It had been presented to her Great Uncle, David Keigwin on his retirement as Executive Officer to the Pilotage Department of Trinity House, in London. David Keigwin was born in 1830 and died in 1919. The tray weighed 2.9 kilos and was roughly estimated to be valued at £1,500, in 1994.

The terms of the Will indicated that tray was to stay in the keeping of Paul Church unless it

closed, when it would be returned to Trinity House. Mrs. Ledbury specifically wanted it to go to Paul Church because of the Keigwin family connections through the years, and the many Keigwins buried in a vault under the floor.

Revd. Harper and the P.C.C. decided that the tray would prove to be an insurance liability, and made a gift of it to Trinity House. Trinity House confirmed by letter that they were pleased to have the tray in their safe-keeping, but were only acting as 'Guardians' and that Paul Church may have the tray back at any time to use in a display of Church Silver. The tray is inscribed with the following:

PRESENTED
TO
DAVID KEIGWIN, ESQUIRE
BY
THE HONORABLE (sic)
CORPORATION OF
TRINITY HOUSE, LONDON
AS A MARK OF THEIR ESTEEM
AND IN RECOGNITION OF DUTIES
FAITHFULLY PERFORMED
DURING 61 YEARS AS AN
EXECUTIVE OFFICER
IN THE PILOTAGE SERVICE
JUNE 1906.

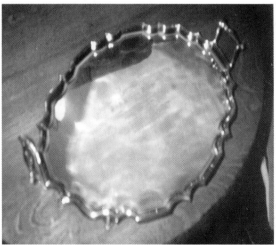

The inscription is centred and, in the case of the name, embellished, and lineaged. According to the latest contact at Trinity House, Mr. Peter Galloway:

'The piece is described as a 20 ½ ins x 15½ ins silver twin-handled oval shaped tray by the Goldsmiths and Silversmith Co, having raised and shaped rim and angled handles, on four scroll feet, with engraved presentation inscription.
London 1905, '92 ozs'.
Its current insured value is £5,560.'

Revd. Aitken

Mabel playing Paul Organ 1898
Helen Barbara Aitken in choir stall
- looking a little bored!
Painting by Frank Bramley

On a Wednesday afternoon, 18th April, 1900, what was described as a '*Fashionable Wedding*' took place in the '*old Parish Church of Paul*' in the presence of a large number of friends and well wishers. The bridegroom was Dr. Ashley Tilsed Jago, of St. Buryan, the youngest son of Mr. Edwin Jago, Paymaster in Chief, R.N. who was well-known and popular in Cornwall—a prominent cricketer, Captain of the St. Buryan Club.

The bride was Miss Mabel Georgina Aitken, the third daughter of the honoured Vicar of Paul, the Revd. R. W. Aitken. She had endeared herself to the inhabitants of the Parish by reason of her kindliness, and thoughtfulness, whilst she rendered much help to the church, especially in the capacity of Organist.

Mabel Jago nee Aitken

The ceremony was performed by the Revd. R. W. Aitken assisted by the Revd. R. J. Martyn, Rector of St. Buryan. The organ was presided at by Mr. F. W. Searle of Penzance who played Mendelssohn's Wedding March with great precision and delicacy of touch. The Service was fully choral. (The best man was Mr. S. J. Lamorna Birch.) There followed a long list of wedding gifts, which made interesting reading; items

Mabel Jago, Sept 1945 at Downs Barn, St. Buryan. She died in 1956, aged 87½.

such as '*a table gong, a set of d'oyleys, a case of meat carvers, silver teapot, silver sugar basin and sifter, and a hand-worked afternoon tea cloth*'. Paul Parish Church Choir gave a silver egg stand; the Parishioners of Paul gave a marble drawing room clock and silver cake basket; and the members of the girls' Bible Class gave a silver mounted biscuit barrel. Mr. Lamorna Birch gave an oil painting. Mr. Cecil Aitken (bride's brother) gave silver teaspoons. The painting to the left shows, incorrectly, tracery in the window of the north aisle east end, it should depict a plain wooden window.

CHAPTER 17 - PARISH MAGAZINES

The Parish Magazine is an important tool of outreach, thus twice a year the whole of Paul Parish, plus some living on the borders, receive a copy. Past magazines are also very important repositories of church history, and I have had the opportunity to look through old magazines, and reproduce extracts in note form thus:

Parish Magazine - September, 1895 – The Revd. Aitken thought it advisable to have Annual Harvest Thanksgiving services in September instead of waiting until Paul Feast as they usually did. The Church was prettily decorated and the choir contributed largely to the brightness of the service, by their efficient singing of both hymns and anthems.

January, 1st 1896 - Copies of the Parish Magazines cost 1/6d, per year. There was a 'Watch-night' service on New Years Eve in the church, the weather cold and rainy and very unhealthy. Before Christmas, Paul Choir spent the evening together at Lamorna, and held a Christmas Concert there in the School, which the Rector of St. Buyran placed at their disposal. Afterwards, they took tea at the Inn. The Vicar reported that they were waiting for the Porthcurnow 'Exiles' Concert, and he hoped to hold a local Musical Evening very soon. Many of the young men are doing Navy drill, and older are getting ready for spring mackerel season. He signs off: *'I am your friend and Minister'*.

August, 1896 - Broccoli planting is over, and the Churchwardens have decided to point the outside walls of the Church, and the interior re-coloured next year. A quiet marriage took place between Miss Beeton and Mr. Charnock. Miss Beeton shrank from the ordeal of a parting scene with those with whom she has been so long and so intimately connected. Her kind help in the Choir will be much missed she came when our present Choir was young and feeble, and did a great deal of hard work for us as our leading soprano her efforts were highly appreciated by the congregation. A Dr. Houston Colisson of Trinity College Dublin gave an organ recital and Mr. Symons, tenor and Mr Percy, baritone, gave some pleasing and effective singing, and the choir closed the proceedings with two pieces admirably rendered. On Wednesday some of the choir and the Vicar went to Perran Uthnoe (sic) to assist at Harvest Thanksgiving Services.

There has been a slight renewal of disagreement between our fishermen, and the East Country fishermen from Scarborough, our men have 'kept their heads so far' and were careful not to commit themselves. A copy of an advertisement from December 1911 Magazine:

'W.J. Waters, Jersey Car and Waggonette Proprietor Churchtown Paul:
A two horse waggonette from Mousehole to Penzance – Every Tuesday 12 noon to 2.00 p.m.
Return from Market Place to Mousehole 12.45 p.m. and 5.30 p.m.'
I think this would be very popular today, with tourists!

Magazine July 1912 - Revd. Frederick J Prideaux, Churchwardens Mr. W. Harris Humphreys and Mr. W. Kneebone, Gwavas, Newlyn. Sidesmen: J. H.S. Osborne, C. Rowe, W. T. Polglase, C. Aitken, J. Nicholls jun and J. Rodda. Parish Clerk Mr. T. E. Wallis Sheffield, Paul, Church constable: Mr. P. Harvey of Trungle. Men's Club open Week-days until 10 p.m. Girls' Club Friday evenings at 7.00. Organist: Mr. W. H. Tregurtha, Belle View Newlyn. Vicar reports signatures to petition against Welsh Disestablishment Bill from Paul reached 400. The pulpit in memory of Revd. Aitken has been put in hand, design of Mr. Sedding has been approved by the committee and indebted to Mr. J Osborne for large amount of time given to this object. Garden Fete 23rd August, 1912. Bazaar to be opened by Mrs. T. B. Bolitho. Total offertories for the month £7.6.11½ d.

Penwith Deanery Mothers' Union Festival 1960s

13 June, 1913 - June 27th Tea at the Vicarage Garden on behalf of Paul & Mousehole Nursing Association. Bazaar and Garden Fete in aid of Tower Fund.

July, 1914 - Magazine price 1d. Churchwardens J. Waters of Kemyell, J. Nicholls of Ragennis. Vicar asked those to support Sunday School Festival on 5th July. The afternoon Service when Rector of St. Buryan the Revd. A. Cornish will visit. The Sunday School is the nursery of the Church. Sunday School Summer Treat and Gala. With the kind permission of Mr. Jarvis at Chywoone, scholars to assemble at the Schoolroom and at 2.00 p.m. headed by Paul band will walk to Chywoone where various sports and games will be held and the band will play. Tea 4.00 p.m. charge 6d.

Paul Horticultural Society hold Annual Show at Chywoone 17th July, all hope for fine weather, special feature the Bread competition. Prize 14 inch engraved Cup mounted on a plinth – 2nd prize 35 lbs Snow Flake Flour!   Cup presented by Beaver Mills Ltd. The Girls' Club annual outing on Friday 26th June, 40 members drove to Mullion and had enjoyable day.

n.b. *This cup used to reside on the mantelpiece in the old Vicarage in Revd. Cadman's time.*

November 1916 on Advent Sunday 3rd December at 3.30 there was a short Service for men only with special hymns and an address on the connection between Advent and the War. Offertories at 11 a.m. for Sick and Needy and at 6.00 for Heating and Lighting the Church.

A Mission from the National Mission visited Paul in November 1916 and 800 helpers were drawn in to sent out personal invitations to every household in the Parish to attend the Mission. Vicar pleased with the way parishioners responded to the appeal. Mr. Foster Morris will come earlier next year to deepen the general impression of the Mission. Hope that the Bishop will come for Confirmation next year as many are unconfirmed in the Parish.

That is the end of the five earlier magazines, now on to those of a more recent date:-

Mark Stubbings

December 1980 – There used to be a Paul Village Christmas Tree in the Square around which Carols were sung. On 21st December at 6.00 p.m. – Festival of Nine Lessons and Carols.

A memorial was written by the Vicar Revd. R. H. Cadman for Mark Stubbings, husband of Elizabeth (Diz), father of Morvah and Demelza, who suddenly passed away at the end of Feast Week. He was described as a 'most charming man, a unique character, deeply spiritual devoted churchman and bell ringer'.

Memorial to Mrs. Catherine Nankervis described as 'a great character' of Sheffield, although living at Gwavas at the time of her death, in November.

October 1981 – The Revd. Cadman extols the merits of Feast week, as reproduced in the Chapter 4 in this book. There was Sunday School Anniversary and Prize Giving on 15th November 6.00 during Evensong, the Vicar exhorts all to come and *'experience what it is, once again, to be young!'*

The Cadmans' Leaving 'do'

The Parish Roundabout sent greetings to: Sally Eustace, Winifred Duckworth, Joan Parsons, Anne Bennets, Willie Polgrean, Maggie Harvey, Gussie Kitchen, Margot Walker, Geoffrey Hyman, Katie Barron and Gwennie Sleeman. This 'Roundabout' remembers those who are ill or who could not attend Church for any reason. A newly formed Paul Church Study Group commenced in the Vicarage on Tuesdays at 7.30. Choral Communion was sung twice a month.

January – 1982 – Proposed Memorial Service at Paul for the dependants of the Penlee Life-Boat Disaster, it was hoped that the Duke of Kent would attend at President of the R.N.L.I.. In memoriam – Margot Walker worshipper at Paul with her husband for a number of years and Harry Pawsey – 'a great soul' sympathy to his wife Ivy.

February, 1982 – Both Duke and Duchess of Kent attended the Memorial Service as above. Mr. George Caunt was appointed organist after Jack Harvey. George was described as having 'a most unflappable temperament'. Revd. Cadman announces that he will continue until the end of April or after Easter, and hoped to see as many as possible for farewells before that date of leaving the Parish. In memoriam:- Geoffrey Hyman, condolences to his wife Joyce. A Parish Dinner was held on Shrove Tuesday 7.30 at the Higher Faugan Hotel.

March, 1982 – Churchwardens E.C. Harvey and J. E. T. Millwood, ask for donations for the Revd. Cadman to be given to P. J. Hutchings P.C.C. Treasurer. There was a special dedication by the Vicar of a new stop on the organ and a plaque in memory of Jack Harvey 'our late organist', during 11.00 Service 14th March. George and Annie Prowse celebrated their Golden Wedding Anniversary. The Choir sang 'Olivet to Calvary' 6.00 p.m. on Palm Sunday.

April, 1982 – Revd. Reg Hugh Cadman and his wife, Alice, (15 years P.C.C. Secretary) and son Hugh say farewell to Paul, and asked all those to call in on him at 'Pendle'. Alice thanked Marion Harvey for welcoming her 16 years ago and teaching her how to make pastry! Alfred Thomas was ill, Leota Pearce was looking after the Sunday School. Elizabeth Stubbings was thanked for putting up Vestry curtains in memory of her husband Mark. The sudden death of Desmond Stone was announced.

Sam Kitchen

August, 1982 – Sam Kitchen to help with the Sunday School and be Superintendent, she is an 'outstanding example of our Sunday School and Church'. Christopher Carter joined the basses in the Choir, and the Choir turned out in full to help celebrate Enid and Cyril's 50 years of marriage. The ferial responses were used while Revd. Harvey was at Paul, he was helping out during the interregnum – and the Choir returned to more familiar setting: by H. Moreton as used at St. Andrew's Church Plymouth.

October, 1982 – The Lord Chancellor approved the appointment of Revd. Geoffrey Harper to be Vicar of Paul. Thanks to Reverends Harvey and Hichens for helping out during interregnum. Sympathy to Doris and John in the passing of Granny Semmens. The sudden death of Cyril Carter took some joy from Harvest Festival singing. For many years Cyril acted as willing taxi driver to Church Services and Choir Practices, bringing Hilary and Enid as well as the Kitchen girls. 'We have always been appreciative of this quiet and faithful service – duplicated by his son-in-law Joe Madron, and we offer our supportive love to the family.

December, 1982 – Institution of Revd. G. Harper. A boy treble joined the Choir – Anthony Howlett of Gwavas. The Parish mourned passing of Willie Polgrean, Churchwarden and member of the P.C.C. for many years. Also Doris Thomas, a faithful worshipper at Paul, especially at early Communion, sympathy to her husband Alfie, and children Nicolette and Paul.

George Prowse

January, 1983 - there was a presentation made to the Revd. W. T. Harvey who helped out during the interregnum, a cheque for £75.00. Revd. Harvey responded thanking Paul for '*many kindnesses, vitualling, transport and friendly greetings*'.
The Church Magazine was increased in price to 10p. In memoriam – George Prowse over sixty years a Choir member, also he was a Churchwarden, Sidesman and P.C.C. member. He and Annie his

wife were responsible for distribution of the Church Magazine for many years. Remember Annie, Keith and Elizabeth in prayers.

February, 1983 - Miss Dorothy Stevens died, a modest contributor to Church finances and had great charm and persistence when running the Cake Stall! The Bell ringers rang 1,260 changes of Plain Bob Minor on 6th December, to welcome Revd. G. Harper.

March, 1983 – the Choir performed 'Behold Your King' on Palm Sunday. The New Lectionary was used for the first time, but the Service was still Holy Communion from the Prayer Book.

April, 1983 – Applications invited for post of Church Caretaker/Verger – duties Cleaning the Church and Church Hall, acting as Verger at Weddings and funerals – salary £360 p.a., plus Verger's fees. Brenda Burton and family were off on a new life in Goldsithney, Rachel was a member of the choir for several years and accompanist for the Sunday School for Alfie and Samantha Kitchen.

May, 1983 – A congregation of 400 took part in Service of Dedication of the memorial to the crew of the Solomon Browne, on Sunday, 24th April. The Revd. Cadman also took part. (See photo in Chapter 7.)
June, 1983 - Johanna Bond was the Rose Queen – crowned on Friday 3rd June, 7.30 p.m. Paul Choir took part in the Penwith Deanery Pilgrimage to Truro Cathedral for Sung Eucharist.

August, 1983 – Sunday morning worship to commence 11.00 a.m. Occasionally, there was a 'Choir Sunday' during which the Choir sang specially prepare music, under Elizabeth Stubbings Choir Mistress. The next Choir Sunday, five-part Preces & Responses by William Smith were to be sung in the Service. A Chubb /Alms box was installed near the South Entrance.
October, 1983 – Feast Sunday Guest Preacher: Revd. Harvey Pentreath, Vicar of Helston.

November, 1983 – A Piano is urgently required for the Church Hall. Remember the sick and housebound – Sally Eustice, Joan Parsons, Anne Benetts, Gussie Kitchen, Mabel Bice, Bertha Harvey, Ester Shaw, Edna Tonkin, William Clift, Annie Prowse, Fred Rodds and Sarah Bond. Enid Carter leaves the choir, thanks for her soprano voice, which will be missed.

December, 1983 – thanks for Special Gift Day – raised £764.20, reports Philip Hutchings, Treasurer. Choir Candle-lit Carol Service should be more candle, less electricity lit, donations of candles requested. Hand-rail fitted to help people down the Vicarage steps safely. Thanks to George and Chris Osborne and Fred Brooks for this new rail. Congratulations to Marion and Eric Harvey on their Ruby Wedding Anniversary. Also to Jack and Olive Waters on their 64th Wedding Anniversary. Jack was Vicar's Warden for many years during incumbency of Revd. Davey. In memoriam – Bertha Harvey – died age 90, cousin to Dawn Pentreath.

January 1984 – memory – Mrs. Mabel Bice died – she was a great 'character'. Resignation of Organist George Caunt, a splendid member of Paul Church, and installation of Mr. Peter Luing organist who teaches music at Humphrey Davy School. Welcome to Joyce Crawford to the soprano line. 300 attended the Carol Service, which was entirely lit by candles! (See photo.)

February, 1984 – The funeral of Frank Leslie Haughton – 23 members of Paul Choir past and present sang at his funeral. He was a gently innovative Choir master, firmly traditional, and thought deeply about every aspect of worship (more about Mr. Haughton in Chapter 12).

April, 1984 – Funeral of Johnnie Waters aged 89 active member of Paul Church for over 40 years, Vicar's Warden, Sidesman, Reader and member of the P.C.C. A loving family man and devoted husband. A.G.M. – Tom Millwood decided not to stand for election as Warden as he had been in office since death of Frank Hodgkinson in 1978. Eric Harvey re-elected and George Osborne as Churchwardens.

June, 1984 – Hutchens' House lost its oldest resident Samuel Tremethick who died at the grand old age of 89. Also Sylvia Webber, a regular worshipper at Evensong. The oldest resident of Sheffield died Millie Ching. All these were remembered with sorrow. Crowning of Rose Queen Joanne Mitchell, crowned by Mrs. Marion Harvey. Attendants Stephanie and Katy Osborne, Emma Mitchell and Lisa Tonkin.

John Harry

July, 1984 – Lizzie Annie is moving from her bungalow by Church Car Park to Hutchens' House, to be taken care of by Lil and Jim. Two new sopranos join the Choir Elizabeth Prowse (rejoined) and Pat Holbury. Memoriam - Irene Vickery formerly ran Fish & Chip shop at Gwavas, once lived in Paul and took an active part in Church life, she was a member of the Mothers' Union. There were major improvements carried out to the Church Hall kitchen.

November, 1984 – The new Organist John Harry was welcomed to Paul Church, he was born at St. Just of an old local family, and worked at Geevor Mine for the last 18 years. John has had a wide experience of music as accompanist for the Penzance Ladies Orpheus Choir, St. Just Opera Group, and the Trencrom Revellers. He has been organist at St. Buryan and St. Just Parish Churches and St. Just Methodist Free Church. A special Choral Evensong was sung to say farewell to Peter Luing, and a Choir party was held at 'Pentreath' with Peter ending with an explosive feast of jazz on the piano.

Sunday 24th November - in Truro Cathedral Mrs. Pat Robson will be licensed by the Bishop as Reader for the Diocese and for the Parish of Paul. Bonfire Celebrations - Sat November 3rd - Trungle Moor. Followed by Supper & Party in the Church Hall, tickets available.

December, 1984 – Penwith One-per-Centers Celebration Eucharist – a rapidly growing number of people from many churches in Penwith who promise to give 1% of their take-home pay to the Third World throughout the year. Celebration Evening follows Eucharist. The Choir lost a great character in passing of George Washington-Cocks, a regular worshipper for many years

In the garden of the Vicarage — c. 1960s at the Fete, some pretty ladies of Paul Church. A few names are: Marlene Ladner, Mary Llewellyn, Barbara Richards, Ruth and Anne Glasson, Pat Polgrean, Sheila Cornthwarta, Decima Carne, Judy Curnow.

Eric Harvey with drum on a tractor pulling the Rose Queen float 1970s

with a useful bass voice. A man of definite tastes fearlessly stating his preferences and acknowledging his prejudices.

January, 1985 – a new order for Matins was printed to make it easier to follow, passed by P.C.C. Three children joined the Choir Kizzy Patrick, Vincent & Steven Coyne. Newlyn Meadery gave special longer candles for the Carol Service.

February, 1985 – In Memoriam of Leon North who died on 14th January he lived at Trungle Farm, until he retired to Newlyn. His father was Leonard North, Churchwarden for some years and in his younger days Leon was in the choir as a boy and later as a man. He played for Paul Cricket Club - sympathies to his wife and family. Alison Maddern was welcomed to the choir, lots of sick members of the choir – Hilary, Dawn, Doris, Pat, Eunice and Charlie.

PAUL BAND – note the familiar large drum

Joyce Osborne, Electoral Roll Officer, asked for forms to be returned to her duly completed.

March, 1985 – Choir – will sing an anthem or hymn between the Collect and the Prayers throughout Lent. The organ was valued at £40,000 - one reason for upgrading heating – maintaining organ.

In Memoriam Edwin Harvey, of Raginnis, who had lived there since 1952 – he, with his tractor and trailer, transported the Choir's piano into the Church for the Summer Festival. Paul villagers will remember him for the nine years from 1968 when he owned the shop. Condolences to his widow Lena.

At the 21st Birthday of Major Simon Bolitho's son Alverne, Edwin was chosen to propose the toast. Sheffield & District W.I. enjoyed a dinner at the New Peninsular Restaurant. The Mothers' Union Festival Service in the Cathedral at 3.00 p.m. a coach took members, from Paul. Mr. Dennis Walsh of Catbells, Trungle Parc is appointed Church Caretaker & Verger from 1st May, 1983. There is a memorial to Mrs. Katie Barron a member of Paul Church *'in every breath she breathed'*. Four new learner ringers started practice: Julie Harper, John and Helen Maddern and Lorraine Gardiner. The Revd. Harper took part in a Peal of 5,040 changes of Surprise Minor on Tuesday 5th April, which took three hours to ring. Alec Jones elected Chairman and Margaret Byrne Treasurer and Secretary of the Penwith Branch of the Diocesan Guild of Ringers.

April, 1985- The passing of George Ernest Riches – one of the regular worshippers at Evensong was sadly noted, he and his wife Jessie will be missed in their favourite pew, they were very generous to the Church. On Friday 19th April the Drama Group will present Joyce Crawford's prize-winning play 'The Strangers' in aid of Paul Church Luncheon Club which had just started.
May, 1985 – A Parish Plan was mooted – with various suggestions for improvements. Charles and Florence Hoare thanked the Vicar and members of the congregation for best wishes on

occasion of Charles' retirement after forty years singing in the Choir, he received a carriage clock from the choristers. The Vicar writes 'his unfailing warmth and friendliness to everyone have been very important for the morale of the choir'. Christian Aid Collections raised £300. Church Heating appeal stands at £1,367, after a coffee morning at the house of Reg and Mary Perrot (raised £288). Mothers' Union Festival Service Truro Cathedral combined with The Overseas Sale. Coach left Paul at 10.00 a.m. Tribute to Sampson Hosking & his music at his funeral.

August, 1985 - Thanks to Joyce and Keith Crawford for the barbecue in aid of the Church Heating Appeal. Mrs Peter Stoffel had a coffee morning at Gwavas Farm on 20th July and raised - £272.62 for the Heating appeal. Thanks to George Osborne and Thornley Renfree for supplying and applying special paint to the Church gates erected in memory of the late Mark Stubbings. Thanks to Marrack Carne for the show case for the display of post cards of the Church *(n.b. he also made the case for the church truncheons, see Chapter 6)*. ***Here endeth the Magazine notes!***

In 2006, in two small locked pew cupboards, there were found several very old Common Prayer and accompanying Hymnal Books. The books are moth-eaten but very interesting, names on the fly-leaves are: J. H. Kneebone, Laurence B. Trehair, Egbert, Trehair, Polly Richards, C. H. Tonkin, Miss Keaster, and Annie Gruzelier. In one is written the following: '*Little drops of water, Little grains of sand, Make a mighty ocean, In a barren land*'. This is from a hymn by Mrs. J. A. Carney 1845, the word '*barren*' should be '*beauteous*'. Maybe there had been a drought!

There was also a leaflet advertising the Church Missionary Society, Penwith Deanery Association arrangements for the Anniversary, 1897. Sermons and Meetings accompanied by '*Lantern Lecture on the South China Mission*'. The meetings involved Sennen School-room, Alverton Hall Penzance, and Paul School-Room (Chairman Revd. R. W. Aitken, Speaker Revd. H. Fuller). The Sermon at Paul was 11.00 a.m. Sunday 16th—Revd. G. Hibbert-Ware; and at 6.00 p.m. Revd. T. Inskip. No month was mentioned. These locked pew cupboards could well have been untouched since 1897, there was nothing to indicate that they had been opened for many years.

Note one new window; the rest are plain church-warden type Wooden Windows circa late 1800s

CHAPTER 18 - MANORS OF PAUL & GEOLOGY

BOLLOWAL (Bellowan 1583 Bolowan 1640)   Bod – dwelling Lowen – happy
BOSSAVA (Botysava 1300)   Dwelling of summer heat
CASTALLACK (Carstallaf 1460)   Car- fort stalaf – swing door (?)
CHYENHALL   House on the moor
CHOONE (Chyunwone 1274)   House on the down
CLODGY   Lazar-House
PARK CLODGEY   Lazar-House field
FAUGAN (Fawgan, Fawgon, Faugan in   Cave Down (fow-gun)
Treveneth Vean 1689)
GLOBBENS (Raginnis field name)   Light-height
GWAVAS (Gwaves 1429)   Winter-dwelling
HALWYN (Helewen – 1327   White or Fair moor
JAGFORD (Jakeford 1278, Jacford juxta   Jak-forth – Jack-way (Lane)
Lulyn 1289 – Lulyn (Newlyn) & Jaghford 1424) As in Newlyn

KEMYEL (Chemiel - Tithing 1185, Kemyel 1250,   Homer K and Middle K
Kymel 1297, Magna Kemyel 1282, Kemyel Pella
1429, Kemyel Drea & Kemyel Crease or Creis mean
respectively
KERNICK (Kernye juxta Porhenys 1310)   Little Corner
KERRIS (Kerismoer juxta Tresfevenik 1300) Kerys – wall, or fence
LEAN CARNE – lyn-carne =   Strip of the rock pile
MARSHALL MANOR (Theisinga Marescalli   Theisinga – Tithing
de Alverton 1260, Decenna Marscoyl et le
Mareschal 1283)

MOUSEHOLE (Musehole 1283, Mosehole 1300,   The various names of Mousehole derive
1309, Mosehol 1301, Mosoyle 1310, Extent of the from a 'messuage' called Mousehole
Borough of Mosehole 1327, Street Kerneke in in Porthenys they were originally
Mowsehole 1573, Street an Garnick in Mowshole two separate places.
1583)

NEWLYN (Nulyn 1278, 1390, Lylyn 1289, 1328, Various names for Newlyn, Paul is
1368 – Four shops at Lylyn 1321, Lulyn juxta | sometimes referred to as PAWLYN
Talcarn 1321, Nenlyn 1431, Newlyn 1436)

PENLEE   Pen-legh –ledge, headland
PENOLVA (Penwoelva 1322)   Watch Head-land
PORTHENYS (Portheness 1267 Porthenys juxta Island Harbour
Mosehole 1309, Porthenes juxta Breweny 1314)
Porthenys Mill 1337
RAGENNIS (Rachenes 1260, Porrhenys and   Opposite the Island
Dour-ragenys watercourse – 1337)
ROSKILLY - ros-kelly   Heath of the grove

STABLE HOBBA	Riding horse stable
STREETANOWAN – stret-an-oghen	Street of the Oxen
TREDAVOE (Trewordavoh 1324)	Homestead on the edge
TRESVENNACK (Tresfevenek 1300, Trefenek 1301)	Longstone
TREVELLA (Drefellou 1460)	Homestead of elms
TREVITHAL (Trewengal 1285, Trevethall 1310, Trevethegal 1314)	Victorious
TREWARVENETH	Homestead on a Hill
TRUNGLE (Trevonglet 1283)	Homestead of the quarry

The meaning of local place names are interesting, and I came across a list of them as above. The notes were abridged from those of Mr. C. Henderson, but a more comprehensive topography of Paul appears in the Annual Report of the Royal Cornwall Polytechnic Society – 1941/42.

In the Parish of Paul, Mousehole and Newlyn were the two main centres of population, while the seats of important families were: Kerris, Kemyel and Trewarveneth. Together with Castallack, Tredavoe, Halwyn and Raginnis, these six were the main **ancient** centres of cultivation when most of the remainder of parish was moor land; the evidence for this is in the old Cornish field names in these areas.

These names are all in the Tithe Map apportionment (ref: DPP 172/ X 355/22) in the Cornwall Record Office. It takes ages to work them all out from the field numbers, as they come under various headings, a such as 'Trungle', and are not in numerical order! This occasioned a lot of eyestrain and to-ing and fro-ing between apportionment and the Tithe Map, which is huge. The main Village of Paul may be seen on a reduced Tithe Map (ref: DPP 172 CN 1853—see Chapter 4) that is certainly easier to read, and doesn't entail being suspended from ropes and pulleys from the ceiling in order to inspect it, but **not to touch**! One may, of course, study this huge carpet-like original Tithe Map (1840) – but it is very fragile, and thus has been put on microfiche for its preservation.

MANORS IN THE PARISH OF PAUL

Kerris, Trewarveneth, Trungle, Brewinney, Alverton Butsava, Fee Marshall, Kemyell, Lanyon, Ragennis, Mousehole and Selena.

BREWINNEY

The lands adjoining, and encompassing Paul Church Town are called in variance: Brewinney, Brewory, Brewoni, Brewony or Bruenny. This Barton has so many different spellings of its name as to be totally confusing. Locally it is pronounced 'Barwinney'.

A Boscawen Deed of before 1300 states '*I, William, son of Nicholas Scutor of Porthenes, have given to Henry, son of Henry of Boscawen Rose, a place which I had in Brewory in front of the Rectory House of Saint Pawlyn,*'

This gives credence to the village of Paul originally being 'Brewinney', before the first Church was dedicated to Saint Paul. The Village then took its name from the Church (see Chapter 4).

Paul Church town (alias Brewinney). It was reported in the 'Cornish Telegraph' for 14th April, 1875 that *'Paul Churchtown was in a sad condition'*. As the Village was entered there were two dangerous ruined buildings opposite Trungle House. The post box, let into a corner house wall, was only accessed over an *'open sewer',* and many and various pigs were allowed to wander at their own *'sweet will'* around the Village! As there were at least five dairy farms in the Village, in the recent past, it was also rare to see the lanes free from cows on their way to being milked.

The Manor of Bruenny consisted in 1777 of: *'60 messuages, 2 grist mills, 60 gardens 1500 acres of lands, 350 acres of pasture, 500 acres of furze and heath and common of pasture with appurtainments in the Parish of Paul Churchtown otherwise Bruenny'* . In this statement is a clue – before the Church was built was the Village of Paul called 'Brewinney'? This is a very interesting concept and may well be true. Supported again by Doble's reference *'Porthenes juxta Breweny 1314'.*

The above land measurements were taken from various legal settlements between Right Hon. John the late Earl of Bute and the Right Hon. Mary Wortley late Countess of Bute and Baronet Mount Stuart. Brewinney Manor was worth £10,000 in 1777.

There is also an Abstract of Title: James Archibald Stuart Wortley and John Stuart Wortley his eldest son to a piece of ground in Paul Church Town – Bruenny and Paul 1823. They were relatives of the Earl and Countess of Bute, and a portion of Bruenny became the school additional burial ground by Deed 29th April, 1817 for the sum of £32.00.

TRUNGLE

Trungle House: once known as The Old Manor House and also The Vicarage

Trungle was once a Village (1788) next to the Village of Brewinney, and has been known as *'Trevolglet in 1283'* and in an Indenture dated 3rd November, 1788 *'Trunglelitch'.*

In 1657 Nicholas Boson of Newlyn married Elizabeth daughter of John Webber. Her marriage settlement brought an annuity for life of £30 per annum from his lands in Trungle and Hellwyn (Halwyn) in Pawle.

The Langfords were a family who owned the Trungle estate, in the 16th century. The family originally came from Wiltshire, and in 1600 this branch moved to Ross-on-Wye, purchasing property there, and later expanding to the Manchester area. In 1715 a direct descendant, Edward Langford, fought for the Jacobites at the Battle of Preston, and then fled to Cornwall. In recognition of his services the Old Pretender (James Francis Edward Stuart son of

James II of England) gave him two filled china tea vases, a rarity in those days; these vases remained with the family until 1840 when they were sold for 500 guineas.

Since all his children were baptized in Madron Church, he must have had a house there. He became a prosperous merchant, and in 1722 married Catherine Nettle from Penzance. In so doing he inherited some tin mines near St. Agnes, later purchasing an estate at Trungle and moving in. By the marriage he had three children, John 1724, Edward 1726, and Constance 1728. John died 1728 and was buried at Madron Church. Constance was married by special licence at Penzance Chapel to Capt. Samuel Pellow, having at least one son (Edward) who, after a distinguished Naval career, became the 1st Lord Exmouth.

In 1772 on the death of his Father, Edward (brother of Constance) inherited the Trungle estates. Circa 1775 he married a widow Elizabeth Nankerville (nee Dansey), whose Father Frederick Dansey came from Plymouth Dock; he died in 1781, and like his Father was buried at Paul Church. The Langford funeral hatchment, hanging in the Church near the north door today, refers to his death. This would have been placed near the family vault but has been moved several times around the church.

On 10th August, 1810, according to Paul Church Burial Records, a Mrs. Nankerville of Truro was buried in the Langford family vault. Therefore it seems that Mrs. Langford reverted to her first dead husband's name when her second husband died. Yet she was buried in the family vault with her second husband, whose name she denied! This does seem very odd especially as she lived miles away in Truro.

Edward Langford must have been a very rich man; he died intestate, and in order to settle the estate, his widow had to visit the Archdeacon of Cornwall who directed that she appoint two trustees who had to 'deposit a bond of £20,000 in good and lawfull money of Great Britain'.

They had one son again called Edward. He sold the estates in 1800 and moved to the area of Bath, becoming Steward for the Poppham family, where another branch of the Langford family resided; from then on the Church and Armed forces feature largely in the family history. (For a photo of the Langford Funeral Hatchment see Chapter 7).

MADRON PARISH REGISTERS: Baptism June 19th 1724 John son of Edward Langford. Baptism – 13th June, 1726 – Edward son of Edward Langford. Baptism – Oct 12th 1728 Constance daughter of Edward Langford. Burial 15th May 1728 John son of Edward Langford. Marriage – 12th May 1752 – Capt. Samuel Pellew to Miss Constance Langford by special licence at Penzance Chapel.

PAUL CHURCH REGISTERS: Burial – 2nd November 1772 – Edward Langford. Burial 26th June, 1781 (son?) – Edward Langford. Burial in family vault – 1810 Mrs. Nankerville.

Trungle was also formerly the seat of the Hutchens, then the Badcocks, then Keigwins in 1868. Also Messrs. Millet, Edwards; and at some time William Pearce, who built a barn there, followed by Revd. Keverne who also leased Trungle for a while in 1763.

Trungle House was the residence of the Curate of Paul for 47 years: this was the Revd. Warwick Oben Gurney, well, his wife lived there, and sometimes he lived in the old Vicarage! As a Curate owned Trungle House, it was sometimes confusingly called 'The Vicarage'.

KERRIS MANOR - '*Kerismoer juxta Tresfevenik 1300*' (ref: Doble)

The barton of Kerris is supposed to have once had manorial rights, as a manor of *Keres* was granted in 1483 to John Duke of Norfolk. The barton was successively the seat of the Chivertons, Hexts, Pearces, and Blewetts, and the property of Mr. Pascoe and others; the old mansion is divided into three farm houses. Kerris *Roundago* is an elliptical structure; the greater diameter being about 52 paces, and the lesser 34; it had four rude pillars at its entrance, each 8 feet high. Little other than the site of this ancient building now remains.

In 1723 an urn was found on this estate; it was in a vault 8 feet long and 6 feet high, the floor paved with stone and the roof arched with the same material. The urn, which was formed of the finest red clay, contained a few brass coins and a quantity of earth.

On the estate of Chy-an-hâl, about a quarter of mile from Kerris Roundago, was an irregularly shaped, unhewn pillar of granite, about 9 feet in height and 8 feet in circumference near the base, tapering wedge-like to the top. This was supposed to be a *Mênheer* or monumental stone. This large Menhir or standing stone, was 9' broad at base, tapering to 7'9". Several small objects have been found in this area from time to time. Walter Borlase records that he only found a pebble and flint, but later a cupped stone was found, and in recent years a pendant of banded sandstone, believe by some experts to be of Egyptian origin.

The Roundago described by William Borlase: '*In the tenement of Kerris there is an oval enclosure. It is about 52 paces from north to south and 34 feet from east to west. At the Southern termination stand four rude pillars about eight feet high, at the foot of which lie some large stones, which I am apt to think did formerly rest upon the Pillars. The plan on which these pillars stand is eighteen feet from north to south and eleven feet wide. I am inclined to think that this was a place of worship and that these stones were designed to distinguish* and dignify the entrance.*'*

The wanton destruction of the Roundago in 1820 is described as follows '*Kerris Round has been of late nearly destroyed and the stones carried to Penzance for rebuilding the pier. There is a report among the inhabitants of the neighbourhood that the horses which were employed in drawing off the stones, and which were young and healthy, died before they had completed their work. It is very probable that the loads were beyond their strength and that they were consequently injured, but superstition is sufficiently alive to attribute it to a supernatural cause.*' The old name for the field, which now includes the Roundago, was 'Dornolds' meaning land of Power.

18th C Front: Kerris Manor

There are also three stones carved with spirals (see Chapter 1); one, built into the wall of a farm building, had a short shaft and a slight neck below its circular head (see photo in Chapter 1).

The second appeared to have been slightly larger, it had at least one more spiral, but has been broken off its shaft and built into the wall of another small building. The third is reported to be somewhere in a hedge, and mislaid.

Medieval fireplace with huge granite lintel

The Architecture of the Manor House at Kerris

Both the north wings of Kerris were medieval buildings, with a courtyard between. The north wing still has the original medieval fireplace, and remains of very early windows and doors – this seems to have been a cross passage house.

The north east wing was probably a Hall house, as there is a very large old chimney in the middle of it. On the north wall beside a chimney is an old wooden staircase. The south of this building has a Queen Anne panelled room made in the time of the second Richard Pearce, when the whole front was given an 18th century Cornish face, built of dressed ashlar.

The southern section of the house which joins these two is of 15[th]C construction, with two gables. The south west gable was a dwelling house, and the south east, a Manorial Courtroom. On the upper floor behind this to the north is a (robing) room with three light mullioned

Kerris Court Room

windows of carved stone from Bath, not granite; this looks out on to the Court Yard. In the room below the courtroom there is a damaged two light window cut from one piece of granite. Both of the upper rooms in these two gables has a tiny Privy window beside the chimney. In the Courtroom the upper edge of plaster moulding is still to be seen. On the inner north wall it has a convex curve or arch, and over the cut granite fireplace on the gable end, it is straight.

Cheveiton Family

Richard Carew wrote in his Survey of Cornwall – '*The name Cheveiton signifieth a house on the green lea, and a castle on a green hill is given by a Gentleman of that name.*' Cheveitons are known, and have lived at a place called Cheverton in West Cornwall since the reign of Henry III, and it seems very probable that this was Kerris. Their name is variously spelt 'Cheveiton/Chiverton'.

One of the Kerris field names was Arron Von, which appears to have the same meaning of 'on the greenwood'.

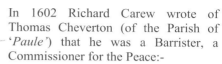

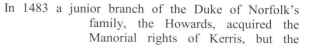
Medieval north wing of Kerris Manor House

In 1483 a junior branch of the Duke of Norfolk's family, the Howards, acquired the Manorial rights of Kerris, but the Cheveitons continued to live there throughout the 16th C.

In 1602 Richard Carew wrote of Thomas Cheverton (of the Parish of 'Paule') that he was a Barrister, a Commissioner for the Peace:-
'Who in a quiet simple life maketh no further use of his knowledge gotten in the laws during his younger age, or that experience where with a long course of years hath enriched him, than may tend without fain, to the advancement of public justice or without fuss to advisement of his private acquaintance.'

Thomas also wrote 'Chiverton's Obits & Burials of Cornish Gentlemen', a lost manuscript, which would have been very useful to Paul Church! Thomas died in 1604; his heir was his brother William, then aged 50, who the same year married Mary, widow of Walter Borlase. She had six children, and C. S. Gilbert wrote that William Cheveiton brought up Borlase's children with great care at his own house, he made Phillipa Borlase his heir. She married William Hicks and their son William was born at Kerris in 1602. In 1628 William Cheveiton, the last of the family, died.

The Hicks Family

Phillipa Hicks, William Cheveiton's heiress, was soon a widow and married into the Gwavas family. By that time she was a very wealthy woman and purchased the impropriation (tithes) of the Church of Paul. William Hicks, Phillipa's son, was a staunch Puritan, although his Borlase cousins were Royalists. The stone crosses remaining in the Parish of Paul are said to have been thrown down by him. (It could be this William who parted the church yard cross from its shaft!) William Hicks died in 1660; he was succeeded by his nephew Thomas. It must have been during the Hicks occupation of Kerris, after William Hicks removed the stone crosses, that one was re-erected at the bottom of the Hill as a boundary mark, and the letters L.A. were cut on it; however by 1850 it had been replaced at Kerris.

Richard Pearce Senior and Junior

1694 Richard Pearce of Penzance (a member of a family who had come from Warwickshire in the time of King Charles I) had married Mary Borlase, a cousin of Phillipa Hicks, and they bought the three parts of Kerris in February, March and October.

1697 He bought more of the land, which had belonged to the Cheveiton family.

1698 Richard Pearce Senior died, leaving his property to his five year old son Richard.

1701 His widow remarried Henry Pendarves Vicar of Paul, in Sancreed Church. Richard Pearce Jnr. grew up and married Maria Jones of Penrose. He extensively altered the house, putting on a Queen Anne front, a new stair case, and panelling in the best parlour; his work was completed in 1721.

1732 He was forced to sell three tenements on the Estate.

1743 Financial difficulties forced Richard Pearce to mortgage the house to John Hawkins of Pennans (Penzance?).

1743 Richard's Mother Mary Pendarves sold her share of Kerris to George Blewett of Marazion but, still unable to keep up the mortgage payments, Richard and Maria were named bankrupt, and John Hawkins came in possession of Kerris by default. 1753 Richard Pearce died.

1750 George Blewett acquired Kerris from the Hawkins family about 1750, and remained in possession until 1797, when George Blewett sold to H. Sandys on condition he could remain as tenant.

1798 Kerris was sold outright to Richard Oxenam of Penzance. He became Colonel of Mounts Bay Militia, and John Jones Pearce, Grandson of Richard Pearce was an Officer under him. Paul Church had a Curate called William Oxnam in 1797; maybe he was the second son who went into the Church! He may, of course, have been no relative, but it's an interesting point; although the spelling is slightly different, this may be a printing error.

1833 Richard Oxenam sold a third part to William Pascoe, and until 1882 the Pascoe family had the principal interest. The house was always divided into three, although some of the time the Pascoe family owned two parts.

29th September, 1848 – Edwin Lay and Thomas Darke mortgaged Kerris Manor Farm to Thomas Simon Bolitho. At a later date the property was acquired by Richard Foster Bolitho Senior and Junior, and conveyed on 25th March, 1870 to James Pascoe. 2nd April 1880 James Pascoe by will left all his property to John Laity of Goldsithney and James Trembath of Castallack as executors, for the benefit of his nephews: James, Nicholas, John and Stephen Pascoe.

29th September, 1882 – Mr. Pascoe sold the Farm to T. B. Bolitho, then on his death in 1915 the Trewidden Estate was settled on Trustees for the benefit of Mrs. Charles Williams. In 1963 Mrs. Williams revoked this trust and conveyed the estate including Kerris Manor, to Barclays Bank and Major Simon Bolitho, for the benefit of Alverne Bolitho (S. E. Bolitho's second son) on his attaining the age of 25 years. Since then Kerris has remained part of the Bolitho Estate. Present tenants are: Mr. and Mrs. A. Sunderland and Mr.and Mrs. J. Giles.

Extracts from a Lease dated 1777

Frances Hitchens let the Southern part of the Barton of Kerris Manor to John Blewett of Marazion, already the owner of the other two parts:- *The Southern Kitchen, the little parlour, and the lower cellars adjoining the said parlour and kitchen, and the chambers and room over the said Parlour Kitchen and Cellar together with stone stairs leading to same.*

The land at Kerris was described as: '*Wheal Gwarra' Park Noneth, The Warren, Don Gregon, Arron Von, Lower Arron Von, Arron Von Croft, the little Goon, Carn Goon, West Moor Goon,*

Carn Moor, with gardens and Orchards adjoining the Warren. The Warren Wall, aforesaid. The landlord reserves the right to use the best commons of pasture, also the best stable and store over.

Kerris became a small community in itself, and once had its own Methodist Chapel.

TREWARVENETH/TREVENETH

In 1320 this was the home of Richard de Trewarveneth, Clerk. The barton of Trewarveneth became the property of a younger branch of the Godolphin family through marriage with the daughter and heiress of John Cowling, the previous owner. Colonel William Godolphin, commemorated in Paul Church (he died in 1689), was the last of this branch; his armour may be seen in Paul Church.

In 1814 Trewarveneth was a farm house, the property of John Legge. The barton was owned by D. P. Le Grice, and the ancient mansion was occupied by the farmer. Now holiday apartments stand on this site. The painter Stanhope Forbes also lived at Trewarveneth.

FEEMARSHALL OR FREEMARSHALL

The manor of Freemarshall, in this parish, some time belonging to the family of Hitchens (*aka Hutchens*) of Trungle, became the property of Mr. George John, of Penzance, by purchase from Mr. Edward Langford. Feemarshall (Fee of Marshal 1384 – Marshall Fee 1399). A Grant of Freewarren was made in 1333 to William Bassett and his heirs forever.

From 1333-1602 there is an unbroken chain of evidence to show the Bassett family enjoyed this Manor which was held in chief of Castle of Launceston. In 1485 it was worth £6, but the extravagance of Sir Robert Bassett, in the reign of Queen Elizabeth I, necessitated the sale of a considerable portion of his patrimony. In 1602 the Manor was sold to Robert Burrington of Sandford. The Burrington family continued to hold Feemarshall until 1692. John Burrington (Grandson of Robert) sold the Manor to Nicholas Burrington. At this time Feemarshall embraced messuages and lands and rents in Trungle, Gwavas, and Nangarden, and in the Parishes of Paul, Sancreed, St. Buryan and St. Erth.

The Manor passed to the Hitchens family and on to Edward Langford through marriage, then to George John who purchased it in early 19th century. In 1819 Rent Rolls included receipts of 2/6d from Gregory Nicholas, who owned a cow that killed Henry Leah of Trelodarvas, a boy of ten years old. George John passed Feemarshall to his daughter Willmot (see Chapter on Burials etc) wife of General John Robyns. It was, up to 1901, the property of Major Cecil Richard Robyns Malone, son of the Revd. Richard Malone of Paul Church.

KEMYELL & BOSAVA

Bottrell states in 'Traditions & Hearthside Stores of West Cornwall 1870' that a common saying was: *'Bossava—was the First House after the Flood',* implying that it was the most ancient habitation of the locality. This was the patrimony of Peter Kemyell who died in the close of the 14th century – his two daughters were the co-heirs. Elizabeth was wife of Geoffrey St. Aubyn, and Alice wife of Ralph Vyvian. Geoffrey St. Aubyn was Sheriff in 1398, and upon this marriage the Manor of Butsava and Kemyell came into the St. Aubyn family. In 1504 Thomas St. Aubyn conveyed it to Richard Pasco, Clerk. Kemyell was held as part of the Manor of Feemarshall.

There are three places with the name of Kemyell: Kymyell-dre – the town; Kymyell-cries – the middle; and Kymyell-wartha – the higher, the latter being the seat of the Kymyell family.

Kymyell-dre and Kymyell-cries were the seats of the Keigwins. Adjoining Kemyell Wartha is Lamorna Cove noted for its fine granite, large quantities of which used to be sent to London. In 1815 a monolith obelisk of granite 22 feet in height, was sent to the Great Exhibition from Lamorna quarry weighing 21 tons! Richard Keigwin (son of Jenkin Keigwin) owned Kymiel crees or Kymiel drea as well as Ragenis, and left Kemiell and Botsava (the spellings continually differ) to his son Richard. Richard Keigwin senior died 21st April 1636

1628 John St. Aubyn paid 12/6d to Robert Burrington on the death of his father Thomas St. Aubyn. The Manor descended through the St. Aubyn family until the Right Honourable John Townsend St. Aubyn, Lord St. Levan.

RAGINNIS

In 1348 Hugh de Trewoef owned this area. I located a Deed, Feet of Fines Number 583, in the Devon & Cornwall Record Society Records, dated 13th October, 1348 (at Westminster): between Drogo de Trebuer, claimant, and Hugh de Trewoef and Nicola his wife, deforciants, for a quarter *'part of the Manor of Ragghenys in Paul'.* For which Drogo gave Hugh and Nicola 20 marks of silver. In Welsh *'rhagynys'* means *'adjacent island'. The* Keigwins owned Ragenis in the 16th century, see above.

PENOLVA

'Penwoelva 1322'. Pen-golva – watch. This area is ideally placed as a look-out point. The farm contains an old building that was used as a look out for the pilchard shoals, this is where a look-out man would signal to a huer who would run through the streets of Newlyn shouting 'Hevva, hevva!' The villagers would then rush out to help fishermen net the pilchards.

THE GEOLOGY OF PAUL

As I was writing about the areas of land, I thought I would look up something about the rock formations beneath the land, which come to the surface in bedrock. I was lucky to find the following information, which is taken from notes of Dr. Boase, with my definitions in brackets to help with comprehension! There is a cavern at Mousehole (original *'Mouse Hole'*) but there is also another cavern of smaller proportions at Carn Kemyel. These are presumably good places (for the adventurous) to inspect bedrock.

There is a narrow belt of slate belonging to the porphyritic series, which bounds the eastern side of the Parish as far as the village of Mousehole. It consists of hard massive (*compact crystalline rock*) and schistose (*pertaining to 'schist' – any metamorphic rock that can be split into thin layers*) varieties of compact feldspar (*any group of hard crystalline materials that consist of aluminium silicates of potassium or sodium, calcium or barium*).

The feldspar is occasionally spotted or intimately blended with actynolite (*which is dark green*) and hornblend (*a complex silicate coloured either green, greenish brown – brown, black or sometimes even opaque*), or with some mineral between them.

The rest of Paul Parish is on granite (*plutonic igneous rock having visibly crystalline texture, generally composed of feldspar, mica and quartz; igneous rock when cooling from the molten state solidifies with or without crystallization*). The quartz can be seen clearly on the granite pillars of Paul Church. At Mousehole slate and granite may be seen in contact with each other (*granite veins in the slate*).

Paul Church 2006.
A haven of peace and spirituality.

CONCLUSION

I have endeavoured to provide a reference point, and to gather together into one volume a wealth of information that is not easily available. Hopefully, this will provide a better understanding of what shaped the Church of Paul, its inception, its role through the years, and its continuing vigorous Christian life. As John Boson wrote:

> *'Neighbour—He that will the Cheifest wisdome finde*
> *Keep right the Holy Church of Paule in Minde*
> *To the pure words of God, Your Lord give Ear*
> *In heart, in mind and Soul be you Sincere.'*

I think a fitting ending for this book would be the Lord's Prayer in Cornish:

> *Agan Tas ni, eus y'n nev,*
> *Bennigys re bo dha Hanow.*
> *Re dheffo dha Wlaskor,*
> *Dha vodh re bo gwyrs, y'n nor*
> *kepar hag y'n nev, - Ro dhyn ni*
> *hedhyw agan bara pub dydh oll;*
> *Ha gav dhyn agan kammweyth, Kepar*
> *Dell avyn nini dhe'n re na eus ow*
> *Kammwul er agan pynn ni; Ha na wra*
> *Agan gorra yn temtashon, Mes delyrv*
> *hi diworth drog. Rag dhiso jy yw an*
> *Wlaskor, ha'n galloes, ha'n gordhyans,*
> *Bys vyken ha bynari.*
> *AMEN*

John George and Roger Bond, Churchwardens

Revd. Gordon and Mrs. Jean Hansford

Revd. Yvonne Hobson Paul Church Curate

A Post-Service Gathering, 2001

PAUL PEOPLE

BELLRINGERS 2006
Captain Margaret Byrne, third from right

CHOIR 2006
John Harry Organist (far left),
John George Choirmaster
(far right)

ACKNOWLEDGEMENTS

I would like to thank those who have supported and encouraged me to write this book. It has been hard work, but jolly good fun too, especially trying to organise my very disorganised mind into some semblance of logical sequence for the myriads of pieces of information about Paul, and its Parish, that came hurtling my way once the book was begun.

I was originally asked to be part of a Committee; and whilst waiting for it to be formed thought I'd look around to see what information there was on Paul Church. From the first visit to the Morrab Library things started to happen. I became like a snowball rolling down hill with great speed, gathering snippets of data at every turn. People came forward with memories, and poured them out, even when I hadn't a pen and paper ready to take them down. Everyone was enthusiastic and eager to put in their snippets. I have had cups of tea and cake with: Marion Harvey, Pat Maddern, Hilary Madron, Gus Kitchen, John Harry (who started telling me so much that I couldn't get it down fast enough). Discussions with Church Wardens Roger Bond, and John George, chats with Mrs. Annie Prowse (sadly recently deceased), Mrs. Mary Barnes, Margaret Byrne, Pam Jones, Elizabeth Stubbings, Mr. and Mrs. Peter Pentreath, Mr. W. B. Cornish, Revd. G. Harper, former Vicar of Paul Church, and Nigel Haward, an expert on geology.

I would like to thank the following:-

Messrs. Scott & Company, and Follett Stock & Company (Diocesan Registrar), who both have lovely offices in wonderful old buildings in Truro, have been most helpful, and have giving me time in quiet rooms to look through their records (Follett Stock have since moved to new offices in Threemilestone). Martin Follett and David Scott, who have both been involved legally and architecturally with looking after Paul Church for some years, supplied me with cups of tea, and put up with me e-mailing and bending their ears with countless questions. Canon M Warner, for his copy of Faculty data. David Thomas of the Cornwall Record Office who shares my excitement for crypts (mine is bigger than yours!), and who has helped me with pieces of information, and looking things up when I couldn't visit the C.R.O. David also proof-read my book for hysterical (historical) mistakes!

Aiden Hicks, historian of Sennen Church, and illustrator of the wonderful front cover; Dr. Jo Mattingly, historian, Ann Preston-Jones, archaeologist; and Matt Mossop, ex-chorister of Paul, for academic direction, and preventing my over fertile imagination from running riot. Professor Nicholas Orme from Exeter University who once again, very helpfully, came to my rescue this time on Cornish Saints. Chris Osborne, Marion Harvey, Elizabeth Stubbings, Pat Maddern, Margaret Byrne and Pam Jones, Mr. and Mrs. Richard Pentreath, and Michael Best for wonderful old photos; also Margaret & Pam for input re the Bells.

Pat Salter of Pinhoe, Exeter, for patiently relaying information from the Devon Record Office by e-mail. My friend, Dr. Christine Hall, for helping me with mediaeval

Latin (again!). The present Vicar Gordon Hansford for being excited with me about the emerging historical picture of Paul, and loaning me Church records. Also the present P.C.C., Robin Young, and Nicholas Hogben my step-son, for their much needed support in getting this into print! Once the book is written, then the hard work begins, little did I know!

I acknowledge permission from the Ordinance Survey Office to reproduce their maps, the British Museum for use of a photograph of the gold Lunula, of which they own the copyright, and the Victoria County History Project for use of unpublished material about the Bells of Paul Church pre-1595, the Cornwall Record Office for allowing me to print photo (P172/2/18/17) now in their collection but once belonging to Paul Church Archives. Also Simon Knight, for use of his aerial photos.

Gillian Trelease—2006
Victoria County History Volunteer (alter ego)
Researcher & Choir Member of Paul Church

Paul Church 2006. Showing main nave, north and south aisles and the 1726 Vicarage in the left background.

REFERENCES

Last time I wrote a church history, for Broadclyst Church near Exeter, I finished the manuscript, and sat back pleased, but exhausted, and an academic friend said 'You have remembered to put in all the references for your information Jill, haven't you?' Well, I hadn't, and it was a real slog having to go back and access my sources again, a hard lesson to learn. This time I remembered to note them, despite my advanced years, and here they are for anyone to research further.

Before I list my references I would like to quote a little verse I found, which I hope sums up my endeavours. Well, I tried!

'For all she did she had a reason
for all she said a word in season
and ever ready was to quote
Authorities for what she wrote!'

Mr. Butler

AITKEN, Revd. R. W. – History of Paul Church – 1910 – ex-Vicar of Paul
ANGLO-SAXON CHRONICLES, THE
BANGOR UNIVERSITY OF WALES – Glebe Terrier of Paul Church –
26th April, 1746 – deposited in 1977
BARING-GOULD, Sabine – The Lives of the Saints
BRITISH MUSEUM – copyright of photo of Lunula
BECKERLEGG, J. J. – Two Hundreds Years of Methodism in Mousehole – 1954
BEDE, The Venerable – The Ecclesiastical History of the English People,
ed. Leo Sherley-Price
BISHOP GRANDISSON – Reg. 1336
BISHOP STAPLETON – Reg. P. 145 – Bruony
BLIGHT, J. T. – Churches & Antiquities of West Cornwall – 1885 (second ed.)
BOASE, G. C. – Collectanea Cornubiesia, 1890
BOXER-MAYNE, W. J. – 'Stray Notes on Paul Parish' – Old Cornwall Soc. Oct 1943
p. 45
CADMAN, Revd. R. H. – History of Paul – Ex-Vicar of Paul Church –
written between 1962-1988
CAREW, Richard – The Survey of Cornwall – 1602
COAT, Miss M. – The Duchy of Cornwall, Its History and Administration in Trans.
Royal Hist. Soc., 4th Series x (1927) pp. 137 et seq.
CORNWALL RECORD OFFICE, Old County Hall, Truro
COX, Charles J. – The Churches of Cornwall – 1912
CUISSARD, Charles M. – 'La Revue Celtique, Vol. V (1883) – (Life of Paul Aurelian)
DEVON RECORD OFFICE
DEXTER, T. F. G. & H. – Cornish Crosses Christian & Pagan
DOBLE, Revd. G. H. – 'Saint Paul of Leon' – 1941. Revd. Doble was Hon. Canon of
Truro Cathedral and Chaplain to the Lord Bishop of Truro
DOMESDAY BOOK
DORSET RECORD OFFICE
DUFFEY, Eamon – The Stripping of the Altars – 1992 – Yale University
DUGDALE, – Monasticon Anglic. – Hailes Abbey & Convent
FEET OF FINES No. 445
FOLLETT, STOCK & COMPANY – Diocesan Registry – Three Milestone, Truro

GASGOYNE, Joel – Map of Cornwall – 1699 RS 1991 (HES ref 912.4237)

GENUKI (Internet)

GILBERT, Davies – The Parochial History of Cornwall, Vol. III – J. B. Nichols, London – 1838

GILBERTS, C. S. – A Historical Survey of Cornwall – 3 Vols. 1817-20

GODOLPHIN, William – legal case Francis Lanyon v Thomas Darrell – Nat. Archives (TNA): C7/208/13 – original research Joanna Mattingly/Catherine Lorigan VCH forthcoming publication.

HENDERSON, C. – Notes on the Topography of Paul – from: The Annual Report of the Royal Cornwall Polytechnic Society – 1914-42

HENDERSON, C. G. – Essays in Cornish History – p. 101-2

HISTORY TIMELINES – Hailes Abbey – Internet

HITCHINS, Fortescue – History of Cornwall – ed. Samuel Drew

INGISTON-RANDOLPH, H. – 1889 P.161.

JOURNALS OF THE OLD CORNWALL SOCIETY – Morrab Library

LACH-SZYRMA, Revd. W. S. (Vicar of St. Peters Newlyn) – Arch. History of Cornwall & Diocese of Truro

LAKES – Parochial History of Cornwall, 1868 (Paul), pp. 48, 56, 225, 233, 427, 451, 464.

LYSONS – History & Topography – 1814

MATTINGLY, DR. Joanna & LORIGAN, Dr. Catherine – 'The Fishing Communities of Mousehole & Newlyn' VCH forthcoming publication.

MIDGELY, L.M. – Ministers' Accounts of the Earldom of Cornwall 1296-97, Vol. 1.

MILES-BROWN, Canon H. – The Church in Cornwall – Penzance Library

MONCRIEFF HOPE, Mr. & BLIGHT, J. T. – Churches & Antiquities of West Cornwall – 1885

MURRAY, J. – Murray's Handbook for Devon & Cornwall (1859), London 1971.

NORDEN – Norden's General Description of Cornwall p. 72-73.

NATIONAL ARCHIVES, The (TNA) – C7/208/13 – Francis Lanyon v Thomas Darrell

OLSON, Lynette – Early Monasteries in Cornwall – 1989

O'NEILL HENCKEN, H. – Archaeology of Cornwall – 1932

ORME, Professor N. I. – The Saints of Cornwall, and enumerable helpful e-mails

PAUL & MADRON – Church Registers in the C.R.O. and Family History Society, Truro

PENDAR, N.M. – Mousehole – 1985

PENN, Peter – Ed. Cornish Notes & Queries 1906 London & The Cornish Telegraph Office, Penzance

PIGOTS – Directory for Cornwall 1830 – index R. Parson.

RHYS, John – Celtic Britain.

ROWSE. A. L. – Tudor Cornwall – 1957

SCOTT & COMPANY, Truro – Records of Paul Restorations

SPARROW, Elizabeth. – The Prices of Penzance – 1985.

THURSTON, Peter – Plans & Specs 1st vol. 1786 – Royal Inst. Cornwall.

TITHE MAP – 1842 – Cornwall Record Office.

TONKINS – Natural History of Cornwall – 1739

VICTORIA COUNTY HISTORY OF CORNWALL – 1831 – C.R.O. and on-line: www.cornwallpast.net

WARNER, Canon F. – Faculties database for Paul Church

WEST PENWITH RESOURCES – Internet

WHITE, Kennett – Parochial Antiquities 1. p. 483

WRMONOC – The Life of Paul Aurelian – A.D. 884. – published by Dom. Plaine in the 'Analecta Bollandiana' in 1882, vol 1. p 208-58

YOUNG. G. – Country Churches

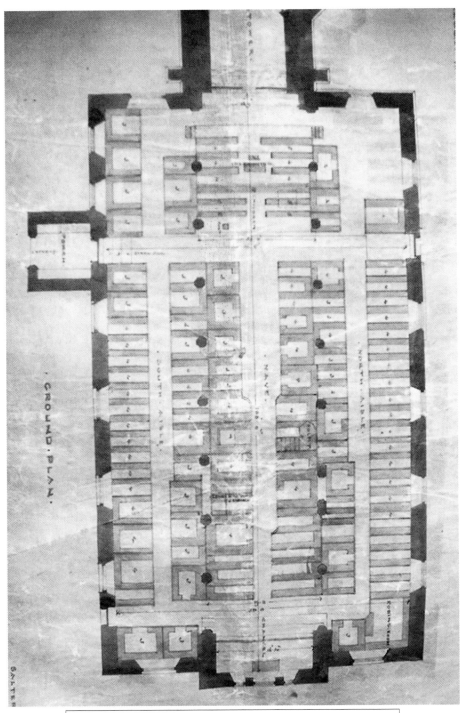

A large plan of the interior of the Church by Salter & Pellow - 1873